Professionalism and Teacher

Amanda Gutierrez · Jillian Fox ·
Colette Alexander
Editors

Professionalism and Teacher Education

Voices from Policy and Practice

Editors
Amanda Gutierrez
School of Education
Australian Catholic University
Banyo, QLD, Australia

Jillian Fox
School of Education
Australian Catholic University
Banyo, QLD, Australia

Colette Alexander
School of Education
Australian Catholic University
Banyo, QLD, Australia

ISBN 978-981-13-7004-5   ISBN 978-981-13-7002-1   (eBook)
https://doi.org/10.1007/978-981-13-7002-1

Library of Congress Control Number: 2019933845

This Springer imprint is published by the registered company Springer Nature Singapore Pte Ltd.
The registered company address is: 152 Beach Road, #21-01/04 Gateway East, Singapore 189721, Singapore

Acknowledgements

In addition to receiving editor feedback, each chapter in this 2019 edition was blind-reviewed to ensure the continued high standard of ATEA publications. We express our sincere appreciation to the following reviewers for their expertise, enthusiasm, and spirit.

Assoc. Prof. Jeanne Allen
Dr. Angelina Ambrossetti
Prof. Tania Aspland
Assoc. Prof. Robyn Brandenburg
Assoc. Prof. Jenene Burke
Prof. Geraldine Castleton
Prof. Carmel Diezmann
Assoc. Prof. Deborah Heck
Prof. Romina Jamieson-Proctor
Dr. Jenny Martin
Dr. Sharon McDonough
Dr. Josephine Ryan
Prof. Parlo Singh
Prof. Simone White

Contents

Editors and Contributors

About the Editors

Dr. Amanda Gutierrez is Senior Lecturer and Professional Experience Coordinator (Secondary Postgrad Courses) in the QLD School of Education at the Australian Catholic University. She is an experienced teacher educator who works in the fields of literacy, professional experience, and partnerships. Her major research interest is professional becoming of preservice and practicing teachers and partnerships, with a minor research interest in critical literacy. She has developed and coordinated multiple partnership programs in Victoria and Queensland.

Jillian Fox is Associate Professor in the Faculty of Education and Arts at the Australian Catholic University. She is an experienced early childhood teacher who has worked with preservice and practicing teachers in both Australia and China. Her areas of teaching and research expertise include work-integrated learning, mentoring, and early years education. In 2017, she won the Vice Chancellor's Award for Innovation for her work on establishing a university-wide work-integrated learning online platform.

Dr. Colette Alexander is Senior Lecturer in the School of Education at the Australian Catholic University. She is an experienced teacher educator who has worked with preservice and practicing teachers across both public and private institutions. Her current research and teaching is focused on research methodology, policy, and assessment. She is Project Lead for the implementation of the Graduate Teacher Performance Assessment (GTPA) across the School of Education and is an early career researcher working with the Institute for Learning Sciences and Teacher Education (ILSTE).

Contributors

Colette Alexander Australian Catholic University, Brisbane, QLD, Australia

Jeanne Allen Griffith University, Brisbane, QLD, Australia

Nan Bahr Southern Cross University, Gold Coast, QLD, Australia

Paulina Billett La Trobe University, Melbourne, VIC, Australia

Theresa Bourke Queensland University of Technology, Brisbane, QLD, Australia

Edgar Burns La Trobe University, Melbourne, VIC, Australia

Jennifer Clifton Griffith University, Brisbane, QLD, Australia

Beryl Exley Griffith University, Brisbane, QLD, Australia

Jo-Anne Ferreira Southern Cross University, Gold Coast, QLD, Australia

Rochelle Fogelgarn La Trobe University, Melbourne, VIC, Australia

Jillian Fox Australian Catholic University, Brisbane, QLD, Australia

Stephanie Garoni La Trobe University, Albury-Wodonga, VIC, Australia

Helen Grimmett Monash University, Clayton, VIC, Australia

Amanda Gutierrez Australian Catholic University, Brisbane, QLD, Australia

Deborah Heck University of the Sunshine Coast, Sippy Downs, QLD, Australia

Jean Hopman Victoria University, Melbourne, VIC, Australia

Kathy Jordan RMIT University, Melbourne, VIC, Australia

Sally Knipe La Trobe University, Albury-Wodonga, VIC, Australia

Glenda McGregor Griffith University, Brisbane, QLD, Australia

Rebecca H. Miles La Trobe University, Albury-Wodonga, VIC, Australia

Minh Hue Nguyen Faculty of Education, Monash University, Clayton, VIC, Australia

Donna Pendergast Griffith University, Brisbane, QLD, Australia

Linda-Dianne Willis The University of Queensland, Brisbane, QLD, Australia

Kenneth Young University of Sunshine Coast, Sippy Downs, QLD, Australia

Chapter 1
Conceptualising Teacher Professionalism

Colette Alexander, Jillian Fox and Amanda Gutierrez

Abstract Recently, Sachs (Teacher professionalism: why are we still talking about it? 22(4):413–425, 2016) posed the question, "why are we still talking about teacher professionalism?" Despite a long history of political and educational discourses about the professionalising of teaching, there remains little clarity about the meaning and intent of terms such as *profession*, *professionalism* and *professionalisation* in the context of teaching. Debates abound in relation to the influence of these discourses on the professionalising, deprofessionalising and reprofessionalising of teachers. Significant to the issues raised is the role and function of teacher education in the professional learning and development of teachers and the promotion of the teaching profession. This chapter explores core issues surrounding professionalism and teacher education with an emphasis on the Australian context. It will: (i) analyse definitions of the concepts of *profession* and *professionalism* and their application to teachers and teaching; (ii) outline core contestations in the spaces between political and educational discourses in contemporary contexts; and (iii) discuss emerging perspectives in teacher education for innovating policy and practice in support of the ongoing maturation of the teaching profession.

1 Introduction

In 2019, we are still grappling with conceptions of teaching as a profession and the contribution of teacher education to the professionalism of teaching. Much has been written nationally and internationally about teaching as a profession, and this has intensified in recent years. Some critical interpretations of issues surrounding teacher professionalism have included Hargreaves' (2000) discussion of the histor-

C. Alexander (✉) · J. Fox · A. Gutierrez
Australian Catholic University, Brisbane, QLD, Australia
e-mail: colette.alexander@acu.edu.au

J. Fox
e-mail: jillian.fox@acu.edu.au

A. Gutierrez
e-mail: amanda.gutierrez@acu.edu.au

© Springer Nature Singapore Pte Ltd. 2019
A. Gutierrez et al. (eds.), *Professionalism and Teacher Education*,
https://doi.org/10.1007/978-981-13-7002-1_1

ical ages of professionalism within socio-political contexts, Evetts' (2008, 2011) alternative discourses and categories of professionalism, and Sachs' (2016) differing interpretations of professionalism in practice. These and other authors, discussed below, have used a range of theoretical positions to provide important insights into teacher professionalism. The contributions to the extensive literature base demonstrates the depth and breadth of thinking about teaching as a profession and how understanding the related language and power relations can provide agentic capacity to teachers and teacher educators in making claims to professionalism.

Significant to the development of agentic capacity are contemporary critiques of the influence of performance cultures, accountability and standards on the way that the teaching profession is framed in contemporary discourses (Sachs, 2016). Australia as a relatively small nation, in population at least, is a microcosm that demonstrates how discourses evident globally are driving reform that ostensibly is working towards the professionalisation of teachers. In the Australian context since 2011, teacher educators have had to grapple with the introduction of the *Australian Professional Standards for Teachers* (APST) (AITSL, 2011a) and two iterations of national program standards for initial teacher education (AITSL, 2011b, 2015). After the review of teacher registration policies in 2018 (AITSL, 2018), it is anticipated that a review of the APST will shortly follow.

The politically driven activity of regulation in initial teacher education highlights the ongoing and intensifying busy work of regulatory compliance that plagues teacher educators across the country and has become a core concern of members of the Australian Teacher Education Association (ATEA) as evidenced by recent conference proceedings. Questions have arisen about the relevance, usefulness and effectiveness of regulation and compliance pursuits for attaining the intended goal of ensuring professional standards of teachers and thereby improving the quality of teaching. This book and its related conference seeks to speak to these issues in relation to policy and practice in teacher education. This chapter sets the scene by providing a discussion of where we are and how we got here and proposes a model for connecting thinking about teacher professionalism in the contemporary context. It then uses Bronfenbrenner's Ecological System theory (1979, 2005) as an emerging construct for organising and exploring the selected projects, contributions and voices from the field that make up the remainder of this book.

2   Defining a Profession

The issue of defining the terms profession and professionalism is a complex one. Take for example buying a property. All kinds of people across various occupations, including the conveyancing solicitor, estate agent, mortgage broker, financial advisor, property maintenance and gardener, and removalist, used the term *professional* to describe their services. As a colloquial or common-sense term, professional is used to represent the competence and expertise of an individual and the quality of the work they do. At this level, it seems logical that the term should be applied to teaching and teachers. But, this common sense use of the term professional contrasts with conceptions and classifications found in political and academic discourses about the professions and claims to teacher professionalism.

Contemporary conceptions of professionalism are contextualised in long-held ideas about the nature and purpose of a profession. Historically, sociological definitions of the term *profession* were used to distinguish professions from non-professions by identifying categories for occupational classification (Gewirtz et al., 2009). The identified archetypal, true or learned professions included divinity, law and medicine whose members professed and applied a specific knowledge base under a moral imperative to work for the benefit of others (Snoek, n.d.; Southwick, 1997). Over time, this categorisation developed in two ways. First, additional disciplinary areas of learning which are applied in service to others sought recognition as a profession. Second, professions and aspiring professions formed associations to self-regulate for entry into and quality practice of the profession to protect the community and the standing of the profession (David, 2000; Southwick, 1997). It is in the context of these developments that teachers and teaching first sought to establish teaching as a profession.

From these initial conceptions, there are three ideas that have been consistent in discourses surrounding the archetypal professions (Bair, 2016; Creasy, 2015; Evetts, 2006; Heck & Ambrosetti, 2018). These are that a profession uses a specific and substantive body of knowledge (Abbott, 1988; Goodson & Hargreaves, 1996); for the service and benefit of others in the community (Southwick, 1997); and establishes self-regulated codes for high quality, moral and ethical practice that serve to control entry into and ongoing practice of the profession (Barber, 1965; Snoek, n.d.). It is argued by many (see, e.g., David, 2000; Etzioni, 1969; Leiter, 1978; Snoek, Swennen, & Van der Klink, 2009; Snoek, n.d.) that teaching does not meet these criteria because teachers do not control entrance to their occupation and have only limited autonomy over their work. Therefore, teaching, like nursing and social work, is often named as a semi-profession (Etzioni, 1969). In contrast, others point to the strong academic knowledge base consisting of formal and technical knowledge (Abbott, 1988; Atkinson & Claxton, 2000; Goodson & Hargreaves, 1996) as evidence of the legitimacy of the claim to teaching as a profession.

Contemporary political agendas and performance cultures focussed on externalised public accountability grounded in regulatory practices are eroding the place of autonomy and self-determination as inherent characteristics of a profession. In the Australian context, the term *profession* is politically defined by the Australian Council of Professions (ACP), a not-for-profit association that advocates on behalf of more than 20 professional associations, including at least one teacher regulatory association. The provided definition is derived from Southwick (1997, p.5) the then President of the ACP and states that a profession is,

> A disciplined group of individuals who adhere to high ethical standards and uphold themselves to, and are accepted by, the public as possessing special knowledge and skills in a widely recognised, organised body of learning derived from education and training at a high level, and who are prepared to exercise this knowledge and these skills in the interest of

others. Inherent in this definition is the concept that the responsibility for the welfare, health and safety of the community shall take precedence over other considerations.

Significantly, this definition does not reflect conceptions described across the literature of autonomous or self-regulated accountability as one of the typical attributes of an archetypal profession (Bair, 2016; Snoek, n.d). Recent political activity in relation to professional accreditation in the Australian context has focussed attention on externalised accountability processes for the professions including the development of:

- *Joint Statement of Principles for Professional Accreditation* in 2016 (Professions Australia & Universities Australia, 2016);
- *Professional Accreditation: Mapping the Territory* report commissioned by the Department of Education and Training (Phillips, 2017); and
- *The Higher Education Standards Panel's advice on the impacts of professional accreditation in higher education* submitted to the Minister for Education and Training (Department of Education and Training, 2017).

Political activity in the regulation of the professions in the Australian context supports an ongoing integrated role for a government body. The Tertiary Education Quality and Standards Agency (TEQSA) fulfils this role, with professional associations, both voluntary and legislated, in accreditation processes for professionally oriented higher education. This points to troubling times for many different professions and the university faculties that support professional learning and development. Whilst politically driven external accountability is meant to safeguard the community and assure quality, it may do so at the cost of democratic and collegial accountability of the professions and their members and in doing so erode the foundations of the very quality it is seeking to assure. Political regulation has also intensified definitions of the professions around the specialised knowledge base that is developed for and used in professional practice for the benefit of the community. This has specific and unique implications for teacher professionalism, for example teacher education in the light of contemporary emphases on evidence-based practice and measurement regimes that undermine the fabric of teachers' innovative use of curriculum and pedagogical knowledge to make professional judgements for the benefit of learners.

3   Teacher Professionalism

In the Australian context dialogue about the potential of teaching as a profession can be traced back to the late 1800s when the first professors were brought in from Britain to advance education in the colonies. Since that time, ideas about the development of the profession have been linked to its relationship with university. As Pearson (1878 as quoted by Garden, 1982, p. 37) stated in possibly the first Royal Commission undertaken to review education on the Australian continent,

> We want the teacher of a primary school to be respected as a man (sic) of fair education throughout the colony. Above all, we wish him to keep the higher prizes of the profession steadily in sight, and to train, if he can spare the time and energy, for the University.

Ironically, it was not until the 1970s and into the 1980s that the political agenda moved teacher preparation or training into an autonomous higher education setting and the era of "teacher education" and a university degree as the minimum expectation for teaching became a reality across the country (Alexander, 2016; Aspland, 2010). This heralded in the beginning of the intensification of political focus on teaching and teacher education through a long line of political reviews (Alexander, 2016; Dinham, 2013). By the 1990s, both political and educational voices were increasingly calling for the nationalisation of quality teaching and learning through professional standards (National Project on the Quality of Teaching and Learning, 1996; Australian Council of Deans of Education, 1998). The standards discourse reflected the "roles, skills, abilities, attitudes, knowledge and understanding required" of teachers (Reynolds, 1999, p. 248). As such, standards were supposed to incorporate the professional qualities and values required of teaching as a profession and to provide an avenue for the professionalisation of teaching.

At the turning of the millennium several national and state reviews of teacher quality, teacher education and the registration of teachers were undertaken in Australia that further sharpened the focus onto teacher professionalism. Notable examples that specifically engaged the issue of teacher professionalism included: (i) the national review, *Australia's teachers, Australia's future* (Committee for the Review of Teaching and Teacher Education, 2003), which called for the professionalisation of teachers; (ii) the *Review of the Powers and Functions of the Board of Teacher Registration* (McMeniman, 2004) in Queensland that resulted in the establishment of the first professional standards for teachers in an Australian context; and (iii) the *Quality Matters, Revitalising Teaching: Critical times, critical choices* (Ramsey, 2000) in NSW that called into question the capacity of teachers to respond collectively to the expectations of a profession. Ramsey (2000, p. 99) stated,

> Teaching is unique when compared with the other professions studied, having no professional registration authority, no mandated system for continuing professional development and no professional oversight of teaching standards or practice.

On this basis, Ramsey (2000) recommended that the NSW government should take responsibility for the profession because, *"teachers either could not or would not be able to so without help"* (p. 14).

As a consequence of this political engagement with teacher professionalism, every state and territory in Australia had an established regulatory authority by 2005. Whilst Queensland and South Australia did so in the 1970s, the other states and territories established boards between 2000 and 2005. This highlights the myopic view taken in the Ramsey (2000) review in that it failed to consider interstate examples in making assumptions about the capacity of the teaching profession. A case in point is Queensland where mandatory registration of teachers commenced in 1975 with the establishment of the Board of Teacher Education (BTE). The BTE was legislated for the regulation of teachers and teaching, and this commitment to the regulation of the profession by the profession has continued in the establishment of the Queensland College of Teachers (QCT) following the contemporaneous McMeniman (2004) review. Yet, Ramsey's (2000) criticism, points to a problem for conceptions of teaching as a profession, in that the core attribute of autonomous self-regulation has never been universally achieved by teachers. Even the Queensland example was driven by political imperatives and supported by legislated establishment of the Board, an initiative of the government not the profession.

In the most recent decade, teacher professionalism has come under increasing pressure through processes of nationalisation in the Australian context. The work of teachers in regard to professional standards of practice and the curriculum they teach has come under increasing externalised regulation with the establishment of national standards or APST (AITSL, 2011a) and a national curriculum (see Australian Curriculum Assessment and Reporting Authority, www.acara.edu.au). Importantly, the APST are developed and maintained by a national authority that is entirely political, owned by the Commonwealth Minister of Education, and a further arms-length away from the state regulatory authorities that continue to be responsible for registering teachers and accrediting initial teacher education. The most recent political review, *Action Now: Classroom Ready Teachers* (Craven et al., 2014), recommended that "the Australian Government establish a national initial teacher education regulator through a reconstituted Australian Institute for Teaching and School Leadership" (p. 12). Such a move would serve to completely severe current links between teachers and the state-based boards that regulate the profession. To date, this recommendation has not been actioned. Yet, the impact of nationalisation on teacher professionalism is reminiscent of the prophetic cautions of academics from the 1990s. These cautions include: (i) shortcomings of competency-based approaches to establishing professional standards for teachers (Louden & Wallace, 1993); (ii) dangers of neglecting complexity, personal judgement and values in standardising of teachers' professional practice (Reynolds, 1999); and (iii) the resultant deprofessionalisation of teaching (Whitty, 1994).

Inherent in conceptions of a profession, as described above, is the importance of self-identification. Professional status for an occupation is dependent upon members' individual identity and collective recognition of their work as a profession. In other words, there is a difference between an individual teacher performing their duties professionally and teachers engaging as members of a profession (Darling-Hammond, 2010). In relation to issues of self-identification, it is not difficult to find evidence of ongoing arguments for teaching not being a profession (Hayes & Hegarty, 2002; Inlow, 1956).

First, arguments against teaching as a profession typically reference the issues of autonomy and self-regulation. As described by Inlow (1956, p. 259),

> Once more the question is asked: Is teaching a profession? The writer feels compelled to answer in the negative. Teaching is moving in the direction of professionalism, but it has not gone the whole way. It still must formulate standards, screen its applicants, and control itself effectively.

It is possible to argue that in the fifty years that have followed, teachers and teaching have moved no closer to recognition as a profession. However, as shown above, the validity of this argument is significantly weakened in contemporary contexts.

Second, arguments about teacher professionalism also reference issues surrounding the body of knowledge the underpins teachers' professional practice. Core to these arguments is the perceived lack of consistency in the body of knowledge that is purported to underpin the teaching profession. It is argued that variance in what is accepted as pedagogical knowledge, what is known or theorised as quality in teaching practice, and what is demonstrated as quality teaching practice is evidence that the knowledge base lacks the robustness required to claim a recognised and organised body of knowledge for teaching. As concluded by Hayes & Hegarty, 2002, p. 35),

> there can be no doubt that professions have a clear knowledge base, connected to theory and research, nor that professionals need to master that knowledge base and be able to express it clearly in the context of everyday professional activity. Teaching must attend to this issue if the goal of authentic professionalisation is to be pursued.

Herein lies a challenge for teacher education, in that the fundamental questions that underpin arguments against the acceptance of teaching as a profession are grounded in issues with the organisation of the *body of learning* that should be *derived from education and training* (Southwick, 1997). In this context, teacher education is meant in its broadest sense as taking in both initial and continuing teacher education through both formal and informal structures. Whilst this is important for understanding the contested nature of conceptions of teaching as a profession, what constitutes the body of knowledge and practice that makes up teaching is not the focus that is taken up here in this book.

Rather, this text is taking up the role of teacher education and engagement of teacher educators in research and practices surrounding teacher professionalism. Critical to the work of teacher educators in researching and supporting teacher professionalism is the capacity to engage with contestations whilst simultaneously supporting teachers' developing professional identities. Despite the real and serious limitations imposed through performance cultures, accountability and standards, teacher educators are still active in thinking about, discussing and promoting teacher professionalism. In the Australian context, there is much evidence, including within this book, that teacher educators are actively working as agents of change within and between the spaces that exist in the guidelines, procedures and standards (AITSL, 2011b, 2015, 2018) that seek to rule over conceptions of professionalism in teaching and teacher education.

4 Contestations in Professionalism

As discussed above, contradictions and contestations of teacher professionalism have flourished across the decades, responding to socio-political agendas, shifting perspectives, competing ideologies and power differentials. It is beyond the scope of this

Fig. 1 Model of Positions in Conceptualising Teacher Professionalism

	Interior/inward	*Exterior/outward*
Occupational	AUTONOMOUS occupational value	DEMOCRATIC ideology
Organisational	MANAGERIAL standards and accountability for individuals	MANAGERIAL performance cultures for schools and systems

chapter to provide a comprehensive review of the total body of research that explores professionalism and we have no intention of adding to the myriad of characterisations. What we would like to introduce is a way of synthesising, and where possible connecting the most prevalent or dominant contestations as a series of domains that describe the discursive positions of teacher professionalism we have identified in the literature. Our cogitations consider the landscape from an inward looking internal and outward looking external lens, where the internal considers the profession from the view of the individual teacher and the external considers this is light of the collective of these individuals. Central to this exploration is the considerations of professionalism from both an occupational and organisational perspective. The model (see Fig. 1) considers the contestations within and across these four domains and demonstrates how various notions of professionalism co-exist in contradictory tension. Each of the resulting positions about teacher professionalism are claimed and counterclaimed by different players in the debate who take on differing perspectives and stances dependent on their role within the context of education.

4.1 Interior/Inward Occupational Perspective

In the *interior/inward occupational domain,* the teacher is characterised as an autonomous professional who possesses occupational value that is recognised as inherent to all who enter and work within the profession. Central to this position is the embodiment of the attributes and characteristics of the archetypal professions, discussed earlier in this chapter. These focus on the teacher's capacity to build trust, competence and therefore a strong occupational presence. Strong individual or internal professional identity is taken to attach integrity and competence to the role and espouses trust in the profession grounded in the internal ethical or moral practice of each member of the profession.

This domain is reminiscent of historical conceptions of a profession, yet it continues to be present as an alternative perspective on teacher professionalism in more recent literature (e.g. Hargreaves, 2000). According to Freidson (2001), education, pedagogical knowledge, experience and ethics are essential necessities for entering the teaching profession. Once achieved, and sometimes licensed, discretion based on these competences is central to the practice of the profession and deserving of autonomous status. The special knowledge and skills that teachers possess advocates the need to trust professionals' intentions in the practice of the profession (Friedson, 2001), and this is reflective of Hargreaves' (2000) second age of a profession. For Hargreaves (2000), this age depicts the "autonomous professional" where teaching embodies judgements and teachers' independent capacities to choose and decide what is best for students. The mandate for autonomous professional practice is supported by Evetts' (2012) definition of a profession as having occupational value. Evetts (2012) defines a profession as having occupational or normative value because the work is something worth preserving and promoting. The characteristics of occupational value are based on trust, competence, a strong occupational identity and co-operation (Evetts, 2014). With this mandate, it is argued that teachers should be allowed to autonomously engage in their profession (Snoek, n.d.).

For some researchers and stakeholders in the profession, the *interior/inward occupational domain* aligns significantly with their ideologies. Ideologically, the principles of autonomy, occupational value and the attributes of the archetypal profession support the inward perception of the teaching profession for individual teachers. The lengthening of teaching degrees, the development of accreditation regimes and the development of the teaching "academy" also contribute to the "licensed autonomy" principle (Alexander, 2016; Hargreaves & Goodson, 1996). Yet, an isolated autonomous approach to the teaching profession can have detrimental impacts. Autonomy favours individualism, an overriding characteristic of teaching as teachers have traditionally taught their classes in isolation, separated from their colleagues. Hargreaves (2000) has attributed stagnated pedagogy, limited support structures and lack of professional dialogue to this approach to teacher professionalism. Furthermore, this domain lacks the collective capacity needed to respond effectively to the challenges and changes imposed by contemporary performance cultures and externalised regulations that prevail in education systems.

4.2   Exterior/Outward Occupational Perspective

The *exterior/outward occupational domain* focuses on the collegial and collaborative aspects of the teaching profession and maintains autonomy for the profession through collective responsibility rather than individually. It recognises teachers' responsibility and commitment to not only their classroom, students and families, but to other members of the profession as well as stakeholders and partners within the wider community. From this position, the profession accepts collective responsibility for quality teaching, outcomes and the progression of the profession. The central emphasis of this position is the democratic action of collaborative, cooperative work amongst teachers and with other educational professionals and stakeholders.

This domain is well articulated and strongly preferenced in contemporary academic discourses. Related terms that theorise this external and collective perspective, include occupational, democratic and collegial approaches to teacher professionalism (Apple, 1996; Biesta, 2017; Evetts, 2008; Hargreaves, 2000; Sachs, 2000, 2003). Evetts (2008) identifies the importance of autonomy combined with discretionary judgement, as described above, but also incorporates collegial authority as essential components of occupational professionalism. This is also reflected in conceptions of democratic professionalism which focuses on collegial relations and collaborative work practices where teachers are advocates and change agents working for the common good of the communities and contexts in which they work (Biesta, 2017; Sachs, 2000). A focus on teacher relationships and collaboration with colleagues, students, their parents and communities for the common good interlinks with Hargreaves (2000) collegial age of professionalism. Hargreaves (2000) describes this age as, "uniting the profession as increasing efforts are made to build strong professional cultures of collaboration to develop common purpose" (p. 166). This type of professionalism sees a shift from the autonomous and individual primacies to a collective, collegial approach and shared responsibility to building the profession. Apple (1996) also suggests that these notions of professionalism seek to clarify professional work and build coalitions between teachers and the educational sector including students, members of the community and managerial systems.

The literature provides strong support for the *exterior/outward occupational domain* as critical for the ongoing recognition and development of the teaching profession. This powerful perspective on professionalism appeals to teachers and teacher educators who inwardly recognise themselves as competent, knowledgeable and ethical practitioners with pedagogical expertise whilst also promoting the benefit of collaborative cultures and communities of practice. Teachers as active contributors to conceptualisations of occupational, democratic and collegial professionalism endorse their professional status maintaining the focus on their shared commitment to progressing teaching. Further, Hargreaves (2000) proposes that this collegial age creates a united approach to education which can respond to change, develop stronger senses of teacher efficacy and create professional learning cultures that respond to contemporary priorities and trends such as globalisation and technological change. In this way, the profession is shown to accept collective responsibility for quality teaching, outcomes and progression of the profession (Brennan, 1996), and it is suggested that resultant trust in teacher competences and knowledge implies that externally imposed rules can be minimised reducing the influence of managerial impositions (Evetts, 2010).

4.3 Interior/Inward Organisational Perspective

The *interior/inward organisational domain* is the first of two domains that reflect an imposed approach to teacher professionalism. Whilst both domains highlight managerial professionalism, they are characterised by an inward or outward perspective—hence the wavy line depicting the seepage between notions. In our model, the inter-connectedness of these two domains is represented by a wavy line to demonstrate the intricate relationship between the domains. In the interior/inward approach to managerial organisation of the profession, the determination of teachers' work moves from teachers to the wider organisational system. This internally oriented management specifically relates to the individual's professional practice as supported through standards and personal accountability.

The impact of internalised or personalised management of the profession is evident in the establishment and use of the APST in the Australian context (AITSL, 2011a). These professional standards and their outworking in practice constructs the work of teaching as a largely independent practice undertaken with students independent of other teachers and unrelated to issues of context. This is outworked in the use of these standards alongside the program standards (AITSL, 2015) for initial teacher education to: (i) develop and assess graduate readiness for any classroom; (ii) enforce responsibility for evidencing readiness with the preservice teacher; and (iii) reward teachers through higher classifications and remuneration based on demonstrating personal competence at higher levels.

Managerial professionalism is widely critiqued within the literature because it is viewed as control constructed from "above" or "outside" the profession and imposed through performance cultures and accountability structures. It is argued that organisational objectives embody socio-political agendas to define practitioner/client relations, create performance indicators, decide quality and impose standards. Thus, organisational objectives, "regulate and replace occupational control of the practitioner/client work interactions, thereby limiting shared decision-making, and preventing the service ethic that has been so important in professional work" (Evetts, 2014, p.41). It is argued that managerial perspectives work to de-professionalise the profession. In the case of this interior/inward position, it is perceived to be countering the democratic and collegial work of teachers by returning focus to teachers collectively but without autonomy. Despite this criticism, this position is also taken up and welcomed by some members of the profession and other educational stakeholders as it is perceived to be a way of improving the status of the profession and rewarding quality teachers.

4.4 Exterior/Outward Organisational Perspective

The *exterior/outward organisational domain* is another position that reflects a managerial perspective. In this domain, the management of the profession focuses on the collection of teachers rather than teachers as individuals. From here, professional judgement shifts from an activity of the teacher working in accountability to professional standards to an activity of the organisation that determines and controls teachers' work. The external management sees control of the profession and the professional work of teachers resting with systems, sectors and school structures within a culture of market-oriented performance and accountability.

Externally mandated organisational professionalism endorses and encourages the standardisation of teacher activity and relies on regulation and accountability incorporating target setting and performance review. The influence of this approach is exemplified in the Australian context in contemporary approaches to curriculum and professional learning. Alongside nationalised curriculum that determines what is to be taught and how, state-based control of classrooms through programs such as Queensland's *Curriculum into the Classroom* (C2C) demonstrates the extent of the external management of the work of teachers. Similarly, the control of teachers' professional learning by schools and systems to ostensibly improve teacher quality and student outcomes through standardised evidence-based pedagogical practice, supported by questionable statistical inferences, is further contributing to the managerial control of the teaching profession (Bergeron & Rivard, 2017). The power to determine how best to achieve quality is given to managers removed from the classroom and pedagogical practice.

Accountability structures and the control of practices and outcomes at a managerial level by actors outside of the profession are seen in all levels of the educational sector (Sachs, 2016). Johnston (2015) argues that portraying teachers and schools as the cause of poor national economic productivity produces a simplified cause-and-effect scenario (Australian Government Productivity Commission, 2012; Marginson, 1999). Corcoran (1995) also discusses how professional development can be a control mechanism when linked to the attempts to develop higher standards of teaching practice. The opportunity for growing teachers' practice and developing contemporary, progressive systems becomes limited if teachers are considered "technicians and implementers of technical knowledge" (Sachs, 2016, p. 8) and not as active participants contributing to their professional development and profession.

It is argued that the position of the *exterior/outward organisational domain* is also working towards deprofessionalising teaching, hence the wavy line in Fig. 1. The APST fail to adequately acknowledge the ethical and moral dispositions of the profession. The use of the standards and curriculum, such as C2C, to control the work of the profession sets up teaching as a simplified technocratic practice. Combined, these agenda are working to return teaching to Hargreaves' (2000) pre-professional age. Organisational professionalism within the exterior domain renders teachers voiceless within the profession and subject to the imposed standards, policies and outcomes deemed by management.

4.5 Seeking an Alternative Position

The four described domains provide insight into the various positions that are present in contemporary literature. They seek to articulate the different ways that teacher professionalism is viewed and discussed, and how this is outworking in contemporary practice. Our interpretations also suggest fluidity in these discourses where competing ideals are debated and opposing conceptions become more or less visible in varying socio-political contexts and times. Empirically, the different discourses of professionalism discussed, whilst competing, do exist together. Together they demonstrate the contestations that prevail in thinking about teacher professionalism.

Whilst our deliberations have identified intersections amongst the contestations, it has also led to the identification of a critical bifurcation that has emerged in the principles, policy and practice surrounding teacher professionalism. This bifurcation is described by Sachs (2016) as, "a chasm between the desires and expectations of teachers and governments to the extent that governments are drawn to and endorse organisational/managerial professionalism, whilst teachers are likely to favour occupational/democratic professionalism" (p. 8). Whilst the implications of this split are described above in relation to the Australian context, it is also played out in global discursive practices. Globalisation has created a competitive state requiring economic rationalisation and policies that build national productivity. Present-day postmodern and neo-liberal society emphasises economic and technological changes (Gewirtz et al., 2009). This changing market-oriented context for society and schools has resulted in changes in the expectations, emphasising accountability, rationality, competitiveness and control (Evans, 2008; Goodson & Hargreaves, 1996; Robertson, 1996). The consequences of which are well described by Hargreaves' (2000) fourth post-professional age and the potential for teacher professionalism to be "diminished or abandoned" (p. 167).

Within this globalised contemporary context, it is argued that appealing to collegial and democratic professionalism that harks back to Hargreaves (2000) age of the collegial professional is no longer sufficient. Rather, teachers and teacher educators need to find and establish new ways to negotiate the socio-political landscape and work towards quality education for all (Alexander, 2016). Hargreaves (2000) suggests a, "postmodern professionalism that is broader, more flexible and more democratically inclusive" (p. 167). Sachs (2003) identifies a new understanding of "transformational" professionalism that constructs its own knowledge, is self-regulated and policy-active, and characterised by inclusivity, public accountability, collaborative activism, flexibility and responsiveness. Herein lies the purpose of the remainder of this book. In contrast, to the doom and gloom that could so easily overwhelm the profession, teachers and teacher educators are keeping the collaborative voices of the profession alive.

5   Emerging Perspectives

Despite the challenges, stakeholders are facing in the current context of contested perspectives, political change, community expectations and often disparaging divisive discourse, there is a continued effort to advocate for teaching as a profession. The chapters in this book provide optimism in a complex time where negative forces erode and remove dialogic spaces to combat deprofessionalisation. The Australian authors share their research, perspectives and ideas about teacher professionalism in current times demonstrating a commitment to contribute to the conversation. The voices reflect characteristics of transformative professionalism, as defined by Sachs (2003), as including (a) inclusive membership, (b) public ethical code of practice, (c) collaborative and collegial, (d) activist orientation, (e) flexible and progressive, (f) responsive to change, (g) self-regulating, (h) policy-active, (i) enquiry-oriented and (j) knowledge building. These characteristics have synergy with democratic professionalism creating professional space and conditions for collegial and collaborative responsibilities and practices.

The chapters provide insight into contemporary research, ideas, policies and standards that influence the conceptualisation of teacher professionalism. A range of methodologies is utilised such as narrative, case studies and document analysis, exploring professionalism contestations within the layers of Australian society. We have chosen to arrange the chapter offerings under three broad themes: (i) social and political context discourse; (ii) partnership engagement and (iii) collaborative professionalism. These broad themes allow us to apply a theoretical lens to the Australian teacher professionalism research space. The manner in which teacher professionalism is perceived, defined, researched and promoted is categorised in this section of the chapter into three broad parts informed by Bioecological Theory (Bronfenbrenner, 1979, 2005).

The Bronfenbrenner model organises contexts of development into five levels of external influence (see Fig. 2). The levels are categorised from the most intimate level to the broadest. We have contextualised the model to relate to "professionalism". The *microsystem* is the inner circle and describes the setting in which professionalism research privileges collaborative pursuits. This layer represents contexts where direct internal relationships work productively to improve teaching and learning and genuinely improve practice. The mesosystem is where microsystems interact (e.g. the relationship between stakeholders). There are cross-relationships between these immediate settings within these layers which conceptualise professionalism as collegial and collective. The interaction between two or more microsystems should produce social capital (Salaran, 2010) empowering individuals. An *exosystem* is an extension of the mesosystem embracing connections between specific social structures. These secondary systems that influence contestations of professionalism include partnerships between educational systems, institutions, and industry. The engagement of a range of stakeholders creating and promoting partnerships provides another voice in the discourse surrounding professionalism. The fourth layer is the *macrosystem*. A macrosystem differs in a fundamental way from the preceding

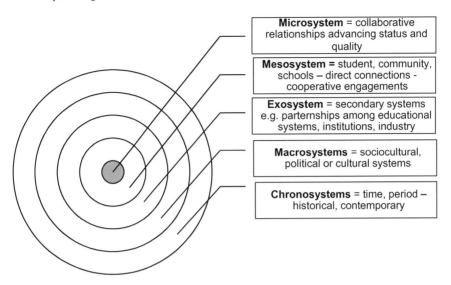

Fig. 2 Bronfenbrenner's Bioecological theory and teacher professionalism

layers in that it refers to the socio-cultural influences on teacher professionalism (e.g., national political policies and agendas, international higher education networks). Macrosystems can be conceived and examined not only in structural terms but as carriers of information and ideology. The *chronosystem* is relevant to the professionalism debate as it relates to time periods and sustained engagement. The development of teacher professionalism in the chronosystem can also be analysed in terms of longevity.

In the case of conceptualising teacher professionalism, it is useful to have a broader picture (or a macrosystem understanding) to contextualise activities in the exosystem, mesosystem and microsystem. For this reason, this book begins with chapters that map the macrosystem through critique of social, cultural and political systems and forces in the Australian context. It then moves to chapters in which authors have explored stakeholder activity and crossing boundaries (predominantly matching exosystem), and the final section provides discussion around direct contributions to teacher professionalism (reflecting the micro- and mesosystems). Each section is outlined in further detail below.

5.1 Social and Political Context—Macrosystem

In a very apt opening to this book, Bourke, in Chap. 2, reflects on her analysis of the 2011 representations of discourse on "what it means to be a professional" in the *Accreditation of Initial Teacher Education Programs in Australia: Standards and Procedures* (AITSL, 2011b) and provides a new analysis of the same discourse in the 2015 iteration of the *Accreditation of Initial Teacher Education Programs in Australia: Standards and Procedures* (AITSL, 2015). To do this, Bourke utilises Foucault's archaeological analysis, in particular focusing on discourse and power to consider inclusions and exclusion of voices, authoritative texts, repetition and any apparent discord across the document. Bourke identifies the competing discourses in professionalism, including a concise discussion of "new professionalism" discourses and "managerial" professionalism discourses. Her analysis of the accreditation documentation suggests a managerial representation of professionalism in which graduates are "positioned as regulated technicians". The chapter illustrates the importance for teachers and teacher educators to have the capacity to work in the space we identified in Fig. 1 of this chapter, interior organisational managerial. This is evident in the way Bourke talks back to authoritative discourses, those exterior organisational managerial discourses that marginalise voices of experienced teacher educators/researchers, restrict definitions of teacher professional discourses and are dominated by "evidence-based" quantitative "impact" data focusing on limited representations of "quality". Bourke's chapter illustrates the agentic capacity of teacher educators to engage with managerial discourses, and Bourke identifies her work as activist professionalism. The chapter argues that teachers and teacher educators need to collaborate to engage with contestations about the profession, and to challenge normalisation of disenabling managerial discourses.

Pendergast, Exley, Bahr and Ferreira, in Chap. 3 focus on the outworking of discourses through contemporary social media and the interplay that influences the positioning of teachers. The chapter speaks back to deprofessionalising performativity discourses perpetuated in the media, particularly about teacher quality and qualifications. It does this through analysing three instances of the authors' own engagement with social media and respondent comments, including the Australian Association for Research in Education blog "Teachers are NOT underqualified and NOT under-educated: here's what is really happening", the piece published in *The Conversation* titled "Seven reasons people no longer want to be teachers", and the article published by ABC Online titled "Teachers can earn more than dentists … and other reasons to enter the profession". Pendergast, Bahr, Exley and Ferreira identify the phenomena and growing power of secondary stakeholders and the forced passivity of those in the teaching profession in relation to contributing to and responding through social media platforms. They also discuss the various risks for teachers that arise as a result of engaging in social media platforms and the need to possess rhetorical skills to successfully communicate in social media genres. The authors send a call to teachers and teacher educators to engage with the social media macrosystem in which secondary stakeholders have growing power and voice. They argue this is an important space for education professionals to develop communication skills which will help the profession speak back to the kinds of deprofessionalising exterior organisational managerial discourses discussed earlier in this chapter.

5.2   *Partnership Engagement—Exosystem*

This section of the book shifts the focus to collaborative and collegial teacher educator work in the exosystem. The three chapters in this section focus on the spaces constructed between university and schools. In particular, those third spaces in which university and school staff cross boundaries to enable preservice teachers to make stronger connections between learning in the academic space and learning/implementing in the practical space. In Chap. 4, Clifton and Jordan utilise third space theory to explore hybrid roles in university–school partnership programs. They illustrate the complexity of this space, particularly the multivarious nature of these hybrid roles. Clifton and Jordan draw on research in their own school–university–system (DET) partnership to outline the various roles required to run the partnership, including new roles and roles that have not significantly changed. They narrow their focus to the new hybrid roles, in particular the teacher educator hybrid roles and their stories from interviews. The analysis identifies the tensions, and increased workload, particularly for those from higher education institutions, as they work to build bridges between multiple stakeholders. It also illustrates the slippages between boundaries that those in the hybrid role negotiate and the multiple questions raised for those trying to define their professional identity in this space.

Gutierrez, Young and Jordan in Chap. 5 provide a cross-institutional interrogation of teacher educators' roles in university–school–system partnerships. They utilise recent modelling on partnerships from an Australian cross-institutional STEM partnership project called STEPS, Science Teacher Education Partnerships. In particular, they reflect on the ideas in the Principles of Partnership Practice and structure individual narratives around the STEPS Interpretative Framework. They then analyse a meta-narrative in which they reflect on their understanding of the various individual narratives. This chapter provides an in-depth understanding of the teacher educators' experiences as they develop, operationalise and try to sustain partnerships. It considers teacher educator roles in boundaries that are not easily defined in traditional university role classifications. The chapter highlights the teacher educators' passion and efforts to bring together stakeholders and partners to develop quality experiences for preservice teachers and progress the teaching profession. It also illustrates the tensions and complications these teacher educators experience as they broker the partnership across multiple spaces and discourses, from the macrosystem of organisational managerial accreditation and standards discourses to the microsystem of PSTs' and teachers' classroom experiences. The chapters presented by Clifton and Jordan, and Gutierrez, Young and Jordan both illustrate the key issues associated with democratic professionalism ideals (Biesta, 2017), particularly in a political environment that foregrounds organisational managerialism (Sachs, 2016). Teachers and teacher educators who align with a democratic view of professionalism in that they promote education as a collective responsibility are often met with restrictive inflexible boundaries impacting sustainability.

In Chap. 6, Miles, Garoni and Knipe present their work as a "professional attachment" model, and they articulate the ways this model assisted preservice teachers as they transitioned into in-service positions around understanding what it means to be a professional in rural and regional teaching settings. They identified the disconnection between initial teacher education and professional experience, perpetuated by traditional models of professional experience. They argue this then continues into the graduate career as they associate theoretical perspective with university perspectives that do not align with practices in their school. In explaining the professional attachment model, the chapter provides an interesting run-down of the various lengths of professional experience programmes across universities, suggesting some universities go beyond the accredited requirements. It provides data from graduate teachers as they reach the 6- to 12-month stage of their in-service career and their supervisors. Miles, Garoni and Knipe argue the professional attachment model enabled the graduates to feel more prepared, more "classroom ready" and confident to teach to diverse student needs, which was reflected in the graduate feedback as well as feedback from their supervisors. They called for the teaching profession to provide stronger support for those entering the profession through more integrated and collaborative transition programmes.

5.3   Collaborative Professionalism—Micro- and Mesosystems

In the final section of this book, the authors in each chapter address the micro- and mesosystems relating to collaborative elements reflecting democratic professionalism at the local level. The section starts with Chap. 7 by Heck, Grimmett and Willis, which explores cogenerative dialogue as a vehicle to reclaim teacher educator professionality through "collaborative development of new possibilities". They analyse cogenerative dialogue in the context of utilising physical materials through LEGO® Serious Play® (LSP) to develop a creative representation of the concept metalogue. The authors track their dialogic interactions, and the contribution the processes and products made to their relational agency. The process allowed a starting point to explore abstract concepts and generated a way to build on each other's ideas. The authors suggested with some minor adjustments, the process would be useful for preservice teachers and would enable them to engage in collaborative conversations, which are critical to their role as professionals in education.

Hopman, in Chap. 8, presents a narrative inquiry in which she explores teacher emotional rules and their impact on teachers' professional agency. She follows seven teachers, including herself, as they progressed through an action research project in which they reflected on their emotional responses in the classroom. The chapter explores discussions by the teachers of critical incidents and the emotions that the teachers identified during these moments. Within this meso-system, Hopman identifies a number of emotional rules that illustrate the chrono and macrosystem restrictions on teachers' outward expression of their internal feelings. Hopman identifies the impact feelings of defeat and failure can have on a teacher's agency, depending on how they learn from the experience invoking these emotions. The chapter argues for teachers to critically reflect on their feelings and understand who they are, as this impacts the ways they react to experiences in the classroom. As was illustrated in Hopman's study, providing a space for teachers to collaboratively explore critical incidents enables teachers to transformatively discuss how emotions and emotional rules influence their professional identities as teachers.

Chapter 9, by Fogelgarn, Burns and Billett addresses the issue of teacher targeted bullying and harassment (TTBH) in Australian schools through a large-scale survey (560) of teachers. The authors argue that the teaching profession is the most likely profession to experience bullying. Further, they identify TTBH as being largely invisible due to chrono and macro socio-cultural and historical discourses that promote individualistic characterisations of teachers, and dominant perceptions of teacher positions of power. They identify the importance of not only students' rights to be safe in classroom and school environments, but also the teachers' professional rights to these same safe environments. The results discussed in this chapter deliver some unsettling findings, such as 80% of the participants having experienced TTBH from parents or students in the last 12 months. This chapter illustrates the impact Biesta (2017) identifies as a distortion of democratic professionalism, in which the clients become the central focus. Fogelgarn, Burns and Billett call for greater consideration in policy and research on the impact of TTBH on teacher professionalism (and teacher attrition) to ensure a safe work environment, and professional agency of teachers.

Allen, McGregor and Pendergast in Chap. 10 discuss their piloting of a professional learning app titled the Student Engagement and Teacher Reflection app (SETRA). This app aims to assist teachers with professional learning on teaching a diverse range of students. In addition, the project hoped to address common professional learning issues for teachers, such as lack of time to physically attend, disconnection between professional learning content and the teachers' classroom realities, and lack of translation of professional learning into teacher practice. The authors identify the pilot study findings which highlighted the reflective capacity of the app for teachers, allowing them continuous and contextualised access to resources on the behavioural, emotional and cognitive dimensions of student engagement. Allen, McGregor and Pendergast argue that the pilot of the app demonstrated the potential of multimodal digital texts to provide rich, collaborative and meaningful professional learning, enhancing teachers' abilities to engage all students in their classrooms. This illustrates the democratic potential of technology to create transformative practices in activist professional (Sachs, 2016) spaces where teachers can share across boundaries and self-regulate their own learning.

The final chapter in *Professionalism in Teacher Education: Voices from policy and practice* provides a microsystem exploration of the EAL teacher identity. In this chapter, Nguyen explores the voices of preservice (PST) and in-service teachers (IST) as they discuss their perceptions of the role of an EAL teacher. The PSTs demonstrate an understanding of knowing their learners and how to implement EAL teaching and support strategies. They also understand the wider aspect of EAL teaching in which the EAL teacher acts as an advocate in the school and community to promote EAL teaching. Nguyen found a missing element of the PSTs understanding relating to developing transition and cultural understanding strategies as EAL students transition into mainstream schooling. In this study, the ISTs demonstrate similar understandings about their roles, but the understandings and strategies utilised are more nuanced. This chapter highlights the complexity and diversity of teaching EAL. It emphasises the importance of EAL teachers understanding their role and the need to collaborate with mainstream teachers, including the senior years of EAL.

As this book moves from the macrosystem to the microsystem, there is an increase in the number of chapters, with the most attention on the meso and microsystems. This is reflective of the nature of the teaching profession, which predominantly focuses on the local contextual issues to improve the quality of student outcomes (and teacher professional learning). We, the editors, hope you enjoy reading the diverse collection of voices, covering various aspects of professionalism and teacher education. They represent the tensions and complexities as teachers and teacher educators try to negotiate a space that is saturated with organisational managerial discourses, and which challenge educators' collaborative agency to define the profession. They also illustrate some of the characteristics of transformative professionalism outlined by Sachs (2003, 2016) as preservice teachers, teachers and teacher educators work together to develop a deeper understanding of the teaching profession and how to productively engage with the organisational managerial discourses which often impact our working lives.

References

Abbott, A. (1988). *The system of professions: An essay on the division of expert labour*. Chicago: University of Chicago Press.

Alexander, C. (2016). *Reforming the reform of teacher education: A critical grounded theory of a social approach to change and continuity* (Unpublished doctoral thesis). University of Adelaide, Adelaide, Australia. Retrieved February 21, 2018 from https://digital.library.adelaide.edu.au/dspace/bitstream/2440/101568/2/02whole.pdf.

Atkinson, T., & Claxton, G. (2000). *The intuitive practitioner: on the value of not always knowing what one is doing*. Maidenhead: Open University Press.

Apple, M. (1996). *Cultural politics and education*. New York: Teachers College Press.

Aspland, T. (2010). Teacher education in Australia: Twisting and turning into the twenty-first century. In K. G. Karras & C. C. Wolhuter (Eds.), *International handbook on teacher education worldwide: Issues and challenges for teacher profession* (Vol. 2, pp. 789–810). Athens: Atrapos Editions.

Australian Council of Deans of Education [ACDE]. (1998). *Preparing a profession: Report of the national standards and guidelines for initial teacher education project*. Canberra: Author.

Australian Government Productivity Commission. (2012). *Schools Workforce*. Canberra ACT: www.pc.gov.au.

Australian Institute for Teaching and School Leadership [AITSL]. (2011a). *National Professional Standards for Teachers*. Education Services Australia: online at http://www.teacherstandards.aitsl.edu.au/.

Australian Institute for Teaching and School Leadership [AITSL]. (2011b). *Accreditation of initial teacher education programs in Australia: Standards and procedures*. Carlton South, VIC: Education Services Australia.

Australian Institute for Teaching and School Leadership [AITSL]. (2015). *Accreditation of initial teacher education programs in Australia: Standards and procedures*. Author.

Australian Institute for Teaching and School Leadership [AITSL]. (2018). *Accreditation of initial teacher education programs in Australia: Standards and procedures.* Author. Retrieved from https://www.aitsl.edu.au/docs/default-source/default-document-library/accreditation-of-initial-teacher-education-programs-in-australia_jan_2019.pdf?sfvrsn=4639f33c_2.

Bair, M. A. (2016). Professionalism: a comparative case study of teachers, nurses, and social workers. *Educational Studies, 42*(5), 450–464. https://doi.org/10.1080/03055698.2016.1219651.

Barber, B. (1965). Some problems in the sociology of the professions. In K. S. Lynn (Edt.), *The Professions in America* (pp. 669–688). Boston: Houghton Mifflin.

Bergeron, P. J., & Rivard, L. (2017). How to engage in pseudoscience with real data: A criticism of John Hattie's arguments in visible learning from the perspective of a statistician. *McGill Journal of Education/Revue des sciences de l'éducation de McGill, 52*(1), 237–246. https://doi.org/10.7202/1040816ar.

Brennan, M. (1996) Multiple professionalism for Australian teachers in the information age? Paper presented at the annual meeting of the American Educational Research Association, New York.

Biesta, G. (2017). Education, measurement, and the professions: Reclaiming a space for democratic professionality in education. *Educational Philosophy and Theory, 49*(4), 315–330. https://doi.org/10.1080/00131857.2015.1048665.

Bronfenbrenner, U. (1979). *The ecology of human development: Experiments by nature and design.* Cambridge, MA: Harvard University Press.

Bronfenbrenner, U. (2005). *Making human beings human: Bioecological perspectives on human development.* Thousand Oaks, CA: Sage.

Committee for the Review of Teaching and Teacher Education. (2003). *Australia's teachers: Australia's future: Advancing innovation, science, technology and mathematics.* Canberra, ACT: Department for Education, Science and Training. Retrieved from http://research.aceredu.au/tll_misc/1/.

Corcoran, T. C. (1995). *Transforming professional development for teachers: A guide of state policymakers.* Washington: National Governors' Association.

Craven, G., Beswick, K., Fleming, J., Fletcher, T., Green, M., Jensen, B., et al. (2014). *Action now: Classroom ready teachers.* Retrieved from https://docs.education.gov.au/system/files/doc/other/action_now_classroom_ready_teachers_print.pdf.

Creasy, K. L. (2015). Defining professionalism in teacher education programs. *Journal of Education & Social Policy, 2*(2), 23–25.

Darling-Hammond, L. (2010). Teacher education and the American future. *Journal of Teacher Education, 61*(1), 35–47.

David, C. (2000). *Professionalism and ethics in teaching.* London: Taylor & Francis Books Ltd.

Department of Education and Training, (2017). *The Higher Education Standards Panel's advice on the impacts of professional accreditation in higher education.* Retrieved from https://docs.education.gov.au/system/files/doc/other/higher_education_standards_panel_advice_on_professional_accreditation_0.pdf.

Dinham, S. (2013). The quality teaching movement in Australia encounters difficult terrain: A personal perspective. *Australian Journal of Education, 57*(2), 91–106.

Etzioni, A. (1969). *The semi-professionals and their organization: Teachers, nurses and social workers.* New York: Free Press.

Evans, L. (2008). Professionalism, professionality and the development of education profession als. *British Journal of Educational Studies, 56*(1), 20.

Evetts, J. (2006). Introduction: Trust and professionalism: Challenges and occupational changes. *Current Sociology, 54*(4), 515–531.

Evetts, J. (2008). The management of professionalism. In S. Gewirtz, P. Mahony, I. Hextall, & A. Cribb (Eds.), *Changing teacher professionalism: International trends, challenges and ways forward* (pp. 19–30). Hoboken, NJ: Routledge.

Evetts, J. (2010). Reconnecting professional occupations with professional organizations: Risks and opportunities. In L. Svensson & J. Evetts (Eds.), *Sociology of professions: Continental and Anglo-Saxon traditions* (pp. 123–144). Daidalos: Göteborg.

Evetts, J. (2011). Sociological analysis of professionalism: Past, present and future. *Comparative Sociology, 10*(1), 1–37.

Evetts, J. (2012). Professionalism in turbulent times: Changes, challenges and opportunities. Paper presented at the ProPEL Conference: Professionalism in Turbulent Times: Changes, Challenges and Opportunities.

Evetts, J. (2014). The concept of professionalism: Professional work, professional practice and learning. In Billett S, C Harteis, H Gruber (Eds.), International Handbook of Research in Professional and Practice-based Learning. Springer International Handbooks of Education.

Freidson, E. (2001). *Professionalism: The third logic.* Chicago, IL.: The University of Chicago Press.

Garden, D. (1982). *The Melbourne teacher training colleges: From training institution to Melbourne State College 1870–1982.* Richmond, VIC: Heinemann Educational Australia.

Gewirtz, S., Mahony, P., Hextall, I., & Cribb, A. (Eds.). (2009). *Changing Teacher Professionalism: International Trends, Challenges and Ways Forward.* London: Routledge.

Goodson, I., & Hargreaves, A. (1996). Teachers' professional lives: Aspirations and actualities. In I. Goodson & A. Hargreaves (Eds.), *Teachers' professional lives* (pp. 1–27). London: Falmer Press.

Hargreaves, A. (2000). Four ages of professionalism and professional learning. *Teachers and Teaching 6*(x), 151–182.

Hargreaves, A., & Goodson, I. (1996). Teachers' professional lives: Aspirations and actualities. In I. Goodson & A. Hargreaves (Eds.), *Teachers' professional lives*, (pp. 1–27). London: Falmer Press.

Hayes, A., & Hegarty, P. (2002). Why teaching is not a profession—and how it might become one. *Education 3–13, 30*(1), 30–35. https://doi.org/10.1080/03004270285200071.

Heck, D., & Ambrosetti, A. (2018). Reclaiming educator professionalism in and for uncertain times. In D. Heck & A. Ambrosetti (Eds.), *Teacher education in and for uncertain times* (pp. 1–13). Singapore: Springer.

Inlow, G. M. (1956). Is teaching a profession? *The School Review, 64*(6), 256–259.

Johnston, J. L. (2015). Issues of professionalism and teachers: Critical observations from research and the literature. *Australian Educational Researcher, 42*(3), 299–317.

Leiter, J. (1978). *The effects of school control structures on teacher perceptions of autonomy.* ERIC.

Louden, W., & Wallace, J. (1993). Competency standards in teaching: Exploring the case. *Unicorn, 19*(1), 45–53.

Marginson, S. (1999). Education and the trends to markets. *Australian Journal of Education, 43*(3), 229–243.

McMeniman, M. (2004). *Review of the powers and functions of the Board of Teacher Registration.* Retrieved from http://www.qct.edu.au/PDF/CSU/btrfinal.pdf.

National Project on the Quality of Teaching and Learning [NPQTL]. (1996). *National competency framework for beginning teachers.* Leichardt, NSW: Australian Teaching Council.

Phillips, K. P. A. (2017). *Professional Accreditation: Mapping the Territory.* Retrieved from https://docs.education.gov.au/system/files/doc/other/professional_accreditation_mapping_final_report.pdf.

Professions Australia & Universities Australia. (2016). *Joint Statement of Principles for Professional Accreditation.* Retrieved from http://www.professions.com.au/images/Joint_Statement_of_Principles_for_Professional_Accreditation_-_2016-03-09_SIGNING.pdf.

Ramsey, G. (2000). *Quality Matters: Revitalising teaching, critical times, critical choices.* Sydney, NSW: NSW Department of Education and Training.

Reynolds, M. (1999). Standards and professional practice: The TTA and initial teaching training. *British Journal of Educational Studies, 47*(3), 247–260.

Sachs, J. (2000). Rethinking the practice of teacher professionalism. In C. Day, A. Fernandez, T. E. Hauge, & J. Moller (Eds.), *The Life and work of teachers: International perspectives in changing times* (pp. 76–90). Abingdon, UK: Routledge Farmer.

Sachs, J. (2003). *The activist teaching profession.* Buckingham: Open University Press.

Sachs, J. (2016). Teacher professionalism: why are we still talking about it? *Teachers and Teaching,* *22*(4), 413–425. https://doi.org/10.1080/13540602.2015.1082732.

Salaran, M. (2010). Research productivity and social capital in Australian higher education. *Higher Education Quarterly, 64*(2), 133–148.

Snoek, M. (no date). *Theories on and Concepts of Professionalism of Teachers and Their Consequences for the Curriculum in Teacher Education*, http://www.hva.nl/kenniscentrum-doo/wpcontent/uploads/2012/04/Theories-on-and-concepts-of-professionalism-Hungarian-publication.pdf.

Snoek, M., Swennen, A., & van der Klink, M. (2009). The teacher educator: a neglected factor in the contemporary debate on teacher education. In B. Hudson (Ed.), *Proceedings of the TEPE 3rd annual conference teacher education policy in Europe: Quality in teacher education,* 288–299. Umeå: Umeå University.

Southwick, J. (1997). *National Competition policy and the professions: Can the professions survive under a national competition policy?* Retrieved from http://www.professions.com.au/advocacy/archives/item/national-competition-policy-the-professions-1997.

Whitty, G. (1994). *Deprofessionalising teaching? Recent developments in teacher education in England.* Deakin, ACT: Australian College of Education.

Dr. Colette Alexander is Senior Lecturer in the School of Education at the Australian Catholic University. She is an experienced teacher educator who has worked with preservice and practicing teachers across both public and private institutions. Her current research and teaching is focussed on research methodology, policy and assessment. She is the Project Lead for the implementation of the Graduate Teacher Performance Assessment (GTPA) across the School of Education and is an early career researcher working with the Institute for Learning Sciences and Teacher Education (ILSTE).

Jillian L. Fox is Associate Professor in the Faculty of Education and Arts at the Australian Catholic University. She is an experienced early childhood teacher who has worked with preservice and practicing teachers both in Australia and China. Her areas of teaching and research expertise include work integrated learning, mentoring and early years education. In 2017, she won the Vice Chancellor's Award for Innovation for her work on establishing a university wide work integrated learning online platform.

Dr. Amanda Gutierrez is a Senior Lecturer and Professional Experience Coordinator (Secondary Postgrad Courses) in the QLD School of Education at the Australian Catholic University. She is an experienced teacher educator who works in the fields of literacy, professional experience and partnerships. Her major research interest is professional becoming of preservice and practicing teachers and partnerships, with a minor research interest in critical literacy. She has developed and coordinated multiple partnership programmes in Victoria and Queensland.

Part I
Social and Political Context

Chapter 2
The Changing Face of Accreditation for Initial Teacher Education Programmes in Australia

Theresa Bourke

Abstract This chapter uses discourse analysis techniques associated with Foucauldian archaeology to ascertain the dominant discourses in the 2015 Australian Initial Teacher Education accreditation document. Findings reveal an overarching discourse of quality assurance anchored within the discursive themes of accreditation, evidence and impact. When these discursive themes are juxtaposed against the academic literature on professionalism, it becomes clear that teacher educators are being discursively repositioned in a managerial discourse. Recommendations are given for how teacher educators can navigate this highly regulated environment.

1 Previous Research—The Policy Context

In previous publications by the current author and colleagues (see Bourke, Ryan, & Lloyd, 2016; Bourke, Ryan, & Ould, 2018), the Australian Institute for Teaching and School Leadership's (AITSL) policy document, *Accreditation of Initial Teacher Education Programs in Australia: Standards and Procedures* (AITSL, 2011) was analysed to ascertain the discourses prioritised in positioning graduate teachers in Initial Teacher Education (ITE). Findings revealed two discourses: (1) a discourse of quality; and (2) a discourse of being professional. Not denying the interrelationship, in light of the theme for this book, only the latter is the focus of this chapter.

Policy analysis of the 2011 accreditation document revealed two themes in the discourse of being professional, namely professional knowledge and professional practice. What we wanted to find out was did the 2011 policy discourse of being professional align with definitions of professionalism from the academic archive and, if so, which ones? Findings revealed "practical" or "flexible" (Goodson & Hargreaves, 1996) professionalism discourses, what Beck (2009) has referred to as "performative professionalism". This discourse, however, has been criticised for relying on tacit knowledge, where educators are cut off from universities. "Democratic", "activist" (Sachs, 2003) and "occupational" discourses (Evetts, 2009) where teachers shape

T. Bourke (✉)
Queensland University of Technology, Brisbane, QLD, Australia
e-mail: theresa.bourke@qut.edu.au

their own lives from within the profession in an "enacted" discourse of professionalism (Evans, 2008, 2011; Evetts, 2009; Hilferty, 2008) were absent. We concluded that graduates were discursively positioned as regulated technicians in a "managerial" professionalism (Sachs, 2003, 2016).

The purpose of this chapter was to continue the story and bring us to the current policy moment by undertaking an analysis of the *Accreditation of Initial Teacher Education Programs in Australia: Standards and Procedures* (AITSL, 2015) document to ascertain if and how things have changed and what the implications might be. This time my interest lies in the positioning of teacher educators, and so the research questions are: (1) how are teacher educators positioned within the 2015 policy document where evidence and impact are prioritised? (2) in what ways do notions of evidence and impact from policy discourses align with the academic literature? and (3) what type of professionalism is being promoted by their positioning? In the spirit of the archaeological approach (Foucault, 1972), recommendations are made for how teacher educators navigate this highly regulated landscape.

2   Background to Accreditation

Education systems in many nations have been subject to the commodification of education to improve teacher quality and efficiency (Solbrekke & Sugrue, 2014). Initial Teacher Education (ITE) is no exception with externally imposed measures of accountability. "Assuring quality" through accreditation is a method that fits well with this market-oriented way of thinking. Some countries have a longer history with these processes. For example, in the USA the National Council for Accreditation of Teacher Education (NCATE) founded in 1954 accredited teacher certification programs in US colleges and universities. Now amalgamated with the Teacher Education Accreditation Council (TEAC), the Council for the Accreditation of Educator Preparation (CAEP) is now the only specialised accreditor of US educator preparation programs. According to Brittingham (2008), American education has become a world leader through successful accreditation processes, and as a result, these moves have become widespread throughout the rest of the world.

Australian teacher educators find themselves entangled in the same accreditation net as their global colleagues. One result has been the need to convince regulatory authorities of program quality. Whilst the commodification of education and the effects on schools has been reported at length, less is documented on the impact on teacher education, especially in Australia. One recent study by Rowe and Skourdoumbis (2017) analysed the Teacher Education Ministerial Advisory Group's (TEMAG) report *Action Now, Classroom Ready Teachers* (Australian Government, 2015), and reported the concepts of quality and readiness anchored within the themes of impact, data and evidence. This chapter takes their analysis further by investigating how these discourses have translated into the 2015 accreditation document for ITE and what effect such has on the professionalism of teacher educators.

According to Cochran-Smith and Lytle (2004), teacher educators have to function simultaneously as researcher and practitioner. In what they refer to as "working the dialectic", the third part of the job is to interrogate all policies that have an impact on education. Therefore, with the revisions outlined in the current accreditation document, using discourse analysis associated with Foucauldian archaeology, it is timely to examine how this policy shapes the professional landscape for teacher educators' work.

3   Theoretical/Methodological Framework

For Foucault (1995), discourses encompass more than what is said; they are also about what is thought, who can speak and their authority. Therefore, discourses are not just about spoken language but are connected to power relations making it necessary to ascertain authorial intentions (Ball, 1990) in accreditation discourses. In policy, Gale (1999) explains the interdiscursivity of discourses where dominant policy actors serve to "oust … others" (p. 400) leading to a particular group's participation being negated (Freeland, 1994). In this way, only certain voices are heard (Ball, 1994). To this end, the voices that are privileged in the 2015 Australian accreditation policy are outlined. Furthermore, Ball (1990) articulated how policy refers to other policies, exercising power through the production of truth and knowledge as discourse. Referring to this as intertextual compatibility (Ball, 1990), the use of supporting texts is also noted. Therefore, the key players and authoritative texts are outlined in the findings before the four steps of archaeological analysis to reveal the dominant discourses begins.

Step 1 is an examination of the 2015 accreditation document for ITE, looking for statements that repeat. According to Foucault (1972), statements are the atoms of discourse so it is necessary to pay particular attention to the repeatability of terms and words, examining their arrangement and co-location within statements. When statements cohere and make repeatable claims of knowledge, they form discursive practices.

Discourses become "discursive practices" or "regimes of truth" as they convey the message about what is normal, here the establishment of the revised accreditation process in Australia. Foucault elaborates by saying that what needs to be looked for is the status of the truth—does the truth rest on "crumbling soil" (1972, p. 137) or on solid foundations? The key question is what has allowed this revised accreditation document to be read as an unproblematic statement of fact?

Step 2 uncovers distances between statements within the document. In this step (Step 2), any words, phrases or statements which contradict the main discourses identified in Step 1 are described.

Foucault (1972) maintained that archaeology is a comparative analysis that is not intended to reduce the diversity of discourses. The intention, rather, is to have a diversifying effect. For this part of the analysis (Step 3), findings are cross analysed with the academic literature on accreditation, evidence, impact and professionalism to highlight the competing discourses in circulation. Additionally, this cross analysis refers to previous research that analysed the 2011 accreditation document to see what changes have occurred.

Finally, the analysis of transformations (Step 4) makes recommendations for teacher educators working within this accreditation environment.

Before outlining the identified discourses from the policy document, the academic literature on accreditation, evidence, impact and professionalism is overviewed so that comparisons can occur later as part of the archaeological analysis (Step 3).

4 The Academic Archives

4.1 Accreditation

While there remains doubt as to what accreditation means (Collins, 2015) in common speak, accreditation is a quality assurance process under which educational institutions' programmes are evaluated by an external body to determine if standards are met. If standards are met, accredited status is granted by the appropriate agency. Many of these agencies such as the Australian Institute for Teaching and School Leadership (AITSL) mention "quality" and "standards" as their mantra and accreditation as the means by which both will be achieved. However, definitions of "quality" and "standards" are hard to agree upon and accreditation as the solution is still a contested space. Many writers over many years have presented arguments for and against the process. Some see accreditation as a mechanism for enhanced transparency and comparability between institutions thus giving university courses legitimacy (Stensaker, 2011). Fertig (2007) also sees the positives, maintaining that undertaking accreditation involves institutional self-analysis which opens up opportunities for innovative initiatives and enhanced professionalism (Collins, 2015). Supovitz and Taylor (2005) and Guskey (2002) concur, saying that if accreditation is done correctly, whole of programme systemic reform can be a powerful tool for effective change.

However, other writers point to the negative aspects of accreditation. Trends (2007) argues that accreditation often focuses on minimum standards instead of excellence. Rather than concentrating on the public good, the social responsibilities of higher education, such as the need for diversity in student recruitment, are overlooked (Stensaker & Harvey, 2006). What results is a self-protecting process, from an institutional perspective, rather than one of societal accountability. Others (see, e.g., Ewell, 2008) further suggest that accreditation processes are neither cost-effective nor value adding; instead, institutions are stifled by top-down, time-consuming bureaucratic processes which increase workloads resulting in staff demotivation. Some such as Shahjahan (2011) go further, saying that accreditation is a form of cultural imperialism in which Western concepts are exported globally.

Stensaker (2011) posits a useful classification for the key policy drivers in accreditation: (1) accreditation as window dressing; (2) accreditation as organisational adaptation; and (3) accreditation as networked governance. The first one has already been discussed—issues around status and legitimacy. However, according to Stensaker (2011), this could equally relate to external agencies' need to "portray themselves as guardians of the public interest" (p. 762). The second two categories (organisational adaptation and networked governance) also refer to the role of external agencies. Often, regulating authorities will turn to accreditation processes as a way to strengthen their control over academe. Deem, Mok, and Lucas (2008) argue that these administrative processes are part of neoliberal economic and business practices, what they refer to as new managerialism.

To date, there has been little evidence of the correlation between educational improvement and accreditation (Shah, 2012) and indeed the ever-shifting landscape of accreditation makes it hard to conduct timely relevant research. This is true in the Australian context where processes and procedures changed remarkably in the period from 2011 to 2015 with an updated version of the 2015 document this year (2018). These changes are outlined later. It is also noteworthy as part of this rapidly changing environment that the Higher Education Standards Framework (Threshold Standards) 2015 is also under review.

4.2   Evidence

In the current era, evidence-based education, policy and decision-making are increasingly capturing the support of many politicians, policy-makers, practitioners and researchers (Biesta, 2010; Shahjahan, 2011). The origins of this trend vary, some attributing it to Western countries' need for greater accountability (Levin, 2003), others relating it to the influence evidence-based practices have had in other professions such as medicine (Biesta, 2007; Simons, 2003). Whatever the origin, like accreditation, evidence-based education has proponents and opponents.

Through the years, governments and teacher educator researchers alike have been critical of research in education. Many phrases have been used for this including "small-scale", "out of touch", "low quality" and of "little obvious policy relevance" (see, e.g., Biesta, 2007; Rowe & Skourdoumbis, 2017; White, 2016). In response to this, proponents for evidence-based practices argue that experimental or randomised control trials are preferable research designs, as they are less biased by researchers' interests (Blunkett, 2000). Indeed, Shahjahan (2011) notes "survey data" as the most common research design for supporting federal policy. This shows that quantitative research (Slavin, 2002) is foregrounded in policy decision-making and promoted "as the only method capable of providing secure evidence about what works" (Biesta, 2007, p. 3).

However, many writers from a critical perspective have argued that the delegitimisation of educational research is not true (see Olson, 2004; Ryan & Hood, 2004; Simpson, 2017) with an emerging body of literature growing that challenges evidence-based policy and practices. Some writers, for example Biesta (2007) whilst acknowledging that evidence-based practices have made improvements in other professions such as medicine, questions their use in education. He argues that interventions to increase effectiveness which are premised on if "we do A, B will follow" (Biesta, 2010, p. 494) would not work in education as there are too many factors to consider in the learning process. Other opponents to evidence-based practices allude to further deficits, for example Luke (2003) maintains that evidence-based approaches further marketise education through textbook production, consultancies and in-service training. Shahjahan's (2011) view is that evidence-based education merely perpetuates a colonial discourse. This writer calls for a deceleration around evidence-based educational policy and practice. In line with this way of thinking, Marilyn Cochran-Smith has highlighted the absence of cultural understandings in approaches to use evidence. With her colleagues from the Boston College Evidence Team, they identify four dimensions for a more nuanced approach to evidence involving: (1) development of a portfolio; (2) recognition that teacher education always poses values and empirical questions; (3) an exploratory, open-ended approach to evidence construction; and, (4) multiple structures for evidence collection, locally and beyond (Cochran-Smith & the Boston College Evidence Team, 2009). With their reference to include values-based questions in teacher education, it appears that they concur with Biesta (2007, 2010).

Basing professional practice on evidence appears as a very sound argument. However, there are many questions for consideration, including what counts as evidence, where does the evidence come from and how is the evidence used? Regardless of which side of the debate you sit on, calls for evidence-based practices in education are persistent.

4.3 Impact

The word impact is Latin in origin stemming from the word impactus, the past participle of impingere which means to push against. The definition that aligns most closely with the rising importance of impact in education is to have an effect or to influence. In the most recent accreditation document, this is spelled out in terms of the impact teacher education programmes based on the Australian Professional Standards for Teachers (APSTs) must have on the learning of preservice teachers. Then as graduates, it is assumed that they will impact on school-student learning.

The approach to "teacher quality" in Australia has been heavily influenced by the work of John Hattie who is the chair/non-executive director of AITSL. Hattie's research focuses on effect size studies which estimate the educational impact of interventions. This has centred on his meta-analyses of learning and achievement (2003, 2009). Hattie (2009) advocates for learning that is visible—in other words, impact that is demonstrated statistically. However, as already mentioned, there are many objections to this way of thinking in education. Recently, Simpson (2017), referring to policy contexts in education, has suggested that "educational policy has fallen prey to metricophilia, the unjustified faith in numerical quantities as having special status as evidence" (p. 14). Moreover, statisticians such as Bergeron and Rivard

(2017) have criticised Hattie's work for being methodologically flawed. Nevertheless, organisations like Evidence for Learning, (with links to Hattie) and their toolkit of 34 evidence-based teaching approaches have entered the Australian educational landscape. This organisation, supported by Social Ventures, Australia, the Commonwealth Bank of Australia and the Education Endowment Foundation from the UK, has limited grounding in education revealing further concerns about market-based approaches in education.

The 2015 accreditation document acknowledges the challenges of measuring teachers' impact on student learning and indeed the Teacher Education Ministerial Advisory Group—TEMAG (Australian Government, 2015) identified a lack of research about what practices result in impact. In the light of this, AITSL released position papers in their 2015 Insights publications detailing strategies for demonstrating impact such as classroom observations, portfolios and satisfaction surveys. Although these strategies were put forward as viable measures for demonstrating impact, many criticisms were posited. For example, classroom observation instruments often lack reliability and credibility (Caughlan & Jiang, 2014), portfolios can privilege good writers over good teachers (Gore, 2015) and satisfaction surveys reveal inadequacies in terms of response rates, biases and power relations (Gore, 2015). In more recent work, the Australian Teacher Educators' Association's (ATEA) publication titled *Teacher Education: Innovation, Intervention and Impact* (Brandenburg, McDonough, Burke, & White, 2016a), presented an array of research projects from all over Australia showcasing strategies for impact such as paired placement models (Gutierrez, 2016), and carefully constructed internships (Jervis-Tracey & Finger, 2016) to name but two. This shows that universities are trialling different teaching approaches for measuring impact. However, the guidelines for the 2015 accreditation document, particularly Program Standards 1.4 and 6.3 list employment data, registration data, principal and graduate satisfaction surveys, student experience surveys, case studies, aggregated assessment data on for example the Teaching Performance Assessment as mechanisms for demonstrating impact. Therefore, it appears that for the most part, evidence of impact is limited to data collections.

4.4 Professionalism

Throughout the years, much has been written on the concept of professionalism, with many attempts to provide a definition for this term, and even more government-led agendas calling for higher degrees of professionalism in education. The academic literature around professionalism has been reported at length elsewhere (see Bourke, 2011; Sachs, 2003, 2016) so will be summarised in the interests of space and confined to discourses from the 1990s onwards as this is when various types of professionalism were posited by writers in response to criticisms of the classical/traditional discourses of professionalism based on medicine and law. Over many years, various nomenclatures have been used for professionalism discourses, but most academics

Table 1 Discourses of professionalism

"New professionalism" discourses	"Manageria" professionalism discourses
Flexible, practical, extended, complex and postmodern (Goodson & Hargreaves, 1996)	Commercialised (Hanlon, 1998)
New and principled (Goodson, 1999)	Managerial (Sachs, 2003, 2016)
Transformative, democratic, collaborative and activist (Sachs, 2003, 2016)	Compliant, controlled (Sachs, 2016)
Enacted (Evans, 2008, 2011; Hilferty, 2007, 2008)	
Occupational (Evetts, 2009)	Organisational (Evetts, 2009)
Deduced, assumed (Evans, 2008, 2011)	Demanded, required, prescribed (Evans, 2008, 2011)
Reflexive (Bourke, Ryan, & Lidstone, 2013)	

agree on two schools of thought on how the concept is viewed—a "new profession-alism" discourse and a "managerial" discourse. These are summarised in Table 1.

"New professionalism" discourses equate to teachers as professionals working with the cognitive dimensions of knowledge and the emotional dimensions of teaching for the greater good of the teaching profession. Alternatively, in response to accountability agendas, professionalism has been colonised by governments, rewritten and redefined in a managerial discourse that sees teachers as unquestioning supporters and implementers of a competency-based, outcome-oriented pedagogy related to the world of work (Robertson, 1996). Nevertheless, despite these competing discourses, there is some agreement between researchers that three criteria are essential for being professional: knowledge, autonomy and responsibility (Leaton Gray & Whitty, 2010). However, as Furlong (2005) reminds us, "the nature of teacher professionalism, [and] what it means to be a teacher [educator], has been a central area of concern for successive governments" (p. 120) for the last 30 years. In 2018, this still appears to be the case in education.

5 Findings—Discourse Analysis of *Accreditation of Initial Teacher Education Programs in Australia: Standards and Procedures*, 2015

5.1 Key Players and Authoritative Texts

The *Accreditation of Initial Teacher Education Programs in Australia: Standards and Procedures* (AITSL, 2015) is an online policy consisting of 31 pages and divided into five sections: the Preamble; Explanatory Information; National Program Standards; Graduate Teacher Standards; and National Accreditation Procedures. Since the implementation of the original accreditation process in 2011, AITSL have conducted a number of reviews. However, there are limited details about what the review processes involved. Apart from saying that the "expertise and vision of teacher educators, employers of teachers, those in the teaching profession, in schools and early childhood settings and the broader education community" (p. 2), stakeholders are not named in the policy. Thanks are given to the expert input from state and territory education authorities, teacher regulatory authorities and the Australian Council of Deans of Education (ACDE) but again with no stakeholders' names it is difficult to determine the authority behind these voices. Interestingly, the expert group were specifically named and acknowledged in the 2011 accreditation document; therefore, authority was known.

With regard to authoritative texts, six are referenced in the 2015 accreditation document, namely the threshold Higher Education Standards as established by the Tertiary Education Quality and Standards Agency Act 2011 (TEQSA Act 2011); the Education Services Overseas Students Act 2000 (ESOS Act 2000); the 2014 TEMAG report *Action now: Classroom ready teachers* (Australian Government, 2015); the Australian Curriculum (Australian Curriculum Assessment and Reporting Authority (ACARA), 2014); the Early Years Learning Framework for Australia (EYLF), 2009); and the Australian Children's Education and Care Quality Authority (ACECQA), 2012) guidelines. These are all either government reports or curriculum documents; there are no references to academic literature.

5.2   *Dominant Discourses in the Accreditation Document*

There is one overarching discourse in the 2015 accreditation document—a discourse of quality assurance. For clarity, the critique of this discourse is divided into four discursive themes, namely (1) accreditation; (2) evidence; (3) impact; and (4) assessment. The latter discursive theme of assessment is minor and confined to the Program Standards so will not be reported here due to word length restrictions.

5.2.1   Discursive Theme of Accreditation

The word accreditation or some form of it, for example "accrediting", appears 100 times in this document leaving the reader no doubt that accreditation is the chosen mechanism for "quality assurance". The repetition of statements (Step 1) such as the "accreditation process" and "accrediting ITE programs" (p. 2) makes it clear that all ITE providers must undertake accreditation "to ensure every program is preparing classroom ready teachers with the skills they need to make a positive impact on school student learning" (p. 2). Described as "essential" (p. 2) and "rigorous" (p. 2), accreditation is said to contribute "to the improvement of the quality of ITE" (p. 3). The notion conveyed is that accreditation will solve the current perceived lack of quality in ITE. This reveals that teacher educators are positioned in a deficit discourse and in need of help from the outside. Statements such as regulatory authorities will "actively lead and implement" (p. 2) the standards support this deficit notion, further marginalising teacher educators from the discourse.

The rhetoric of agreement at a national level in accreditation is evident in statements such as "nationally accredited", and "nationally consistent assessment of evidence", "assuring robust and nationally consistent decisions" (p. 3). However, education in the federation of Australia has always been the realm and the responsibility of the state governments. Even though it is explained that "jurisdictional teacher authorities … in their local (state) context" will be in charge (p. 2), the messages appear to be in contradiction to each other. The burning question is: can we be sure that all state-based regulatory authorities and their panels, interpret and evaluate evidence in the same way?

In the Explanatory Information and National Accreditation Procedures sections, accreditation is mentioned a further 62 times co-located (Step 1) with "application for accreditation" (p. 26), "panel" (p. 27), "report", "recommendation" (p. 28), "decision(s)" (p. 28, 30) and "status" (p. 30). What is clear from the repetition and co-location of words is that accreditation is a defined procedure and ITE providers must apply to gain accredited status. This is in contradiction (Step 2) with the use of the word "flexibility" (p. 3) where providers are encouraged to be "innovative" (p. 3) in their practices.

5.2.2   Discursive Theme of Evidence

In the preamble, evidence is mentioned five times (Step 1) specifically pointing out two distinct but related types of evidence: (1) evidence of preservice teacher performance from within a programme; and (2) evidence of graduate outcomes collected at the completion of a program. Throughout the rest of the document, evidence is mentioned 45 times in total (Step 1) with various co-locations: "interpretation of the evidence … collected" (p. 5); "evidence of program impact" (pp. 7, 29); "evidence of the validity and reliability of the teaching performance assessment" (p. 8); and "evidence supplied against the … standards" (p. 30). The lexical linking across these statements reveals that not only do teacher educators have to deliver quality courses and graduates but they have to provide reliable evidence of doing so. This evidence must show impact on outcomes and be measurable against the standards, locking academics in a never-ending cycle of reporting their worth. While there are no specific contradictions within this discursive theme, what is noteworthy is that the word "data" is often used interchangeably. Co-located with words such as "publically available" (p. 2), and "aggregated" (p. 7) and mentioned 27 times in the programme standards, data collections such as satisfaction surveys and employment and registration data are prioritised as mechanisms for showing impact. Teacher educators must use data to provide evidence of "what counts".

5.2.3 Discursive Theme of Impact

The word impact is mentioned 38 times (Step 1) and prioritised as a principle linked to the first two discourses—accreditation and evidence. Co-located eight times with "demonstrating", the notion conveyed is that ITE courses must have a "positive impact" (p. 3) on preservice teachers' performance and graduate outcomes so that they in turn will have a "positive impact on school student learning" (p. 2) "throughout their career" (p. 9). It appears that the taken-for-granted solution to produce impact is using evidence through accreditation processes, where impact, for the most is narrowly defined as numbers.

5.3 Cross-Analysis: Structural Changes and the Key Players and Authoritative Texts in the Accreditation Document—2011 to 2015

The 2015 accreditation process is made up of the same elements as the 2011 document, namely the National Graduate Teacher Standards, National Program Standards and the National Accreditation process. However, there is a distinct change in the order of these elements. The 2011 document foregrounds the Graduate Standards, whereas the Program Standards are given priority in 2015. This shift foregrounds teacher education and represents a direct intervention into the programmes delivered by universities in terms of development, design, entry, structure, content, outcomes and the reporting of such.

There is also a move towards a more prescribed process with the addition of an Explanatory Notes section and a guidelines manual (*Guidelines for Accreditation of Initial Teacher Education Programs in Australia (2016)*) outlining in more detail than ever before what ITE institutions have to do to obtain accredited status. It is clear that these notes/guidelines with associated templates eliminate state variations and put forward compulsory ways of working at a national level so that regulatory authorities can steer at a distance on behalf of the government. Rowe and Skourdoumbis (2017) describe the use of "numerous, sizeable, lengthy documents" as "confounding" in accreditation processes (p. 8). However, as revealed in *Insights: Outcomes of the 2015 National Initial Teacher Education Accreditation Panel Review, November 2015* this prescription was requested by teacher educators "to support a consistent layout and ordering of content to enable panels to more efficiently navigate applications" (p. 5). However, what often results from such prescription is a genre focused less on improvements in quality, the espoused aim and more on the management of the accreditation process. Obtaining accreditation becomes operational and more about how effectively ITEs can follow the guidelines (Rowe & Skourdoumbis, 2017).

What the 2011 and 2015 documents do have in common are short consultation times. Commentators such as Louden (2000) have criticised short timeframes contending that time must be taken to consult to the depths required. Although different policies are used as supporting texts, like in 2011, they are all government documents continuing the self-referential policy cycle of accreditation as the truth; academic research is absent. On closer analysis of, for example, the authors behind TEMAG, one of the authoritative texts, it becomes apparent that only two members of the Advisory Group have ever had any classroom experience—as Rowe and Skourdoumbis (2017) report, the "specialism of education, with a professional knowledge base that requires expertise and first-hand experience, is largely omitted" (p. 7). All these moves position teacher educators as deficit. This logic of deficiency then allows the so-called necessary intervention of accreditation. Ball (1995) maintains that this indicates a transition away from "intellectual intelligence to technical rationalism" (p. 267) reshaping the professionalism of teacher educators.

5.3.1   Competing Discourses in Circulation (Step 3)

When the identified discourses from the 2015 accreditation document are juxtaposed against the accreditation academic archive, the intent of this document becomes clear—quality assurance. Here, accreditation is not seen as a contested space but as the taken-for-granted solution to assuring "quality" and "being professional" (the discourses from 2011) in ITE. Using Stensaker's (2011) classification, it is obvious that organisational adaptation and networked governance are adopted by regulatory authorities to position themselves as powerful actors, the document categorically stating that they will "lead" and "implement" (p. 2). They are the ultimate authors as they approve or reject applications. There are also elements of accreditation as window dressing: regulatory authorities portraying themselves as the gatekeepers of the public good. This is evident in statements such as [re]"accreditation will provide assurance of graduate teacher quality and building public confidence in the profession" (p. 3).

   In terms of evidence, it is very clear that regulatory authorities determine "what counts" as evidence—here narrowly defined as evidence of preservice teacher performance and graduate outcomes. The language used is that of performativity which privileges measurable outcome goals (Ball, 2003). "Data" and evidence are used interchangeably, foregrounding quantitative ways of working. Rowe and Skourdoumbis' (2017) analysis of TEMAG (an authoritative text) revealed that evidence was mentioned 134 times and data/data sets mentioned 82 times in statements such as "preservice teachers must learn how to collect, use and analyse student data to improve student outcomes and their own teaching" (p. 20). This is indicative of a clinical practice model for teaching which TEMAG openly advocates. As already pointed out, Biesta (2007, 2010) warns that evidence-based practices and medical model approaches are not appropriate in education. He maintains that evidence cannot replace value judgements by autonomous professionals. Moreover, Biesta (2015) contends that defining education as achievement alone is one-dimensional, negating the other purposes of education like socialisation (ways of being and doing) and subjectification (student as person). The language of performativity, calculation and effectiveness in this document sees value replace values (Ball, 2003; Biesta, 2010).

However, when the discourse of evidence is viewed in the light of work by Cochran-Smith and colleagues from the Boston College Evidence Team (2009), the inclusion of Teaching Performance Assessments (TPAs) as a type of portfolio fulfils some of the principles for a more nuanced, exploratory, open-ended approach to evidence gathering.

The last discursive theme from the accreditation document for cross analysis is that of impact. To recap, "teacher quality" has been defined in terms of the impact teacher education programmes have on preservice teachers (PSTs) who, as graduates, will impact on school-student learning; impact defined as qualification only (Biesta, 2015). However, the circular logic portrayed here is problematic as it assumes a simple and simplistic continuity from initial teacher education to school-student learning (Fenstermacher & Richardson, 2005) which is difficult if not impossible to identify (Meiers & Ingvarson, 2005). As Brandenburg, McDonagh, Burke, and White (2016b) argue, "the research, policy and practice connection is often non-linear, complex and cyclical" (p. 1). Biesta (2010) reminds us that education is a moral non-causal practice with a lot of factors in need of consideration in the learning process.

So far, we have seen that teacher educators have been silenced, positioned as lacking and in need of help from external authorities to improve quality, in effect marginalised from the policy discourse. We have also ascertained that the policy discourses around accreditation, evidence and impact promote accreditation as quality assurance, evidence and impact as quantifiable. This short summary answers the first two research questions: (1) how are teacher educators positioned within the 2015 policy document where evidence and impact are prioritised? and (2) in what ways do notions of evidence and impact from policy discourses align with the academic literature? The next section responds to the third research question: what type of professionalism is being promoted by their positioning?

Professionalism was once seen as a discourse of resistance or the "enemy" of economic rationalism and the discourse of performativity (Sanguinetti, 2000, p. 241). However, as can be seen in this analysis, governments, through the use of various policy technologies such as intertextuality and interdiscursivity, have hijacked and remodelled the notion to promote their redefined version of professionalism—a managerial, controlled or compliant professionalism (Sachs, 2016). Evetts (2009) refers to this as organisational professionalism or professionalism from above. This is visible in the top-down bureaucratic standardised work procedures imposed by external authorities to make teacher educators auditable and accountable. Accreditation anchored in evidence/data and impact discourses and enshrined with distrust for academics is a blatant attempt to codify the work of teacher educators so that they can be controlled from a distance, what Beck (2009) refers to as performative professionalism. A decade ago and in reference to teachers, Evans (2008) named this as a process of de-professionalisation at work. Teacher educators are now in the same position.

The last step in archaeology is the analysis of transformations (Step 4) which makes recommendations for teacher educators working within this highly regulated environment.

6 Recommendations

It is important to stress that academics should be held accountable but how this is achieved will make a difference for the preferred version of professionalism for teacher educators. Accountability according to Halstead (1994) can be either contractual or responsive. Contractual accountability is bureaucratic and usually takes the form of standards and is measurement driven. Responsive discourses rely on self-regulation and are process oriented: a democratic culture of accountability. Writers such as Ravitch (2010) maintain that a good accountability system needs professional judgement; one of the major characteristics of professionalism, not just a score based on achievement. So what discourses of professionalism can teacher educators promote despite prescription by accreditation?

Research by Furlong (2013) and Ellis and McNicholl (2015) argues that teacher education has to "re-tool" in this highly accredited environment. By this they mean working in collaboration with education stakeholders for knowledge mobilisation and research. Furlong (2013) promotes Hoyle's (1974) notions of extended professionality and Hirst's (1996) practical theories to advocate for practical wisdom. This means teachers and teacher educators partnering to develop state-of-the-art practices underpinned by research.

One way of doing this is by working with partners—teachers in schools—to implement the new elements of the 2015 accreditation process, for example primary specialisations. Research around the enactment of these new policy elements will be crucial for bridging the divisions between teacher education at university and practices in schools. These collaborative partnerships will result in collective wisdom with associated transfer of knowledge to inform teaching practices in original and creative ways for the good of universities and schools. Collaboration and collegiality are key characteristics of new or collaborative professionalism, to use Sachs' (2016) terminology.

A second way is within the university itself. Rather than academics working in silos which has often been commonplace, a process of "joint inquiry" (Stosich, 2016) should be adopted where teacher educators work together across courses for teaching the knowledge and skills necessary for the TPA, for example. Rather than seeing the TPA as a compliance mechanism, it could be a chance for innovation, improvement and effective change (Guskey, 2002; Supovitz & Taylor, 2005). All policies are interpreted and translated in local contexts so teacher educators have "wriggle room" to craft and maintain a strong sense of local identity and integrity of practice. In this way, transformative professionalism discourses are dominant, where inquiry, discretionary judgement and being policy active are foregrounded (Sachs, 2003).

Recently I have been part of my university's panel to assess the TPA which includes an oral dimension. Not only did the preservice teachers' presentations display knowledge and skills to demonstrate impact, Evans' (2011) three components of professionalism, namely behavioural, intellectual and attitudinal, were clearly evident. New professionalism discourses (Goodson, 1999) embrace the emotional as well as the cognitive dimensions of teaching and should not be excluded just because they are difficult to measure. We cannot lose sight of the moral and social purposes of education.

Rowe and Skourdoumbis (2017), in response to recent educational reform in Australia including accreditation, set a challenge stating:

> It is important ... for scholars to disrupt and interrupt these proposed imaginaries, by endeavouring to influence not only how they become established as policy truths but also by exposing the power relationships that they exert on people and particular fields of scholarship like education. Scholars need to consistently illuminate the discrepancies within these reforms to the broader public. (p. 12)

This chapter has responded to this challenge through the lens of activist professionalism (Sachs, 2003, 2016) by revealing repetition and co-location in policy documents, the silencing of academic voices and self-referential policy cycles as the strategies to establish accreditation as a discursive practice, a productive form of power. Teacher educators have been discursively repositioned as being out of touch, side-lined and condemned to window dressing the implementation of top-down directives from regulatory authorities. By "working the dialectic" (Cochran-Smith & Lytle, 2004), the truth of accreditation as necessary rests on shaky ground. However, the discourses around accreditation, evidence and impact have been normalised, the regime of truth for quality and professionalism in tertiary education. Sachs maintained that all teachers should be involved and respond to issues that relate to education and schooling, reclaiming the professional agenda to "make things happen rather than to let things happen to them" (Sachs, 2003, p. 144). The paper provides a strong argument that echoes this call to action and urges teacher educators to become part of the culture that expects to challenge and interrogate taken-for-granted practices and enter the public sphere in doing so.

References

Australian Children's Education and Care Quality Authority (ACECQA). (2012). *National quality framework*. Sydney: ACECQA.

Australian Curriculum, Assessment and Reporting Authority (ACARA). (2014). *Australian curriculum*. Sydney: ACARA.

Australian Government. (2015). *Australian Government response: Teacher Education Ministerial Advisory Group, Action now: Classroom ready teachers*. Canberra: Australian Government Department of Education and Training. https://docs.education.gov.au/node/36789.

Australian Institute for Teaching and School Leadership (AITSL). (2011). *Accreditation of initial teacher education programs in Australia: Standards and procedures*. Melbourne: AITSL.

Australian Institute for Teaching and School Leadership (AITSL). (2015). *Accreditation of initial teacher education programs in Australia: Standards and procedures*. Melbourne: AITSL.

Ball, S. (Ed.). (1990). *Foucault and education: Disciplines and knowledge*. London: Routledge.

Ball, S. (1994). *Education reform: A critical and post-structural approach*. Buckingham: Open University Press.

Ball, S. (1995). Intellectuals or technicians? The urgent role of theory in educational studies. *British Journal of Educational Studies, 43*(3), 255–271.

Ball, S. (2003). The teacher's soul and the terrors of performativity. *Journal of Education Policy, 18*(2), 215–228.

Beck, J. (2009). Appropriating professionalism: Restructuring the official knowledge base of England's "modernised" teaching profession. *British Journal of Sociology of Education, 30*(1), 3–14.

Bergeron, P. -J., Rivard, L. (Trans.). (2017). How to engage in pseudoscience with real data: A criticism of john hattie's arguments in visible learning from the perspective of a statistician. McGill Journal of Education/Revue des sciences de l'éducation de McGill, [S.l.], v. 52, n. 1, july 2017. ISSN 1916-0666. Available at: Date accessed: 04 mar. 2019.

Biesta, G. J. (2007). Why "what works" won't work: Evidence-based practice and the democratic deficit in educational research. *Educational Theory, 57*(1), 1–22.

Biesta, G. J. (2010). Why "what works" still won't work: From evidence-based education to value-based education. *Studies in Philosophy and Education, 29*(5), 491–503. https://doi.org/10.1007/s11217-010-9191-x.

Biesta, G. J. (2015). What is education for? On good education, teacher judgement, and educational professionalism. *European Journal of Education, 50*(1), 75–87. https://doi.org/10.1111/ejed.12109.

Blunkett, D. (2000). Influence or irrelevance: Can social science improve government? *Research Intelligence, 71,* 12–21.

Bourke, T. (2011). *Teacher professional standards: Mirage or Miracle Cure. An archaeology of professionalism in education.* Ph.D. thesis, Queensland University of Technology, Brisbane, Australia.

Bourke, T., Ryan, M. E., & Lidstone, J. (2013). Reflexive professionalism: Reclaiming the voice of authority in shaping the discourses of education policy. *Asia-Pacific Journal of Teacher Education, 41*(4), 398–413.

Bourke, T., Ryan, M. E., & Lloyd, M. M. (2016). The discursive positioning of graduating teachers in accreditation of teacher education programs. *Teaching and Teacher Education, 53,* 1–9.

Bourke, T., Ryan, M. E., & Ould, P. (2018). How do teacher educators use professional standards in their practice. *Teaching and Teacher Education, 75,* 83–92.

Brandenburg, R., McDonough, S., Burke, J., & White, S. (Eds.). (2016a). *Teacher education: Innovation, intervention and impact.* Singapore: Springer.

Brandenburg, R., McDonough, S., Burke, J., & White, S. (2016b). Teacher education research and the policy reform agenda. In R. Brandenburg, S. McDonough, J. Burke, & S. White (Eds.), *Teacher education: Innovation, intervention and impact* (pp. 1–14). Singapore: Springer.

Brittingham, B. (2008). An uneasy partnership: Accreditation and the federal government. *Change, 40,* 32–38.

Caughlan, S., & Jiang, H. (2014). Observation and teacher quality: Critical analysis of observation instruments in preservice teacher performance assessment. *Journal of Teacher Education, 65*(5), 375–388.

Cochran-Smith, M., & Lytle, S. L. (2004). Practitioner inquiry, knowledge, and university culture. In J. J. Loughran, M. L. Hamilton, V. K. LaBoskey, & T. Russell (Eds.), *International handbook of self-study of teaching and teacher education practices* (pp. 601–649). New York, NY: Springer.

Cochran-Smith, M., & The Boston College Evidence Team. (2009). "Re-Culturing" teacher education: Inquiry, evidence, and action. *Journal of Teacher Education, 60*(5), 458–468.

Collins, I. (2015). Using international accreditation in higher education to effect changes in organisational culture: A case study from a Turkish university. *Journal of Research in International Education, 14*(2), 141–154.

Deem, R., Mok, K. H., & Lucas, L. (2008). Transforming higher education in whose image? Exploring the concept of the 'World-Class' University in Europe and Asia. *Higher Education Policy, 21,* 83–97.

Department of Education and Training. (2009). Belonging, being and becoming: *The Early Years Learning Framework for Australia* (EYLF). Canberra: Australian Government.

Ellis, V., & McNicholl, J. (2015). *Transforming teacher education: Reconfiguring the academic work.* London: Bloomsbury.

Evans, L. (2008). Professionalism, professionality and the development of education professionals. *British Journal of Educational Studies, 56*(1), 20–38.

Evans, L. (2011). The 'shape' of teacher professionalism in England: Professional standards, performance management, professional development and the changes proposed in the 2010 White Paper. *British Educational Research Journal, 37*(5), 851–870.

Evetts, J. (2009). The management of professionalism: A contemporary paradox. In S. Gewirtz, P. Mahony, I. Hextall, & A. Cribb (Eds.), *Changing teacher professionalism: International trends, challenges and ways forward* (pp. 19–30). London: Routledge.

Ewell, J. (2008). *US accreditation and the future of quality assurance*. Washington, DC: The Council for Higher Education Accreditation.

Fenstermacher, G. D., & Richardson, V. (2005). On making determinations of quality in teaching. *Teachers College Record, 107*(1), 186–213.

Fertig, M. (2007). International school accreditation: Between a rock and a hard place? *Journal of Research in International Education, 6*(3), 333–348.

Foucault, M. (1972). *The archaeology of knowledge* (Trans.: A. M. Sheridan Smith). London: Tavistock.

Foucault, M. (1995). *Discipline and punish: The birth of the prison* (Trans.: A. Sheridan). New York, NY: Random House.

Freeland, J. (1994). *Teacher education in the late 1990s: Fighting for a place on the post pluralist policy agenda*. Paper presented at the 24th Teacher Education Association (ATEA) Conference, July, Brisbane, Australia.

Furlong, J. (2005). New labour and teacher education: The end of an era. *Oxford Review of Education, 31*(1), 119–134.

Furlong, J. (2013). *Education—An anatomy of the discipline. Rescuing the university project?* London: Taylor and Francis.

Gale, T. (1999). Policy trajectories: Trending the discursive path of policy analysis. *Discourse: Studies in the Cultural Politics of Education, 20*, 393–407.

Goodson, I. (1999). *Towards a principled professionalism for teaching*. Keynote address presented at the New Professionalism in Teaching Conference, January, Chinese University of Hong Kong.

Goodson, I., & Hargreaves, A. (1996). *Teachers' professional lives*. London: RoutledgeFalmer.

Gore, J. (2015). *Insights: Evidence of impact of teacher education programs: A focus on classroom observation*. A paper prepared for the Australian Institute of Teaching and School Leadership. http://www.aitsl.edu.au/docs/default-source/initial-teacher-education-resources/ite-reform-stimulus-paper-2-gore.pdf.

Guskey, T. R. (2002). Professional development and teacher change. *Teachers and Teaching: Theory and Practice, 8*, 381–391.

Gutierrez, A. (2016). Exploring the becoming of pre-service teachers in paired placement models. In R. Brandenburg, S. McDonough, J. Burke, & S. White (Eds.), *Teacher education: Innovation, intervention and impact* (pp. 139–155). Singapore: Springer.

Halstead, M. (1994). Accountability and values. In D. Scott (Ed.), *Accountability and control in educational settings* (pp. 3–14). London: Castell.

Hanlon, G. (1998). Professionalism as enterprise: Service class politics and the redefinition of professionalism. *Sociology, 32*(1), 43–63.

Hattie, J. (2003). Teachers make a difference. What is the research evidence? *Interpretations, 36*(2), 27–38.

Hattie, J. (2009). *Visible learning: A synthesis of over 800 meta-analyses relating to achievement*. Abingdon: Routledge.

Hilferty, F. (2007). Contesting the curriculum: An examination of professionalism as defined and enacted by Australian history teachers. *Curriculum Inquiry, 37*(3), 239–261.

Hilferty, F. (2008). Theorising teacher professionalism as an enacted discourse of power. *British Journal of Sociology of Education, 29*(2), 161–173.

Hirst, P. H. (1996). The demands of professional practice and preparation for teaching. In J. Furlong & R. Smith (Eds.), *The role of higher education in initial teacher training* (pp. 166–178). London: Kogan Page.

Hoyle, E. (1974). Professionality, professionalism and control in teaching. *London Educational Review, 3*(2), 13–19.

Jervis-Tracey, P., & Finger, G. (2016). Internships in initial teacher education in Australia: A case study of the Griffith Internship. In R. Brandenburg, S. McDonough, J. Burke, & S. White (Eds.), *Teacher education: Innovation, intervention and impact* (pp. 157–174). Singapore: Springer.

Leaton Gray, S., & Whitty, G. (2010). Social trajectories or disrupted identities? Changing and competing models of teacher professionalism under New Labour. *Cambridge journal of education, 40*(1), 5–23.

Levin, B. (2003). *Improving research-policy relationships: Lessons from the case of literacy.* Paper presented at the OISE/UT International Literacy Conference: Literacy Policies for the Schools We Need, November 8, Toronto, Canada.

Louden, W. (2000). Standards for standards: The development of Australian professional standards for teaching. *Australian Journal of Education, 44*(2), 118–134.

Luke, A. (2003). After the market place: Evidence, social science and education research. *Australian Educational Researcher, 30*(2), 87–107.

Meiers, M., & Ingvarson, L. (2005). *Investigating the links between teacher professional development and student learning outcomes.* Barton, ACT: Australian Government, Quality Teacher Program.

Olson, D. R. (2004). The triumph of hope over experience in the search for 'what works': A response to Slavin. *Educational Researcher, 33*(1), 24–26.

Ravitch, D. (2010). *The death and life of the Great American school system: How testing and choice are undermining education.* New York, NY: Basic Books.

Robertson, S. L. (1996). Teachers' work, restructuring and postFordism: Constructing the new 'professionalism'. In I. Goodson & A. Hargreaves (Eds.), *Teachers' professional lives* (pp. 28–55). London: RoutledgeFalmer.

Rowe, E., & Skourdoumbis, A. (2017). Calling for 'urgent national action to improve the quality of initial teacher education': The reification of evidence and accountability in reform agendas. *Journal of Education Policy.* https://doi.org/10.1080/02680939.2017.1410577.

Ryan, K. E., & Hood, L. K. (2004). Guarding the castle and opening the gates. *Qualitative Inquiry, 10*(1), 79–95.

Sachs, J. (2003). *The activist teaching profession.* Buckingham: Open University Press.

Sachs, J. (2016). Teacher professionalism: Why are we still talking about it? *Teachers and Teaching, 22*(4), 413–425. https://doi.org/10.1080/13540602.2015.1082732.

Sanguinetti, J. (2000). An adventure in 'postmodern' action research: Performativity, professionalism and power. In J. Garrick & C. Rhodes (Eds.), *Research and knowledge at work: Perspectives, case-studies and innovative strategies* (pp. 232–249). London: Routledge.

Shah, M. (2012). Ten years of external quality audit in Australia: Evaluating its effectiveness and success. *Assessment and Evaluation in Higher Education, 37*(6), 761–772.

Shahjahan, R. A. (2011). Decolonizing the evidence-based education and policy movement: Revealing the colonial vestiges in educational policy, research, and neoliberal reform. *Journal of Education Policy, 26*(2), 181–206. https://doi.org/10.1080/02680939.2010.508176.

Simons, H. (2003). Evidence-based practice: Panacea or over promise? *Research Papers in Education, 18*(4), 303–311.

Simpson, A. (2017). The misdirection of public policy: Comparing and combining standardised effect sizes. *Journal of Education Policy.* https://doi.org/10.1080/02680939.2017.1280183.

Slavin, R. E. (2002). Evidence-based education policies: Transforming educational practice and research. *Educational Researcher, 31*(7), 15–21.

Solbrekke, T. D., & Sugrue, C. (2014). Professional accreditation of initial teacher education programmes: Teacher educators' strategies—Between 'accountability' and 'professional responsibility'? *Teaching and Teacher Education, 37,* 11–20.

Stensaker, B. (2011). Accreditation of higher education in Europe—Moving towards the US model? *Journal of Education Policy, 26*(6), 757–769.

Stensaker, B., & Harvey, L. (2006). Old wine in new bottles? A comparison of public and private accreditation schemes in higher education. *Higher Education Policy, 19*, 65–85.

Stosich, E. (2016). Joint inquiry: Teachers' collective learning about the common core in high poverty urban schools. *American Educational Research Journal, 53*(6), 1698–1731.

Supovitz, J. A., & Taylor, B. S. (2005). Systemic education evaluation: Evaluating the impact of systemwide reform in education. *American Journal of Evaluation, 26*(2), 204–230.

Trends, V. (2007). *Universities shaping the European higher education area*. Brussels: European University Association.

White, S. (2016). Teacher education research and education policy-makers: An Australian perspective. *Journal of Education for Teaching, 42*(2), 252–264.

Theresa Bourke is a Senior Lecturer and Academic Program Director at the Queensland University of Technology. She teaches into a number of curriculum and discipline units specifically in geography. Her research interests include professional standards, professionalism and accreditation processes especially using the theories of Michel Foucault. Other research areas include assessment in geographical education and teaching to/about diversity.

Chapter 3
Social Media and Teacher Professionalism: Getting in on the Act

Donna Pendergast, Beryl Exley, Nan Bahr and Jo-Anne Ferreira

Abstract In this chapter, we examine our collective experiences with a relatively new medium of communicating academic research, that of social media postings. We draw on three instances of professional blogging about the topic of teacher professionalism, all undertaken during 2018. The three professional blogs were accessed, read and shared on various social media sites and key ideas were tweeted. Others self-selected as responders. In this way, the blogosphere provided the means for fast, direct multimodal representations and dialogic communication with an extraordinarily wide audience about a topic of national significance. An analysis of the content and responses from a range of participants concluded that Government regulators, teacher education providers, employing departments and teacher unions, for example, no longer held an exclusive position as producers and transmitters of assumptions about teacher professionalism. Indeed, the general public, activist groups, individual teachers, teacher educators, publishing companies and the like provide the voice of the new wave of public discussion about the topic of teacher professionalism. Not all stakeholders are represented. Many teachers and school leaders are rendered voiceless by their employers. We also note that being active within the blogosphere is time-consuming, intellectually and emotionally exhausting, and at times, risky business. The reality is that many members of the teaching profession have to rely on a smaller number of networked professionals to contribute points of view on their behalf. A question remains about how the profession can overcome this forced passivity.

D. Pendergast (✉) · B. Exley
Griffith University, Brisbane, QLD, Australia
e-mail: d.pendergast@griffith.edu.au

B. Exley
e-mail: b.exley@griffith.edu.au

N. Bahr · J.-A. Ferreira
Southern Cross University, Gold Coast, QLD, Australia
e-mail: nan.bahr@scu.edu.au

J.-A. Ferreira
e-mail: jo-anne.ferreira@scu.edu.au

© Springer Nature Singapore Pte Ltd. 2019
A. Gutierrez et al. (eds.), *Professionalism and Teacher Education*,
https://doi.org/10.1007/978-981-13-7002-1_3

47

1 Introduction

On 24 September 2018, a commentary entitled *Teachers are NOT underqualified and NOT under-educated: here's what is really happening*, was published on the Australian Association for Research in Education (AARE) blog. It attracted the most interest of any blog ever published on the site with more than 11,000 readers and many shares through social media on Facebook, Twitter, WordPress, Linkedin and Reddit (AARE, 2018). The article directly refuted claims by policy makers and more generally the media and the wider community about professional issues related to teachers and their work. Importantly, the article made the claim that 'Australian teachers are doing well. They are not under-qualified and they are certainly not under-educated' (Bahr, Pendergast, & Ferreira, 2018) and built a series or arguments to defend this position.

This blog is one of several online publications in 2018 by the chapter authorship team to directly contest assumptions about the teaching profession. Earlier in 2018 and this time in a broader media space rather than one dedicated to education, on 16 April Bahr and Ferreira's (2018) article entitled *Seven reasons people no longer want to be teachers* was published by The Conversation. Shortly following this, on 20 April, Pendergast and Exley's (2018) article entitled *Teachers can earn more than dentists ... and other reasons to enter the profession* was published by ABC Online. This article was designed as a direct response to the Bahr and Ferreira (2018) online publication. Both publications were read and shared extensively to a broad audience.

As academics, we are committed to publishing research as an important part of our work. Indeed publishing for impact is regarded as a crucial part of the work of members of the academy. However, engaging in social media commentary style publication remains a relatively new way of considering the notion of impact and certainly one that remains contested in terms of a range of issues such as: its validity, ethics, perceptions of self-promotion, potential impact on workload, balance between information and entertainment, to name a few of the complexities around publishing in this medium. Lupton's (2014) study of over 700 academics further revealed tensions in relation to boundaries between the professional (work) and the personal (life), and the role of academics in a medium that enables participatory democracy of thought.

Given this context we set out to achieve the following in this chapter. First, we consider the key elements of the three featured commentaries in terms of what appears to interest the readership and therefore—to an extent—may be regarded as proxies for discussion about teacher professionalism in the wider community. Second, we explore the role and value of social media, drawing upon these recent blogs to consider how employing social media might be a strategy to raise discussion about teacher education professionalism. We share numerical data about the commentaries in terms of readership data and sharing frequency and reveal the breadth and scale of the written responses to the blogs. Finally, we look broadly to social media and the interactions with multiple stakeholders and the challenges and opportunities this makes available to the profession.

2 Social Media and the Rise of Secondary Stakeholders

Social media is a relatively new yet powerful means of communication for producing and transmitting assumptions about the teaching profession and teacher professionalism. Since the move away from print to digital communication, and the arrival of Web 2.0 technology towards the end of the first decade of the new millennium, literally millions of people throughout the world have access to a seemingly unlimited amount of press about others' assumptions on these topics. At the time of writing this manuscript, five popular English social media sites for Western audiences were Facebook, YouTube, Instagram, Twitter and Reddit. The interactive features of Web 2.0 technology provide the means through which people could express assumptions on these topics. For this reason, social media is considered by many to be a vehicle of democracy because of the potential to foster 'decentralized citizen control as opposed to hierarchical, elite control' (Meraz, 2009, p. 682).

Social media has multiple formats, all of which promote ties between users and mobilises information via a news sharing or discussion function. The popularity of these social media platforms is in part fuelled by their interactive formats, and their relatively limited barriers of entry (Meraz, 2009). Yet to attract attention, social media users need to build and maintain credibility in an era when accusations of fake news are aplenty (Smith, Kendall, Knighton, & Wright, 2018).

Despite these points of similarity across social media platforms, each social media platform has its own specialised social purpose and social structure (Halpern, Valenzuela, & Katz, 2017). Two commonly used social media platforms are Facebook and Twitter. They each carry their own measure of participation and thus concepts of efficacy. From a comparative viewpoint, Facebook users have 'friends', thus forming a relatively symmetrical relationship of reciprocity with other users. Twitter, on the other hand, operates with 'followers' who share a particular interest but without being required to reciprocate. In this way, Facebook is more attuned to multi-way social connectedness, whereas Twitter is more attuned to the one-way sharing of information. Facebook's profiles are customised with personal information fields, whereas Twitter allows users greater anonymity (Halpern et al., 2017).

3 The Featured Commentaries

The three commentaries utilised in this chapter were all published in digital format online and were available to be re-posted and included in social media such as Twitter, Reddit and Facebook. Paper 1 was first published in the AARE Blog, Paper 2 in The Conversation and Paper 3 in ABC News Online.

Paper 1, *Teachers are not under-qualified and not under-educated: Here's what is really happening* (Bahr, Pendergast et al., 2018), was published on the AARE blog, *EduResearch Matters*. The blog was established in 2013 to connect Australian educational researchers directly to the broad audience of Australians who are interested in education, including parents, teachers, politicians and journalists. Around one post is published each week in everyday language. Articles published on the AARE blog include republish links to email, Facebook, Twitter and other social media.

Paper 2, *Seven reasons people no longer want to be teachers* (Bahr & Ferreira, 2018), was published in *The Conversation* which was established in 2011 and aimed at 'making the knowledge of scholars and researchers accessible to the general public by having journalists commission and edit analytical and opinion pieces written by academic experts—and delivering the resulting stories online. This turned out to be a new form of journalism' (The Conversation, 2017, p. 3). In the 2017 Annual Report, the largest month of individual users to come to The Conversation site was reported to be 6.7 million in the month of October. Articles published in The Conversation include republished links to email, Facebook, Twitter and other social media.

Paper 3, *Teachers can earn more than dentists… and other reasons to enter the profession* (Pendergast & Exley, 2018), was published in *ABC News Online* which is part of the Australian Broadcasting Corporation (ABC) national news service in Australia produced by the News and Current Affairs division. The ABC was established in 1947 and online in 2010. In 2016, the average monthly reach of ABC Online in Australia was 7.6 million (ABC, 2016). Items published online include republished links to email, Facebook, Twitter and other social media.

The diversity of these publishing sites is of itself interesting in that the publishers chose whether they believed the article would be relevant and interesting to their audience, which would be expected to be different—but intersecting—audiences. AARE readers are more *likely* to be educators and those interested in education as members of the Association and hence have direct access to the blog. The Conversation readers tend to be more educated than the general public as the concept behind this website is sharing academic research, even though the writing style makes it more accessible. ABC News Online readers are more likely to be educated than the general public, and looking for items that are news rather than information.

Table 1 provides an overview of the three social media publications we refer to in this chapter in order to firstly consider what appears to interest the readership and therefore may be regarded as proxies for discussion about teacher professionalism in the wider community; and secondly as a focus for exploring the role and value of social media with regard to the teaching profession.

4   Analysing the Papers and Responder Posts

In order to consider the publications, we first analyse characteristics of the articles and second, the comments posted online in response to the articles. For the first stage, for each article, we consider the title and opening paragraph and how this positions the article as positive, neutral or negative; the range of subject matter covered; the image/s accompanying the article; and the most frequent words used in the article. For the latter step, we employ a method developed by Pendergast (2013) which involves the content being analysed for frequency to develop a taxonomy. Functional lemmas

Table 1 Details about the 3 social media publications

Title	Teachers are not under-qualified and not under-educated: Here's what is really happening	Seven reasons people no longer want to be teachers	Teachers can earn more than dentists… and other reasons to enter the profession
Abbreviation	Paper 1	Paper 2	Paper 3
Publisher	Australian Association for Research in Education (AARE) Blog	The Conversation	ABC News Online
Authors	Bahr, Pendergast and Ferreira	Bahr and Ferreira	Pendergast and Exley
Date	24/09/2018	16/04/2018	20/04/2018
Links	https://www.aare.edu.au/blog/?p=3197	http://theconversation.com/seven-reasons-people-no-longer-want-to-be-teachers-94580 https://www.abc.net.au/news/2018-04-16/seven-reasons-people-no-longer-want-to-be-teachers/9661878	https://www.abc.net.au/news/2018-04-20/seven-reasons-people-still-want-to-be-teachers/9675864

are removed (e.g. is, that, were, are, and, etc.), and the remaining words are presented as word clouds with words presented in font size proportional to their frequency, with the larger text being terms used more often. This is presented as a word cloud for visual impact. Each of these characteristics of the content of the articles is analysed and reflections about how this might serve as a form of proxy about current interest in the teaching profession is proffered.

For the second stage, we conduct an analysis of the comments posted in response to each article. Data about the posts such as the specified gender of the author; average posts per person; and an analysis of the frequency of terms used in the comments provide insight into the nature of the responses to the articles. Again we utilise Pendergast's (2013) method of text analysis to present word clouds visually representing the frequency of terms used. We also provide insight into the altmetrics of the social media sites.

5 Findings

Stage 1 of the analysis focused on the characteristics of the commentaries. The titles and opening sentences presented in Table 2 provide a summary of each and indicate clearly the valence (positive, neutral or negative) of what follows with regard to the

Table 2 Title and opening sentences of the 3 social media publications referred to in this chapter

Paper 1	Paper 2	Paper 3
Teachers are not under-qualified and not under-educated: Here's what is really happening	Seven reasons people no longer want to be teachers	Teachers can earn more than dentists… and other reasons to enter the profession
Australian teachers are doing well. They are not under-qualified and they are certainly not under-educated, as some media stories would have you believe. They are doing an admirable job managing exhausting workloads and constantly changing government policies and processes. They are more able than past generations to identify and help students with wide ranging needs. They are, indeed, far better qualified and prepared than those in our nation's glorious past that so many commentators reminisce wistfully about[a]	The oldest profession—teaching—is no longer attractive. The Queensland Deans of Education revealed there have been alarming drops in first preference applications for this year's teacher preparation courses. Queensland has experienced an overall 26% drop. Most alarmingly, UQ reported a 44% plunge. QUT saw a 19% drop These figures reflect a national trend. ACU's is down 20% for campuses in Queensland, New South Wales and Victoria. This follows disappointing interest in 2017. VTAC reported a 40% drop in 2017 compared to 2016. So why don't people want to be teachers anymore? There are at least seven reasons people aren't so keen[b]	Teaching is a complex profession, so very dependent on the people who take on the role of teachers Yes, the profession of teaching is at another set of crossroads. One certainty is that the profession of teaching is not static; the rhythms of the profession don't play the same tune for long before another wave of innovation hits the spotlight And given the importance of the work of teachers, this is no surprise In their recent piece, Seven reasons people no longer want to be teachers, Nan Bahr and Jo-Anne Ferreira raised a few points that warrant discussion which, hopefully, can lift prospective teachers out of the quicksand of despair and towards a future of opportunity and career fulfilment Here, we acknowledge the ebb and flow of teacherly life by identifying seven new crossroads for aspiring teachers but focusing the lens on why people do choose to be teachers, and why teaching is a most satisfying career choice[c]

Source
[a]Bahr, Pendergast, et al. (2018)
[b]Bahr and Ferreira (2018)
[c]Pendergast and Exley (2018)

teaching profession. Paper 1 and 3 are positive valence papers while Paper 2 is a negative valence paper. None of the papers were neutral.

Table 3 provides a summary of the content of the three papers. When looking across the content of the articles, there is considerable overlap related to *teacher education* including references to entry, qualifications and quality of programmes. There is also overlap related to the *teaching profession* with a focus on negative perceptions including references to salary, public perceptions and workload. The content takes different directions; however, the issues remain relatively consistent.

When considering the content of the three papers, we present a series of word clouds that provide a visual presentation of the words used in the paper with their frequency represented by the relative font size. In generating the images words with three letters or fewer were removed and words with plurals and tenses have been matched so that, for example, *teacher* and *teachers* are combined as *teacher*; *admin*, *administer*, *administered* and *administration* are combined as *administration*. This word grouping is consistent with the methods outlined by Pendergast (2013).

Figures 1, 2 and 3 present the word clouds for the three papers with the greater frequency of words used represented in larger font.

A summary of the most frequently used words across each of the papers is presented in Table 4, and quite unsurprisingly, the words *teacher, teach* and *education* feature as having high levels of usage in all three papers. The words *need, tests* and *report* feature in Paper 2, which takes a more negative stance about the teaching profession.

The papers were each accompanied by images selected by the publishers without consultation with the authors. A summary of features of these images is presented in Table 5.

One of the reasons to incorporate images is the persuasive ability of images to reinforce the claims made in text (Hayne, 2018). Using Lister and Well's (2001, p. 77) 'sociological concept of convention' and drawing on the 'sign systems and codes ... of dress, style, architecture, objects, body language', the stock photographs used in Papers 1 and 2 signal cultural markers of white middle class which perhaps says more about the editor of each site than the paper or the authors, given they had no influence on the selection of the images.

The ABC photographs show both teachers and students in the same image and in two of the images the teachers are named, giving a sense of authenticity and newsworthiness to the image choice. While the majority of the students portrayed appear to be Caucasian, these photographs do include teachers and students of different races, and for the most part, the children and teachers seem to be engaged and interacting. As Käpplinger (2015, p. 174) notes, these 'real' photographs 'differ a lot from so-called stock photos, with their rather artificial atmospheres, although these might invoke the impression of "professional" images'.

For stage 2, we analysed the comments posted in response to the papers, a capacity enabled by the digital format which encourages participatory democracy. Table 6 provides a summary of the frequency and demographic information available for the posts (responder comments) made in response to each paper and the comment trail.

Table 3 Analysis of the content of the 3 social media publications referred to in this chapter

Title	Teachers are not under-qualified and not under-educated: Here's what is really happening	Seven reasons people no longer want to be teachers	Teachers can earn more than dentists…. and other reasons to enter the profession
Abbreviation	Paper 1	Paper 2	Paper 3
Content	(Paragraph sections) • Teacher qualifications • Entrance to teacher education courses • Quality of teacher education courses and teacher educators • Teacher workload	(Numbered reasons) • Teacher education competency fixation • Standardised testing obsession • Lack of autonomy • Work intensification • Negative public images • Teacher bashing • Teachers' salaries are poor	(Numbered reasons) • We now ask them why they want to be teachers • They need more qualifications, but see benefits • The world-class national curriculum *does* include creativity • The pay's actually not bad • Teachers rise above the negativity • They're not just looking for a fall-back (same as 1) • Teachers can influence others to teach

Fig. 1 Paper 1 Word cloud with text size representing frequency

Fig. 2 Paper 2 Word cloud with text size representing frequency

Fig. 3 Paper 3 Word cloud with text size representing frequency

Table 4 Most frequent words used in Papers 1, 2 and 3 (alphabetical order, conjunctions removed)

	Paper 1 (%)	Paper 2 (%)	Paper 3 (%)
Aspiring			1.05
Career			1.35
Course	1.04		
Education	3.24	1.45	
Need		1.27	
People			1.05
Profession	1.04		1.94
Programme	1.04	1.27	
Qualification	1.43		
Report		1.27	
Student		1.27	
Teach	1.30	2.91	3.74
Teacher	5.97	5.64	5.23
Tests		1.09	

Table 5 Summary of images included in the Papers

Paper	Description of image	Caption	Source
1	Close up of face of androgynous white, young adult holding a whiteboard marker	No caption—used as banner image	Stock
2	White, female, older head on hand looking tired and despondent	Banner image with the text—The programmes are long and intense, the creativity and relationships aspect of the vocation has been eroded, there is pervasive negativity in the media, and comparatively poor salary and working conditions	Stock
	Girl in uniform at desk alone writing	Standardised tests, like NAPLAN, contribute to lack of enthusiasm to take up teaching	Stock
3	3 children in uniform, sitting, raising hands, no adults	The inaugural Australian Curriculum is futures driven, exciting to teach and has all the hallmarks of a world-class curriculum	Original
	White, female, older teacher in big chair with storybook and one child standing close by, children sitting on floor observing reading	Teacher Delena Clarke and Jasmine Smith telling the kindergarten class about what to expect at Beef Week 2015	Original
	White, male older teacher sitting at a flip chart with children sitting on floor observing	Grade 1 class at Fairfield Public School	Original

Table 6 Postfrequency for Papers 1 and 2

Paper	Paper 1 (AARE Blog)		Paper 2 (The Conversation)		
Number of comments	18		261		
Unique number of people commenting	14		94		
Gender	M	F	M	F	X[a]
N (%)	6 (43%)	8 (57%)	61 (65%)	19 (20%)	14 (15%)
Number of posts	9 (50%)	9 (50%)	154 (59%)	89 (34%)	18 (7%)
Average posts per person	1.5	1.13	2.52	4.68	1.29

[a]Gender not disclosed

These data are available for Papers 1 and 2 but not for Paper 3 as the ABC News Online social media site does not allow for audience comment.

Paper 1 published on the AARE blog attracted comments of almost equal proportion of male and female; however, males were more likely to add more than one comment. Paper 2 published on The Conversation had 261 comments made by 94 unique responders, of whom 65% were male and just 20% female (15% did not disclose). However, on average female responders made more than double the number of comments (4.68) than males (2.52).

We also produced word clouds of the comments for each paper (Paper 3 ABC Inline did not have a comment facility, so no word cloud is generated for this paper) (Figs. 4 and 5).

As presented in Table 7 and quite unsurprisingly, the words *teacher, teach, school, student* and *education* feature as having high levels of usage in the comments. The words *great* and *criticise* also feature, highlighting the dual nature of the responses .

Because of different publication sites and the availability of different analytic data, our information about the reach and impact of the papers is not directly comparable, nor is the source consistent, but a story can be told about each paper. Altmetrics data, that is the measure of attention articles receive online through social media such as Twitter, Facebook and Google, are partially available for each of the Papers, some sourced directly from the publisher. Altmetrics data are also complicated by the time of data collection, as the life of the publications continues indefinitely and hence the impact is constantly growing. For example, Paper 2 was published on 16 April 2018. By 24 April 2018, it had attracted 255,426 readers. It was 'republished' 9 times through The Conversation site. The article was commented on through Twitter (117 tweets and retweets) and shared through Facebook (8400 shares). By 29 April, the paper had 263,252 reads, 229 comments, 187 tweets and retweets and 8796 Facebook shares (Bahr, Graham, Ferreira, Lloyd & Waters, 2018). A summary of altmetrics available at the time of preparing this chapter is presented in Table 8.

Fig. 4 Paper 1 18 comments presented as word cloud with text size representing frequency

Fig. 5 Paper 3 261 comments presented as word cloud with text size representing frequency

Table 7 Most frequent words used in Paper 1 and Paper 2 comments (alphabetical order, conjunctions removed)

Word	Paper 1 comments (%)	Paper 2 comments (%)
Australia	1.02	
Criticise	1.02	
Education	1.91	
Great	1.15	
School	1.15	1.27
Student	1.02	
Teach	2.04	1.36
Teacher	4.83	2.76
Work	1.91	
Year		1.20

Table 8 Altmetrics data available for each paper

Paper	Site	Twitter	Facebook	Views on day	Total views	Shares
Paper 1	AARE	92[d]	1K+[d]	6000[a]	11,300+[a]	1200[a]
Paper 2	Conversation	187[c]	8K+[c]		310,967[c]	386[b]
Paper 3	ABC News	27[e]				

[a] According to AARE email
[b] According to Bahr, Graham et al. (2018)
[c] According to The Conversation website
[d] According to AARE website
[e] According to   to   https://twitter.com/search?f=tweets&q=Teachers%20can%20earn%20more%20than%20dentists%E2%80%A6%20and%20other%20reasons%20to%20enter%20the%20profession&src=typd

6   Discussion

As the previous examples in this chapter demonstrate, primary stakeholders of the teaching profession (e.g. government regulators, teacher education providers, teacher employing authorities, teacher unions and so forth) no longer have an exclusive position as producers and transmitters of assumptions about teacher professionalism. With the coming of the social web, the asymmetry of influence of information and subsequent action has changed. A widening group of highly influential secondary stakeholders (e.g. the general public, activist groups, individual teachers, individual students, employer groups, publishing companies and so forth) have entered the public conversations. The secondary stakeholders are amassing huge audiences which they use as leverage for promoting counter assumptions and influencing change. The social media repositories gain their momentum by collecting multiple forms of evidence about a particular assumption. According to the research from Jurgens, Berthon, Edelman, and Pitt (2016), sometimes it is the mass of evidence, rather than the weight of evidence, that can be used to advantage. In addition, secondary stakeholders can produce and transmit their own assumptions which implicate the power of primary stakeholders to maintain control of the agendas. Jurgens et al. (2016, p. 12) identify that secondary stakeholders now have (i) an increased ability to gather, analyse and share information, (ii) frame issues so as to garner greater appeal and a larger audience, and (iii) capitalise on the mobilising structures of the social web. These mobilising structures allow secondary stakeholders to reach and organise larger populations of people more rapidly, for linked networks to take action, and thus effect the production of assumptions at local and global levels.

The significant shifts in the ease and frequency of accessibility, the masses of people involved and society's increasing appetite for social media communication presents both challenges and opportunities for those trying to positively affect assumptions about teacher professionalism. Despite the widespread appeal of social media, many in the teaching profession do not actively contribute to this medium of communication. As we'll see, some contribute more than others. The next section overviews the reasons why some hesitate to get into the social media act. The final section considers existing and future opportunities for social media in positively affecting assumptions about teacher professionalism.

6.1 Challenges of Getting into the Social Media Act

A number of reasons exist as to why it is a challenge for some stakeholders to get into the social media act.

The first challenge is that many teacher and school leadership stakeholders are forced into a passive position by their employers. By way of background, aside from our positions as teacher educators within universities, we four authors have all undertaken a range of volunteer positions with state-based and national teacher professional associations. In these forums, we often work alongside volunteer pre-service teachers, teachers and school and system leaders. We are aware of the wave of activity on social media pertaining to the teaching profession and teacher professionalism. We appreciate the importance of canvassing and, at times, contributing to the social media conversations. We have all had firsthand experience with how time-consuming and intellectually and emotionally exhausting these social media interactions can be. However, we are also struck by the reality that some of our industry colleagues feel as though they cannot publically contribute to these social media conversations. Despite being highly experienced and deeply knowledgeable teachers and school leaders, and indeed utterly committed to their profession and the topic of teacher professionalism, their workplace agreements institute codes of conduct that variously require employees to be impartial, promote the public good and publically commit to the system of government and the like. We also each know of individuals who have participated in some social media conversations about the teaching profession and teacher professionalism and have been reprimanded by line managers for doing so. Thus, workplace codes of conduct mean that many who might otherwise wish to contribute to the agendas on these topics are rendered voiceless. Their workplace codes of conduct limit them to the role of passive receivers of the assumptions that are being produced and transmitted by empowered primary and secondary stakeholders. There is an inherent issue when so many members of the profession have to rely on a smaller number of networked professionals (such as those who work in teacher education or teacher unions) to contribute conversations that represent the disparate voices of the profession. A question remains about how the profession can overcome this forced passivity.

The second challenge relates to personal risk. Those who have the right to enter into the social media conversations that produce assumptions about the teaching profession and teacher professionalism also do so with some risks. Like any public communication activity that requires one to make oneself 'manifest' through self-disclosure, there is risk of a disappointing outcome, a risk of loss of reputation or a risk of loss of network followers (Smith et al., 2018).

The third challenge relates to the sophistication of the means of communication. To become involved, one must become proficient with a great range of social media communication strategies. While on the surface social media communication seems efficient, it is not without its own sophisticated rhetorical strategies for constructing content and digital literacies for communicating content (Jurgens et al., 2016). Ideograms, such as emojis, are not standardised language with all users. Their use is platform and culturally specific (Ge & Gretzel, 2018). When adults involved in a social media conversation do not have the requisite confidence to use rhetorical strategies (Exley & Willis, 2016) or the digital interface (Willis & Exley, 2018), they may hesitate and thus withhold their contributions or make ineffective contributions. Similarly, if users do not subscribe to the social media language, their ideas will not resonate with the other social media consumers. Talking the language, so to speak, is of utmost importance for engaging within Facebook or the twittersphere (Ge & Gretzel, 2018).

A final challenge to be discussed in this chapter relates to the depth of the matter. Meraz (2009) comments that abstract issues are more difficult to transfer via social media when compared with more concrete issues. This is especially the case for micro-blogging platforms such as Twitter where communication is limited to 240 characters. This reality raises an epistemic matter for topics related to the teaching profession and teacher professionalism. If social media compromises abstract messages and continues to give priority to easily reduced and communicated empirical messages, then, we contend, the discipline suffers. Bernstein (2000, p. 162) was quite clear on this point: It is only access through new ways of thinking that 'new possibilities for a fresh perspective, access to new questions, a new set of connections, a new problematic and a new set of speakers emerge'. A longitudinal study into teachers' professional knowledge bases demonstrates that teachers bring deep theories and abstract thinking to their teacherly work (Exley, 2005). Thus, relegating such weighty topics to a medium that might be only able to manage reductive assumptions may be counter to the mission of advancing the teaching profession and teacher professionalism.

6.2 Opportunities for Getting into the Social Media Act

In contrast to the challenges noted above, social media use brings multiple opportunities for changing assumptions about the teaching profession and teacher professionalism. The first benefit of people from the profession adopting social media use is the increased speed and convenience of communication. 'Liking', 'sharing' and 'tweeting' are all time efficient functions, so much so that they have become part of human daily interaction for trillions of users (Brems, Temmerman, Graham, & Broersma, 2017). Social media can also facilitate connections across settings, such as between the profession and the public, and between geographically dislocated members of the profession.

The second opportunity of people from the profession adopting social media use is that they can be closer to the pulse of assumptions held by a wide range of primary and secondary stakeholders (Ge & Gretzel, 2018). Being closer to these more personal networks puts people from the profession in a better position to appreciate how others see the issues, and augments the likelihood of both learning about opportunities to participate, and being asked to participate in the production of professional assumptions (Halpern et al., 2017). As a point of interest, Halpern et al.'s (2017) literature review identified studies that reported that when network size increases so too does a participant's probability of interacting with new information and/or following their friends' lead to engage in social action. This is an important point to consider when attempting to bring into relief topics that do not have wide spread uptake but are nonetheless important.

When people from the profession adopt social media use, a third opportunity arises, that of the potential to restore the balance of power around matters for the teaching profession and teacher professionalism. Instead of secondary stakeholders having the monopoly of power over the assumptions that are produced and transmitted, the agenda setting is in the hands of the people from the profession (Meraz, 2009). In this way, secondary stakeholders will struggle to be central gatekeepers over matters important to the profession. The people of the profession can collaborate to promote the profile of an individual who represents the collective cause. In spite of the seemingly chaotic fashion with which social media interactions take place, certain topics manage to get an inordinate amount of attention, thus bubbling to the top in terms of popularity and contributing to new trends for public and professional notice. Two compelling cases come to mind.

Recently, a mathematics teacher from Cherrybrook Technology High School in Sydney, Eddie Woo, won the Australia's Local Hero Award on 25 January 2018. He was the first teacher to give the Australia Day address in New South Wales. In his address, Eddie spoke out about the teaching profession and matters that impact teaching professionalism: 'Education has been one of Australia's greatest assets but things won't stay that way unless we give educators the cultural and capital support they need to do their jobs. Valuing education isn't about awards or accolades, it's much more about trust and respect' (Gock, 23 January, 2018). Vignettes of his address went viral and some ten months later, a Google search for <Eddie Woo teacher>

returns 3.35 million hits. Eddie Woo's professional Facebook page has in excess of 10 thousand 'friends' and his twitter account, @misterwootube, has 17 thousand followers. One twitter follower with the handle @mesterman tweeted to @mister-wootube about a Head of Department Mathematics vacancy @OLMCParramatta, encouraging Eddie that staff at @OLMCParramatta would love to work with him. Another twitter follower with the handle @KerrieQ tweeted that she 'felt blessed to have heard today's guest lecture @westernsydneyu for our preservice teachers. Thank you for taking the time to inspire our new teachers'.

Gabbie Stroud, a former teacher, appeared on the ABC television panel show 'QandA' in early October 2018. Gabbie spoke about her passion for teaching, and the causes and effects of demoralisation and why she felt compelled to leave the teaching profession. Gabbie was scathing of the effects of standardised testing on the professional teaching standards. Gabbie lamented: 'I think we're seeing a time where education in Australia, we must be getting close to rock bottom, because I think there are teachers that are suffering, there are students that are suffering…' (Bedo, 9 October, 2018). Within six weeks of her appearance on 'QandA' a Google search for <Gabbie Stroud teacher> returns 35 thousand hits. Gabbie Stroud's professional Facebook page has in excess of three and a half thousand 'likes' and her twitter account @GJ_Stroud has in excess of one and half thousand followers. One twitter follower with the handle @EducatorSTEM motivated @GJ_Stroud with the hashtag #preachit. Another twitter follower with the handle @megsamanda, a music and digital technologies teacher, tweeted that she bought Gabbie's book as her birthday treat.

It would seem that monologues from Eddie Woo and Gabbie Stroud resonate with their followers, even though neither generates an inordinate amount of content on their social media profiles. Regardless, people of the profession have linked to Eddie Woo and Gabbie Stroud to automatically receive the content that they generate. In this way, Eddie Woo's and Gabbie Stroud's monologues are transformed into social dialogues. On this occasion, people of the profession were able to overcome the barrier of passivity and put these two advocates for the profession on pedestals. In doing so, the people of the profession have assisted in bringing two human faces to represent the work of teachers. These two advocates have come to represent a critical stakeholder group and bring into social dialogue matters pertaining to the teaching profession and teacher professionalism.

Smith et al. (2018) purport that social media influencers demonstrate 'personality traits that include being verbal, smart, ambitious, productive and poised' (p. 10). Smith et al. (2018) details research that shows that when individuals are officially or unofficially assigned as 'brand ambassadors', their personality traits carry over onto the brand and further influence the actions of others. For example, brand ambassadors often enter into mediation, gatekeeping, advocacy and/or boundary spanning roles for their respective associations (Smith et al., 2018). Successful brand ambassadors, however, are unique. They are not necessarily 'created or developed' by the association, rather tending to 'self-select into their organisation connection' (Smith et al.,

2018, p. 15). This good news story now leaves another challenge for the profession. When Eddie Woo and Gabbie Stroud self-select out of their brand ambassador roles, from where will our next brand ambassador come?

7 Conclusion

In this chapter, we set out to consider the key elements of the three featured articles, looking towards high-frequency word use in the articles and in comments alongside the key topics. We also reflected on the choice of images included in the papers. We then explored the role and value of social media drawing upon these recent publications to consider impact on the teacher professionalism context. Finally, we reflected more broadly on social media and the interactions with the multiple stakeholders of the challenges and opportunities of this form of engagement.

For the four of us, flirting with social media as a means to generate interest in, and challenge assumptions about, the teaching profession has been a departure from our mainstream academic publishing programme. And it has been a rewarding departure. Most notably, the speed of reach to literally hundreds of thousands of readers is in deep contrast to the highly specialised readership of academic journals where we typically publish after a long and arduous peer review process that may take 12–18 months and our papers may be read by just hundreds. However, we must affirm that both have a place for us as academics. We also discovered that the challenge of the personal and the professional intersecting was also real for each of us as we received Facebook and Twitter feeds into our personal accounts, with both affirmations and criticism. The feedback from our colleagues and the wider community with an interest in the teaching profession has been phenomenal compared to feedback associated with our other academic work, with opportunities for follow-up interviews and speaking engagements flowing from interest in our papers. What we have learnt is that there is a place for publishing using social media, and we are keen to develop our capabilities in this space.

References

Australian Association for Research in Education. (2018). *Personal email communication.*
Australian Broadcasting Commission. (2016). *ABC annual report, 2016.* http://www.abc.net.au/corp/annual-report/2016/c2-online.html. Accessed December 21, 2018.
Bahr, N., & Ferreira, J. (2018). *Seven reasons people no longer want to be teachers.* The Conversation. http://theconversation.com/seven-reasons-people-no-longer-want-to-be-teachers-94580. Accessed November 21, 2018.
Bahr, N., Graham, A., Ferreira, J., Lloyd, M., & Waters, R. (2018a). *Promotion of the profession.* Bilinga, Australia: Southern Cross University.

Bahr, N., Pendergast, D., & Ferreira, J. (2018). *Teachers are NOT underqualified and NOT under-educated: Here's what is really happening.* Australian Association for Research in Education (AARE) blog. http://bit.ly/AARETeacherEd.

Bedo, S. (2018, October 9). Education experts lash out at Australian schooling system. *News.com.au.* Available from https://www.news.com.au/entertainment/tv/current-affairs/education-experts-lash-out-at-australian-schooling-system/news-story/f9b159e4c0bc5f0ae44dee522776e559.

Bernstein, B. (2000). *Pedagogy, symbolic control and identity: Theory, research, critique* (Rev. ed.). Maryland, USA: Rowman & Littlefield Publishers.

Brems, C., Temmerman, M., Graham, T., & Broersma, M. (2017). Personal branding on Twitter. *Digital Journalism, 5*(4), 443–459.

Exley, B. (2005). *Teachers' professional knowledge bases for offshore education: Two case studies of Western teachers working in Indonesia.* Unpublished thesis, Queensland University of Technology.

Exley, B., & Willis, L.-D. (2016). Children's pedagogic rights in the web 2.0 era: A case study of a child's open access interactive travel blog. *Global Studies of Childhood, 6*(4), 400–413.

Ge, J., & Gretzel, U. (2018): Emoji rhetoric: A social media influencer perspective. *Journal of Marketing Management.* https://doi.org/10.1080/0267257x.2018.1483960.

Gock, K. (2018, January 23). A lesson from Eddie Woo: Be a mathematician on Australia Day. *Sydney Morning Herald.* Available from https://www.smh.com.au/national/nsw/a-lesson-from-eddie-woo-be-a-mathematician-on-australia-day-20180123-h0mway.html.

Halpern, D., Valenzuela, S., & Katz, J. (2017). We face, I tweet: How different social media influence political participation through collective and internal efficacy. *Journal of Computer-Mediated Communication, 22*(6), 320–336.

Hayne, J. (2018). How fake news can exploit pictures to make people believe lies. *ABC News.* Retrieved from https://www.abc.net.au/news/2018-11-22/fake-news-image-information-believe-anu/10517346.

Jurgens, M., Berthon, P., Edelman, L., & Pitt, L. (2016). Social media revolutions: The influence of secondary stakeholders. *Business Horizons, 59,* 129–136.

Käpplinger, B. (2015). Addressing 21st century learners—A comparative analysis of pictures and images in programs of adult education providers in Canada and Germany. In *Proceedings of the 34th CASAE/ACEEA Annual Conference* (pp. 171–177), Montreal.

Lister, M., & Wells, L. (2001). Seeing beyond belief: Cultural studies as an approach to analysing the visual. In T. van Leeuwen & C. Jewitt (Eds.), *Handbook of visual analysis* (pp. 61–91). London: Sage.

Lupton, D. (2014). *'Feeling better connected': Academics' use of social media.* Canberra: News & Media Research Centre, University of Canberra.

Meraz, S. (2009). Is there an elite hold? Traditional media to social media agenda setting influence in blog networks. *Journal of Computer-Mediated Communication, 14,* 682–707.

Pendergast, D. (2013). An appetite for home economics literacy: Convergence, megatrends and big ideas. *The Journal of Asian Regional Association for Home Economics, 20*(2), 57–65.

Pendergast, D., & Exley, B. (2018). *Teachers can earn more than dentists … and other reasons to enter the profession.* ABC Online. http://www.abc.net.au/news/2018-04-20/seven-reasons-people-still-want-to-be-teachers/9675864.

Smith, B., Kendall, M., Knighton, D., & Wright, T. (2018). Rise of the brand ambassador: Social stake, corporate social responsibility and influencer among the social media influencers. *Communication Management Review, 3,* 1.

The Conversation. (2017). *The conversation 2017 annual stakeholder report: A year of record audience growth.* https://cdn.theconversation.com/static_files/files/14/2017_Stakeholder_Report_The_Conversation.pdf?1518052945. Accessed November 20, 2018.

Willis, L.-D., & Exley, B. (2018). Using an online social media space to engage parents in student learning in the early-years: Enablers and impediments. *Digital Education Review, 33,* 87–104.

Professor Donna Pendergast is Dean of the School of Education and Professional Studies at Griffith University. Her research expertise is educational transformation and efficacy with a focus on: middle year's education and student engagement; initial and professional teacher education; and school reform. In 2015 she received the Vice Chancellor's Research Supervision Excellence Award; in 2017 a National Commendation from the Australian Council of Graduate Research for Excellence in Graduate Research Supervision and in 2018 the Australian Council for Educational Leadership Miller-Grassie Award for Outstanding Leadership in Education.

Professor Beryl Exley is Deputy Head of the School of Education and Professional Studies at Griffith University with special responsibility for Learning and Teaching in Initial Teacher Education and Professional Studies Programs. Her areas of teaching and research expertise focus on English Curriculum and Literacies Education and the affordances and challenges of using multimedia to advance the educational agenda. She currently serves as the National President of the Australian Literacy Educators' Association (ALEA) and has chaired AITSL Accreditation Panels for Initial Teacher Education programs since 2016.

Professor Nan Bahr is Deputy Vice Chancellor (Students), Professor and Dean of Education at Southern Cross University. In this role she is responsible for oversight and strategic management for improved engagement, experience and retention of students across the University. Professor Bahr also has specific responsibility, as Dean of Education, for the quality of the Teacher Education programmes, research and service in the field of education for Southern Cross University.

Professor Bahr has a national and international profile for educational research. She has impact and an established reputation as a public advocate for improvement of the professional status of teachers in Australia. Key research has been in the fields of music education, educational psychology, teacher education, adolescence, resilience and teaching innovation in higher education. As a University Teacher, she has been awarded the University of Queensland Award for Excellence in Teaching, has been a finalist (twice) for the Australian Awards for University Teaching, and has been awarded for extended service with the Australian Defence Force.

Associate Professor Jo-Anne Ferreira is Director of the Centre for Teaching and Learning and Academic Director, SCU Online at Southern Cross University. She is responsible for enhancing teaching quality and the student learning experience, both face-to-face and online. Prior to this, she was Director, Teaching and Learning in the School of Education at Southern Cross University. She began her teaching career as a secondary English and Geography teacher in South Africa and Australia.

Jo-Anne has developed and delivered award winning professional development programmes in Australia, South Africa and across the Asia-Pacific region to teachers and student teachers. She has also taught in universities in South Africa and Australia. Her research interests are in online education and the sociology of education with a special interest in post-structuralist theories of identity, embodiment and power, in systems-based change, and in environmental and sustainability education. She has most recently led a decade-long research project on systems-based change as a strategy for embedding sustainability education in teacher education.

Part II
Partnership Engagement

Chapter 4
Who Is the Hybrid Teacher Educator? Understanding Professional Identity in School–University Partnership

Jennifer Clifton and Kathy Jordan

Abstract Teacher education has long been criticised for a perceived disconnect between university-based and school-based learning, and literature often proposes closer integration of these two spaces as central to bridging this disconnect (Allen and Wright in Teachers Teach Theory Pract 20:136–151, 2014; Darling-Hammond in J Teacher Educ 57:300–314, 2006); third space theory is one way to frame this integration (Zeichner in Educ Researcher 28:4–15, 2010). Third space theory provides a theoretical premise that has the potential to reconceptualise the connection between universities and schools through disrupting binaries and encouraging the continual negotiation and reinterpretation of identities (Bhabha in The location of culture. Routledge, London, 1994). Through reconceptualising the spaces of, and between, schools and universities, third space theory encourages new ways of thinking about partnerships, shared knowledge and ways of working, and in doing so creates hybrid roles which challenge traditional roles or positions within both spaces. Drawing on interviews with several hybrid teacher educators, this chapter discusses the fluid roles and responsibilities of these emerging roles and considers implications for shifting professional identities in teacher education.

1 Introduction

Teacher education has long been challenged to reconceptualise the connection between theory and practice, with better connections often identified as necessary to support prospective teachers to develop theoretical and practical skills for teaching (Grossman, Hammerness, & McDonald, 2009; Taylor, Klein, & Abrams, 2014). The *Top of the Class* report from The House of Representatives Standing Committee on Education and Vocational Training (2007) referred to the lack of connection

J. Clifton (✉)
Griffith University, Brisbane, QLD, Australia
e-mail: j.clifton@griffith.edu.au

K. Jordan
RMIT University, Melbourne, VIC, Australia
e-mail: kathy.jordan@rmit.edu.au

© Springer Nature Singapore Pte Ltd. 2019
A. Gutierrez et al. (eds.), *Professionalism and Teacher Education*,
https://doi.org/10.1007/978-981-13-7002-1_4

between schools and university as a weak link (p. 71). The Teacher Education Ministerial Advisory Group report, *Action Now: Classroom Ready Teachers* (2014), took an even stronger stand, arguing that the most significant action to be pursued is "the integrated delivery of initial teacher education" (p. vii).

In her national study of teacher education in the United States, Darling-Hammond (2006) identified several ways in which greater links can be made between theory and practice, including developing well-designed professional experience (also referred to as practicum or placement) as well as closer connections between school and university staff. She also suggested (Darling-Hammond, 2010) that models of teacher education need to be underpinned with stronger relationships with schools "that press for mutual transformations of teaching and learning to teach" (p. 227). Several researchers suggest that this mutual transformation could be achieved by drawing on the concept of third space theory (Taylor et al., 2014; Zeichner, 2010).

The notion of a third space stems from hybridity theory which considers that individuals draw on multiple discourses to understand the world (Bhabha, 1994; Zeichner, 2010). Third space theory has been used in a variety of disciplines including geography, the arts, postcolonial studies, feminist studies and education (see, e.g., Gutiérrez, 2008; Moje et al., 2004; Soja, 1996). It is essentially used to explore the spaces "in-between" two or more discourses, conceptualisations or binaries (Bhabha, 1994). A hybrid space is often defined as a space that combines two spaces (in this case, schools and universities) that bring together formerly separate domains, creating alternative/new spaces which are "fundamentally different from either individual domain" (Klein, Taylor, Onore, Strom, & Abrams, 2013, p. 28). In their influential paper, Moje et al. (2004) summarised three main ways in which theorists have conceptualised third space and how this can be applied within an educational space: as a bridge between knowledge, where there is space to acknowledge contradictions and/or bridge competing understandings; as a navigational space that enables crossing or drawing upon different binaries, discourses or discursive boundaries; and as a transformative space that enables competing knowledge to be brought into "conversation", leading to new understandings, new forms of learning and knowledge projection (Moje et al., 2004).

The potential for this research is that third space theory challenges binaries that have typically populated teacher education, including university/school, theory/practice and teacher educator/school-based practitioner (see, e.g., Gaffey & Dobbins, 1996; Guyton & McIntyre, 1990; Zeichner, 1999) and integrates these binaries in new ways so that "an either/or perspective is transformed into a both/also point of view" (Zeichner, 2010, p. 92). Questioning the binaristic thought which has typically shaped university/school relationships, and encouraging alternative ways of working and learning, have given rise to new roles and positions which merge and/or reimagine what is considered academic and practitioner knowledge. This in turn shifts academic and practitioner identity, challenges traditional roles and produces complex hybrid roles (Zeichner, 2010). While there is some research about these hybrid roles (Akkerman & Bakker, 2011; Bullough, Draper, Smith, & Birrell, 2004; Jennings & Peloso, 2010; Martin, Snow, & Franklin Torrez, 2011; Sandholtz & Finan, 1998), little is known about their stories; in particular: How did they become involved in hybrid roles? What is the hybrid teacher educator's professional identity? What are some of the benefits and challenges faced by people in hybrid roles? How might this hybrid work be captured within the existing professional administration and organisational frameworks?

Drawing on interviews with several hybrid teacher educators who were part of an innovative practicum model based on partnerships and a coaching model, this chapter unpacks some of these evolving roles within teacher education. It begins by discussing third space theory and how this philosophy shapes our understanding of hybrid roles. It then outlines the emerging roles and the stories of some of the hybrid educators. Finally, it concludes by discussing some of the implications for these new hybrid educator roles.

2 Hybrid Teacher Education Roles in Third Space Constructs

> If we are to move toward more egalitarian social practices and relations to enhance the educative value of student teaching experiences, we will need to understand more about how hybrid teacher educators go about establishing multiple relationships and negotiating the challenges and tensions of complex social contexts. It is time to focus more on new kinds of roles for university-based teacher educators. (Martin et al., 2011, p. 31)

While third space theory may not have originated in education, it has been adopted by educational researchers in various ways, including exploring the intersections and disjunctures between everyday and school-based literacy (Moje et al., 2004), examining the art of migrant students (Elsden-Clifton, 2006) and researching the stories of bilingual students in schools (Harman & Khote, 2018). It has also been adopted in teacher education (Flessner, 2014; Gannon, 2010; McDonough, 2014) and more specifically within professional experience as it has the potential to disrupt many of the binaries which have structured this complex space (Cuenca, Schmeichel, Butler, Dinkelman, & Nichols, 2011; Wood & Turner, 2015). Zeichner (2010) discusses some of the approaches that have been used to facilitate third spaces in teacher education such as campus-based laboratory schools, modelling of practice through coursework, simulated classrooms or use of practising teachers in programs. Zeichner's argument is that the concept of hybridity enables greater connection:

> This work in creating hybrid spaces in teacher education where academic and practitioner knowledge and knowledge that exists in communities come together in new less hierarchical ways in the service of teaching learning represents a paradigm shift in the epistemology of teacher education programs. (2010, p. 89)

Similarly, Klein et al. (2013) argue that teacher education underpinned by third space theory attempts to "address the major criticisms of teacher education, from the theory-practice divide, to the unequal status of practitioner and academic knowledge as well as the teacher and learner knowledge, and to the nature of school-university partnerships" (p. 51).

Creating these paradigm shifts necessitates new roles within teacher education, which has the potential to bring "academic, practitioner and community-based knowledge together in the teacher education process" (Zeichner, 2010, p. 92). This view is shared by Klein et al. (2013, p. 28) who argue that in third space, the roles and responsibilities for academic and school-based teacher educators will be in effect "redefined", and by its very nature, it challenges the hierarchies which have shaped the professional roles, titles and/or position descriptions in both schools and teacher education. The literature refers to third space teacher educators in different ways, including as boundary spanner (Burns & Baker, 2016; Sandholtz & Finan, 1998; Scanlon, 2001; Weertx & Sandman, 2010), boundary crosser (Akkerman & Bakker, 2011) or hybrid teacher educator (Jennings & Peloso, 2010; Martin et al., 2011; Williams, 2014).

As suggested by Martin et al. (2011) in this section's opening quote, as teacher education embarks upon hybrid roles, there needs to be more discussion on how these alternative or new understandings and practices and roles influence teacher education and narratives from the people who take up these hybrid positions. This chapter is designed to add to the field exploring hybrid educators and the important and complex roles they play within and between schools and universities. We are mindful that third space is not easy, quick or completed, and these roles are shaped by "time-honored institutional regularities and customary imbalances in authority and power" (Klein et al., 2013, p. 28). Therefore, in this chapter, we also explore the changing identity of those who engage with the third space and how instructional structures, histories and traditions shape the work that hybrid educators do and the way in which they understand their role (Klein et al., 2013). Specifically, this chapter explores the narratives of hybrid teacher educators and how they bridged or navigated spaces and encouraged transformed or alternate conceptualisations of professional identity.

3   Facilitating Hybrid Teacher Educators

This chapter is concerned with examining the hybrid teacher educator roles involved in the design and delivery of the course, *Professional Experience: Connected Classrooms,* which was underpinned by a third space design. Beginning in 2015 and with the support of the Department of Education and Training, Victoria, a partnership involving the School of Education, RMIT University, 13 primary schools, and industry was formed, underpinned by a third space theoretical premise. The initiative was formed around a second-year course/unit in the Bachelor of Education. This course blurred many of the traditional binaries in teacher education programmes, including university/school, theory/practice and university-based teacher educator/school-based teacher education. For instance, course content was co-designed by school and university teaching staff and taught both on campus and on site in partner schools. Preservice teachers (PSTs) were taught by a suite of hybrid teacher educators including school coordinator, school-based coach and project leaders. For more information about the specifics of the model, please refer to Elsden-Clifton and Jordan (2016).

Recorded interviews were held with a range of stakeholders involved in this course over a 12-month period (June 2017–2018) with ethics approved by Department of Education, Victoria and the university. Three interviews with hybrid teacher educators form the basis of this chapter. Each interview was semi-structured, with questions and prompts framed by the recommendations of Patton (1990). Each interview was conducted along the same lines, with the researcher opening each interview with general conversation and then moving into set interview questions. Prompts and questions were rephrased where necessary and questions asked as judged relevant at the time, to keep the interview running smoothly. Interviews used open-ended questions based on the following themes:

- The hybrid role undertaken and how these were different from other roles they had in university and/or school spaces;
- Reasons for being in a hybrid role and the characteristics they felt were desirable for this role;
- Perception of PSTs, teacher mentors and university and school leadership of their role;
- The impact of the hybrid role on their personal and professional identity; and
- The changes in the attitudes, approaches or practices at university and schools because of this role.

Interviews concluded with the interviewer asking if there was anything else the interviewee wished to add, or whether the interviewee wished to clarify or elaborate on something that was said earlier. Later, transcripts of the interviews were made which were then read by the researchers and reviewed against the recording, checking for accuracy. Transcripts were then re-read and key themes identified. The data were coded by recognising, matching and analysing patterns and themes. This involved using a cyclical approach in which we identified broad themes related to the theoretical premise and then used a more in-depth coding cycle in which smaller or more precise themes were then identified following the first cycle of the coding process. These themes were later used as a framework or scaffold for discussion (Merriam, 1988). Data with similar characteristics or properties were then grouped together under each theme. Pseudonyms were used to ensure the confidentiality of participants.

4 Emerging Hybrid Roles

In the design of the practicum course informed by third space constructs, it became obvious that new roles needed to be created to undertake various tasks or to support the interplay between placement, site-based learning, university-based learning, PST development and teacher mentor support. While some roles remained largely the same, others became more fluid as customary boundaries between roles and responsibilities were redefined (Zeichner, 2010). These roles are outlined in Table 1.

Table 1 Roles and Duties

Role	New or standard role	Key duties	Remuneration
School-based coach	New role	Refers to a practising teacher who usually taught at the placement school and is released from normal teaching duties to support PST learning during placement	Project funding and University funding
School coordinator	New role	Refers to an academic staff member who supports the partnership school during the placement, troubleshoots, and provides advice to coaches and teacher mentors and "at risk" support to PSTs	Project funding
Project leader	New role	Refers to an academic staff member who oversees the project, including staffing, courseware development, delivery and assessment	Project funding
School leader	Standard role	Refers to principal or assistant/deputy principal in the placement school. Nominates staff to act as school-based coaches and can influence selection of site coordinator and teacher mentors	Nil
Academic teaching staff	Standard role	Refers to an academic staff member who coordinates the course, develops, delivers (taking lectures and tutorials), and assesses course content and administers course, including PST queries	University funding

(continued)

Table 1 (continued)

Role	New or standard role	Key duties	Remuneration
Site coordinator	Standard role	Refers to the person within a school who manages the PST programme including allocation of teacher mentors and who liaises with PSTs and the university	University funding
Professional experience administrator	Standard role	Refers to the person within the university who administers the placement of PSTs, liaises with site coordinators and teacher mentors, and oversees reports and record keeping	University funding
Pre-service teacher	Standard role	Refers to the person undertaking an initial teacher education program	Nil
Teacher mentor	Standard role	Refers to the person within a school who supervises and assesses the PST during placement	University funding

As many of these roles are new or redesigned, the emerging hybrid roles and how they interact with other roles is now explained in more detail to provide context to the data.

4.1   School-Based Coach

The role of the school-based coach was a new role developed to closely connect university and school-based learning. The role was designed to be undertaken by a practising teacher at the partner school. This teacher was released from their normal teaching duties to perform this role (funded by the project) for the duration of the placement (4 weeks). Across the 15 partner schools, there were a total of 23 coaches, as some schools had two or three coaches.

Coaching models originate from business/corporate, sporting or counselling backgrounds (Fletcher & Mullen, 2012; Lord, Atkinson, & Mitchell, 2008). Though there is an increase in coaching in educational settings, the literature tends to focus on its use in improving students' learning outcomes, such as literacy coaching or peer coaching (Gill, Kostiw, & Stone, 2010). Literature that investigates the use of coaching within professional experience in education, or work-integrated learning in higher education generally, is relatively scant. The literature makes a general distinction between coaching and mentoring, defining coaching as short term, goal orientated, and performance driven, and mentoring as longer term and developmentally driven, with no specific goal (Fletcher & Mullen, 2012). This is reflective of the distinction between the role of the teacher mentor and the school-based coach that we describe in this chapter.

The placement and course were framed around PSTs setting goals. During their 20-day placement, PSTs were supported by a school-based coach to achieve these goals. Like teacher mentors, they also supported building the teaching capacity of PSTs: observing them teaching, providing feedback and having professional conversations around their practice and addressing issues as they arose in the school. In performing this role, the coach, however, focused on the PSTs and their professional learning needs rather than on the learners (school students), which is often the focus of the teacher mentor. Coaches also had a teaching role, teaching the course content on-site in partner schools and supporting PST learning, including helping them refine and revise their goals based on the school context and learning needs of students they were teaching.

The coaches also knew the teachers at the school site and, as they knew the PSTs' specific learning goals (that had been set during coursework), were able to help influence this decision-making to select "best fit" mentors for them. Coaches were also in regular contact with key university staff, checking in and providing feedback, and were instrumental if there were any PSTs at risk. Thus, the school-based coach played an important role in creating a third space that bridged and connected theory to practice.

4.2 School Coordinator

Having a university staff member work directly with schools became the defining role of the school coordinator, another new role that we created for this model. There was one school coordinator, and this role was undertaken by an academic staff member (full-time academic staff with a Ph.D.) as we wanted someone who knew the university processes—such as the Student Code of Conduct and expectations of placement—and who had the required knowledge and authority to intervene if there were issues so they could assess students "at risk" and/or terminate placements. Many of the duties involved were atypical of what is conventionally associated with an academic, such as liaising with school leaders and teachers and having specific knowledge of the partner schools, including their school history, programs and priorities, and the student cohort. The school coordinator visited each school during the placement to check in with the coaches and to trouble shoot issues.

They also played an important role in the partnership work involved in this third space. The school coordinator, along with the project leaders, was paramount in the establishment of the initial partnership development. During the year, they also facilitated partnership "work" such as attending meetings with school leaders, presenting at staff meetings and learning more about the school. As their relationships with schools developed, there were often times they were asked to work more closely with the school; for instance, they were invited to present awards, facilitate professional learning or be a member of the school board.

The school coordinator role was one of the more complex and hybrid in nature, as they had to intersect with many other professionals. It involved answering questions about professional experience from PSTs, teacher mentors and school-based coaches.

4.3 Project Leaders

The role of a project leader generally relates to performing tasks associated with the project's leadership. The project leaders' team comprised of two academics, two school leaders and one industry partner. However, very quickly it was realised that this leadership involved more than just the project. The project leaders were the faces of the project and needed to be able to relate with all those involved and assume the discourse of those involved. For the school-based teacher educators, this meant fulfilling a traditional school leader role, but also involved meeting with other school leaders at meetings or regional gatherings to discuss the project and contribute ideas and school perspectives.

For the university teacher educators, this meant fulfilling a traditional academic role, defending workload allocation, explaining the project and justifying design decisions made to the university. It meant being able to liaise with schools and talk a different talk about why forming partnerships was effective for teaching and learning and how it benefited schools and the university. The project leaders in many respects became people managers, liaising with all professionals involved in the partnership. Project leaders also became event managers, hosting professional learning events including a Think Tank Day working with schools to co-design the course that underpinned this project, and the professional learning event at the end of each year celebrating successes and sharing practices. The project leaders also played a strategic role in developing the model and negotiating with university staff such as head of school and programme directors. They appointed key staff, collected research data, attended key meetings and worked directly with industry such as the Department of Education, Victoria.

5 The Hybrid Teacher Educators

Several interviews were conducted as part of a broader project around models of professional experience (eight interviews in total with various hybrid teacher educators). This chapter uses data from three of these interviews to represent the three hybrid roles described above.

5.1 Lara, School-Based Coach

Lara has been teaching for almost 10 years and is a leading teacher and ICT coach. She taught at one school and while she was on maternity leave this school used her as a coach. After returning from leave, she took a position at another school and became the coach at her previous and current partner school concurrently. She also lectured and tutored the course at university and on-site. When asked about the coaching role and whether it was different from her school teaching role, Lara commented, "*I don't see them all that differently,*" as both involved coaching, "*improving practice and sharing my knowledge and expertise in different areas.*"

Lara's interview reveals how complex her role was. When asked about what a typical day would look like for a school-based coach she responded:

> Every day is different, which is why I loved the role and it always looked different and this is hard, as I go from the two roles of being a coach and teaching my Year 5 s at times if something was happening in my normal class. But if I had to try to capture it, before school I would often touch base via email with the other school-based coach, first teaching block I might observe the beginning of a lesson by PST #1, I then may observe PST #2 who was teaching a small group. In the second teaching block I might meet and conduct a 20 min coaching session with PST #2. Hopefully the teacher mentor also has release time to attend, and I can help them work on their mentoring skills and then in the third teaching block I might be in my own classroom teaching reading. After school I may do a 15 min coaching session with PST #1 and then touch base with the school and site coordinator or action things if there are any issues, but in saying that it could all look different the next day! So yeah it is pretty complex.

Lara spoke at length about one aspect of coaching which involved working with PSTs one-on-one each week to *"just touch base, see how they're going"*. As she reflected:

> I think it was a great time for them to be able to sit down and reflect on what had happened this week, what questions they still had and then also just to have a time to sit with me and say this is not working or I'm really having trouble with this mentor, have you got a strategy that I can work with?

She would also have a one-on-one coaching session with them around teaching practices that they wanted to work on, especially those involving digital technologies, the emphasis of the course. Lara commented on how valued she felt as a coach, with PSTs often commenting favourably on how she had supported them. As she relayed, *"they've said to us that it's nice to have a face at the school that you can confide in and that it's someone separate from your mentor"*.

Lara spoke at length about how she felt that she had an important role to play in bridging the university and practice in schools. She returned to this position several times throughout the interview. As she commented, *"as I said before they could be struggling with their mentor, and it's also someone that has a link between the uni assignments and what's expected"*. Lara elaborated on this, commenting that she thought she performed a useful role in bridging the expectations of the university and the school; that while teacher mentors may have some understanding of PST expectations while on placement, they do not have a lot of time to know its details, whereas she as the coach does. As she notes: *"My role then was to filter some of the information to my mentors."* Later in the interview she returns to this point about the importance of having someone in the school who *"unpacks it like we [coaches] do"* and how *"I think it does mean more because its's coming from someone that they know and respect within the school and think well I need to make this work"*. As she later adds, *"having that person there in the school I can then touch base … I can literally walk into any classroom and say hey what's going on"*. And this: *"I think again just having that link between a university person that actually really understands the course and understands the assignments, understands some of the issues that come with going into a new school and having that time to be able to sit with all of the other PSTs"*.

Lara also spoke about how important it was for a coach to have relationships with other staff at the school, particularly teacher mentors. As she commented, sometimes her role involved mediation with a teacher mentor. She spoke about a time when a PST came to her concerned about the lateness in feedback that her teacher mentor was giving her on her planning, leaving her feeling very confused about expectations, quite stressed and upset. As Lara elaborated, *"I had to go in and speak and negotiate on both of their behalf, to say this is a bit unrealistic and this is how we can go forward from here"*.

Lara spoke too about how being a coach has impacted on her own practice. She commented for example that talking with teacher mentors, *"has helped me to think about my practice and what I do to help other people to improve their practice"*. Later she returns to his point, commenting that being a coach has *"helped to make links between current research and what's happening and making links between new teachers that are coming out and what's expected from mentors and things like that within the classrooms".*

5.2 Jackie, a School Coordinator

Jackie was a teacher educator who had been teaching at the university for some time. Coming from a teaching background, she mainly taught in the Bachelor of Education program, teaching across all year levels and course types (educational studies as well as curriculum studies and professional experience). Alongside the project leaders her role involved working closely with the partner schools to ensure the 4-week placement block ran smoothly. Jackie commented that she took on the role because she thought she would enjoy it and it would enable her to reconnect with schools: "*I haven't been in the school classroom for a long time. This just made sense to me*". Yet as she went on to explain, the role was more complex than she had initially thought:

> When I first took on the role, I thought that it was fairly straight-forward. I was accustomed to making school visits to visit PSTs while on placement and to observe them teach. I had taught within prac courses before, so I went in fully aware of the workload and issues, but I guess I thought it would an extension, or just like this work. So, I thought this was what I would be doing, but to be honest, I probably didn't think that much about it. I just thought it sounded like a great opportunity to work with schools, to follow the PSTs from my classroom into the school classroom and to gain some currency and connection with schools. However, I had greatly underestimated the extent of partnership and relationship work that was involved in the role and it did start to be not reflective of the workload allocated to this position.

As she commented, part of this role was organising visits to each school. "*Yeah, I thought, visit each school. Simple. But you know, it isn't that simple.*" As Jackie then explained, "*sometimes was a bit of a problem. Who should I visit first? Who should I visit last? Who do I organise the visit with, school leaders or coach it was a bit political in some school?*" As Jackie commented, though, the visits needed to go smoothly:

> Sometimes I felt a bit of pressure, yeah, sure. You know these partnerships are important to us [university]. I need to make them work. I was aware of the literature that partnerships are easy to form, but they are harder to sustain. Layered on the fact this was a new model that I could see real value in so yeah I was acutely aware of the high importance of this role.

She later spoke about this skill set as being akin to being a public relations manager:

> It was a lot more than just the liaison work I had done in the past. It was more of a public relations exercise. I needed to really know the school, who are the main people, what coffee they drank [laughs] because schools can easily tell, you know they can tell if you're not a teacher, if you're not really that interested, or if you are trying to fake it.

Many schools she visited asked her to go on a tour to look round the school: "*This was really important. I had a lot of fun doing this. They are really proud of what they've done and what they've been able to achieve"*. As she added, *"they really want you to see the school, you know, really see it"*. She spoke about how sometimes she felt a bit of unease when visiting schools because she did not know them well, *"look I know our program and I know how to teach. But, you know, visiting schools and talking with them, that was a different experience"*. As she also commented, the schools she was visiting were all very different and she needed to change her identity and presentation depending on the school:

> These schools are so different. And yes, I know that, but I also didn't know that, if you know what I mean. Some of the schools I visited were huge. Over two thousand students at one. Some of them were quite small and had undergone a lot of change. These were the older schools, who now had declining numbers. So each school I had to approach in slightly different ways.

She spoke about one visit in particular:

> I remember this one visit to the school. I'd arrived early, so I was sitting in the outer office, when a staff member, well I'd assumed it was a staff member, spoke to me. I explained who I was and what I was doing. I hadn't realised that I was talking to the principal. But before I knew it, I was in her office, sharing a coffee and talking about her staffing issues. You just had to be mindful that you were constantly "on".

This toll and the emotional work were a feature of a lot of the stories told by Jackie. As she explained, being the school coordinator had some challenges, including when she needed to address PST performance issues:

> I was often the first port of call, like the coach would email to say they were worried about this one student – it might be because they aren't settling in, or teaching isn't for them, or a breakdown in relationship with the mentor teacher or the PST is too anxious to continue – so that would involve a visit to the school, intense meetings with at-risk students and follow up with all the school leader, supervising teachers, coach, uni and course coordinator – everyone! There was a lot of emotional work involved.

Jackie commented that a lot of this work she considered *"unseen"* and that other staff members questioned if she was working, as *"I was away from the workplace for weeks at a time, and there was a lot of time out of the normal workplace, so it felt a pressure, I suppose it was like I was 'missing' from the workplace"*. At the end of the interview Jackie reflected, *"while it was difficult at times, exceeded the allocated time provided, I felt it is the most rewarding part of my year. It reminds me why I became a teacher educator in the first place"*.

5.3   Patricia, a Project Leader

Patricia had been a teacher educator at the university for some time and had managed various funded research grants previously. She had volunteered to lead this project, being involved from its initial scoping, the formal expression of interest submitted, and the development of the project implementation plan. As she commented:

From the outset I really believed in this project. I've been convinced for some time that we needed to have closer connections with schools. We also needed to work with schools more and this project provided the perfect mix of research, innovation, working in new ways with schools and teaching differently at university.

As Patricia explored in some detail, this project involved some 200 second-year PSTs, and some 15 partner schools. As she added, "*And you know there were only the two of us from the university*". Patricia explained that while she had had various conversations about the intent of the project when it was being scoped, she felt a bit unsure whether the Head of School at the university recognised what was involved and whether requested support would be realised. "*I thought if we were organised we'd be right. You know project mange it. Work out what needs to be done, by whom and by when.*" As she elaborated, while this planning and management were important, "*we would not have got the project off the ground if we hadn't done the grunt work, for instance, my colleague had to do the role of school coordinator in the first year or two just to make sure any issues could be ironed out*".

During the interview, she made several comments about how leading this project was different from other projects she had managed. "*For a start, you're dealing with schools not just as a site of research, but as an equal partner with a voice and input that you are trying to encourage. You're dealing with people. It's all real*". And this, "*you know it sounds so easy. Form partnerships with schools, do some time in schools with support from a coach. But what does this really mean? We were totally unprepared for this*". And further, "*We're academics. Yes, we manage our classes. We teach. But this is different*". Patricia explained that the main difference was the relationship aspect of the third space model, "*relationships. That's what it is all about. And how do you get trained for that? We just had to learn on the job*"; however, this was also problematic, "*but you know the real problem was that others didn't really appreciate this, but to be fair even we had underestimated the true time and investment in relationships we would have to make*".

6   Discussion

A third space construct in teacher education makes visible the connections between schools and universities, including key personnel. This chapter explores the narratives of hybrid teacher educators who have bridged and navigated the spaces occupied by theory and practice. The interviews highlighted the complexity of the hybrid teacher educator role within third spaces and suggest there are a number of considerations for university–school partnerships that have implications for schools, universities and broader contexts.

6.1 Complexities and Tensions Within Third Space

All interviewees noted a tension of being "in-between": Jackie outlined the need to think politically to navigate visits; Patricia noted the difficulty of implementing a project and research agenda while still encouraging input and shared responsibility; and Lara spoke about having to negotiate relationships between PST and mentors.

Brookhart and Loadman (1992) discussed three areas where they see difficulties or tensions with university–school partnerships: the theory-practice divide, issues of time and power, and finally, the different institutional structures and conditions for employees at university and schools. Given several design features were employed to honour third space principles from the beginning of the project (e.g. shared responsibility, co-constructed material), a disconnect between theory and practice featured very little in the interviews. Smoothing out connections was certainly the role of the school-based coach. For instance, Lara spoke several times about being a bridge between schools and universities, saying at times this was between PSTs and the university and how she was the *"link between the uni assignments and what's expected"*. At other times this was between the university and school/supervising teachers, *"my role then was to filter some of the information to my mentors"* and between mentor teachers and PSTs, *"I had to go in and speak and negotiate on both of their behalf"*. However, tensions around time and different structures did feature in the interviews.

All three noted that bridging boundaries and navigating within this boundary-spanning territory increased their workload, or that their workload was higher than expected. Lara, the school-based coach, spoke about juggling her own classroom with PST obligations when she outlined her role on a *"typical day"*; Jackie commented that she had *"underestimated the extent of partnership and relationship work that was involved in the role and it did start to be not reflective of the workload allocated to this position"*. Some of these tensions around time may be due to what Martin et al. (2011) describe as "institutional and economic structures" (p. 4) that can constrain new and emerging hybrid teacher education roles.

While the interviewees had a philosophical belief in partnerships and saw many benefits, each of them outlined how a hybrid role was fundamentally different from the roles they had previously held in schools or universities, which seemed to be more problematic for those who had primarily come from higher education. For instance, Lara noted that she did not really see a difference as both school-based and university-based teaching involved *"improving practice and sharing my knowledge and expertise in different areas"*, whereas Jackie spoke about how being within the third space meant she felt *"unseen"* or away from the workplace and Patricia spoke about how she felt the work she had completed was unappreciated and undervalued. This may be because school-based coaches were released from normal duties for the duration of the placement, but for Jackie and Patricia this work was absorbed into their university work under broad categories such as research, teaching or administration. It may also be because there is currently a lack of status and understanding of these roles within university contexts. Further work is needed to account for third space labour in institutional workplaces for this to be considered valued and sustainable work.

6.2   Relationships Within Third Space

Martin et al. (2011) in their description of a hybrid teacher educator described the role as being in a "web of relationships" including "relationship with individuals, relationship with similar groups of people, relationships across groups of people and interactions" (p. 7), and this web was similar for the interviewees. Patricia explicitly made this point in her description of what made this role different from other project roles she had undertaken. Jackie spoke about having to be constantly "*on*" and describing having to be continually attentive to multiple people, akin to a "*public relations exercise*".

Jackie also acknowledged the toll of playing an active and pivotal role in cultivating a third space where various stakeholders are valued and thus each school needed to be approached in "slightly different ways". She also explained how this role involved juggling the multiple obligations she had to consider from the school, "*I was often the first port of call*", university, "*You know these partnerships are important to us [university]. I need to make them work*", and PSTs, "*I just thought it sounded like a great opportunity to … follow the PSTs from my classroom into the school classroom*".

6.3   Professional Identity

Taylor et al. (2014) noted that hybrid teacher educators must position themselves at times in "unfamiliar and uncomfortable" (p. 7) ways, acknowledge the privileging of academic knowledge, and be mindful of their language and actions. Most of the interviewees noted that at times they had to venture into unfamiliar territory. Jackie talked about thinking it would be like other roles she had performed associated with practicum courses where she was familiar with the roles, responsibility and identity in the traditional triad of PST, mentor teacher and university liaison. However, she explained how the school coordinator role went beyond this and how there was a difference in what she had to do in terms of partnership and relationship work. Patricia spoke at length of how her identity as project leader shifted in a project based on third space theory and Lara outlined how her role became about helping navigate terrain for PSTs and teacher mentors.

Of interest emerging from the data was the fluidity of these roles; there were slippages between these hybrid roles. For example, Lara fulfilled the coach role at two partner schools and lectured at university and Jackie had been a project leader and a one-time school coordinator. The literature often refers to boundary spanners or hybrid teacher educators as a singular group, but this research demonstrates that there are multiple versions of hybrid teacher educators and it is hard to capture or define "one type" of boundary spanner. This has implications for workforce policy and planning to ensure that it can accommodate flexible and non-traditional professional roles that sit within, alongside, and between schools and university.

The narratives are testament to the evolving space of partnerships in teacher education that go beyond the traditional triadic relationships of PST, teacher mentor and university liaisons. There is a growing array of roles that are needed as teacher education moves towards partnership models proposed by policy rhetoric. In destabilising what counts as knowledge and "official" roles and conventions, some interesting dilemmas and questions are raised. However, more research will be needed to fully realise the complexities around new position descriptions, workload models that account for the complexity of the relational work. There will also need to be further consideration of the philosophical and practical actions that are needed to maintain third spaces in teacher education, as well as, the workplace supports needed for key hybrid educators to be "housed" at both sites including union, workplace health and safety, well-being and policy implications. The question of who should take on the role of hybrid teacher educator, including what qualifications and experience need to be considered, alongside how workplaces and institutions recognise the role of boundary spanners.

It does raise questions and dilemmas around the sustainability of these redefined roles and has ramifications for the workforce and professional identity: Who is the teacher educator and how is this role morphing and slipping in current times? What are the career risks for those who navigate binaries and take up third spaces? Within these roles, to whom does the hybrid teacher educator report—is it schools, universities, both, or none, and if so, how? What is the career trajectory for those within third spaces? Are we ready for third spaces and the professional roles that they create?

7 Conclusion

For some time, reviews and reports into teacher education in Australia have lamented the theory-practice divide, often proposing partnerships with schools and well-structured professional experience programmes as ways to achieve greater connection. There is also perhaps increasing impatience for what is perceived to be teacher education reluctance to change, and failure to work with schools to realise a shared commitment to teacher education. Researchers such as Zeichner (2010) and Klein et al. (2013) have proposed new ways of thinking about the epistemology of teacher education in which both practitioner and academic knowledge are valued. Such researchers have suggested that third space offers a useful means of reconceptualising this relationship, as it values multiple perspectives rather than the binaries of theory/practice and academic/practitioner that have characterised traditional teacher education.

In this chapter, we have proposed that the traditional role of the teacher educator is evolving and that new hybrid roles are emerging as educators bridge and navigate across these university and school spaces. New hybrid roles include school-based coaches, who traverse the dual role of practitioner and teacher educator when they teach PSTs on-site in schools; school coordinators, teacher educators who act as boundary spanners across universities and school sites in support of forming and sustaining relationships with schools; project leaders, teacher educators primarily, who appropriate the role of relationship manager into their tool kit as they oversee the many and varied roles stakeholders adopt in this project. As this small data set shows, a third space construct in teacher education makes visible the connections between schools and universities, including key personnel. This chapter explores the narratives of hybrid teacher educators who have bridged and navigated the spaces occupied by theory and practice. It highlights the potential of hybrid teacher educators to bring together theory and practice in meaningful ways, but also considers the challenges that these roles bring. It suggests that teacher education needs to exist across multiple spaces and not be confined to university sites removed from the practice of schools. Furthermore, it suggests that new hybrid roles are needed in this new hybrid space where multiple stakeholders can engage in the enterprise of teacher education.

References

Akkerman, S. F., & Bakker, A. (2011). Boundary crossing and boundary objects. *Review of Educational Research, 81*(2), 132–169.

Allen, J. M., & Wright, S. E. (2014). Integrating theory and practice in the pre-service teacher education program. *Teachers and Teaching: Theory and Practice, 20*(2), 136–151.

Bhabha, H. (1994). *The location of culture*. London: Routledge.

Brookhart, S. M., & Loadman, W. E. (1992). School-university collaboration: Across cultures. *Teaching Education, 4*(2), 53–68.

Bullough, R. V., Jr., Draper, R. J., Smith, L., & Birrell, J. R. (2004). Moving beyond collusion: Clinical faculty and university/public school partnership. *Teaching and Teacher Education, 20*(5), 505–521.

Burns, R. W., & Baker, W. (2016). The boundary spanner in professional development schools: In search of common nomenclature. *School-University Partnerships, 9*(2), 28–39.

Cuenca, A., Schmeichel, M., Butler, B. M., Dinkelman, T., & Nichols, J. R. (2011). Creating a "third space" in student teaching: Implications for the university supervisor's status as outsider. *Teaching and Teacher Education, 27*(7), 1068–1077.

Darling-Hammond, L. (2006). Constructing 21st-century teacher education. *Journal of Teacher Education, 57*(3), 300–314.

Darling-Hammond, L. (2010). Constructing 21st century teacher education. In H. Valerie & C. W. Lewis (Eds.), *Transforming teacher education: What went wrong with teacher training, and how we can fix it* (pp. 223–248). Herndon, VA: Stylus Publishing.

Elsden-Clifton, J. (2006). Constructing "Thirdspaces": Migrant students and the visual arts. *Studies in Learning, Evaluation, Innovation and Development, 3*(1), 1–11.

Elsden-Clifton, J., & Jordan, K. (2016). Reframing professional experience: Adopting a distributed open collaborative course framework to facilitate third spaces. In A. Bertram & T. Barkatsas (Eds.), *Global Learning in the 21 Century*. Sense: Rotterdam.

Flessner, R. (2014). Revisiting reflection: Utilizing third spaces in teacher education. *The Educational Forum, 78*(3), 231–247.

Fletcher, S., & Mullen, C. A. (Eds.). (2012). *Sage handbook of mentoring and coaching in education*. London: Sage.

Gaffey, C., & Dobbins, R. (1996). *Tertiary teacher educators: Do they make a difference in practicum*. PEPE Monograph, No. 1, 105–122.

Gannon, S. (2010). Service learning as a third space in pre-service teacher education. *Issues in Educational Research, 20*(1), 21–28.

Gill, J., Kostiw, N., & Stone, S. (2010). Coaching teachers in effective instruction: A Victorian perspective. *Literacy Learning: The Middle Years, 18*(2), 49–53.

Grossman, P., Hammerness, K., & McDonald, M. (2009). Redefining teacher: Re-imagining teacher education. *Teachers and Teaching: Theory and Practice, 15*(2), 273–290.

Gutiérrez, K. D. (2008). Developing a sociocritical literacy in the third space. *Reading Research Quarterly, 43*(2), 148–164.

Guyton, E., & McIntyre, D. J. (1990). Student teaching and school experiences. In W. R. Houston (Ed.), *Handbook of research on teacher education* (pp. 514–534). New York: Macmillan.

Harman, R., & Khote, N. (2018). Critical SFL praxis with bilingual youth: Disciplinary instruction in a third space. *Critical Inquiry in Language Studies, 15*(1), 63–83.

House of Representatives Standing Committee on Education and Vocational Training. (2007). *Top of the Class: Report of the Inquiry into Teacher Education*. Retrieved from http://www. aph.gov.au/parliamentary_business/committees/house_of_representatives_committees?url=evt/ teachereduc/report/fullreport.pdf.

Jennings, G., & Peloso, J. M. (2010). The underutilized potential of the hybrid educator in teacher education. *The New Educator, 6*(2), 153–162.

Klein, E. J., Taylor, M., Onore, C., Strom, K., & Abrams, L. (2013). Finding a third space in teacher education: Creating an urban teacher residency. *Teaching Education, 24*(1), 27–57.

Lord, P., Atkinson, M., & Mitchell, H. (2008). *Mentoring and coaching for professionals: A study of the research evidence*. London: NFER.

Martin, S. D., Snow, J. L., & Franklin Torrez, C. A. (2011). Navigating the terrain of third space: Tensions with/in relationships in school-university partnerships. *Journal of Teacher Education, 62*(3), 299–311.

McDonough, S. (2014). Rewriting the script of mentoring pre-service teachers in third space: Exploring tensions of loyalty, obligation and advocacy. *Studying Teacher Education: A Journal of Self-study of Teacher Education Practices, 10*(3), 210–221.

Merriam, S. B. (1988). *Case study research in education. A qualitative approach*. San Francisco: Jossey-Bass Publishers.

Moje, E. B., Ciechanowski, K. M., Kramer, K., Ellis, L., Carrillo, R., & Collazo, T. (2004). Working toward third space in content area literacy: An examination of everyday funds of knowledge and discourse. *Reading Research Quarterly, 39*(1), 38–70.

Patton, M. Q. (1990). *Qualitative evaluation and research methods*. Newbury Park, CA: Sage.

Sandholtz, J. H., & Finan, E. C. (1998). Blurring the boundaries to promote school-university partnerships. *Journal of Teacher Education, 49*(1), 13–25.

Scanlon, L. (2001). *The boundary spanner: Exploring the new frontiers of a school-university partnership as a community of practice*. Paper presented at the AARE Conference, Freemantle.

Soja, E. W. (1996). *Thirdspace: Journeys to Los Angeles and other real and imagined places*. Malden, MA: Blackwell.

Taylor, M., Klein, E. J., & Abrams, L. (2014). Tensions of reimagining our roles as teacher educators in a third space: Revisiting a co/autoethnography through a faculty lens. *Studying Teacher Education, 10*(1), 3–19.

Teacher Education Ministerial Advisory Group (TEMAG). (2014). *Action now: Classroom ready teachers*. Retrieved from https://docs.education.gov.au/system/files/doc/other/action_now_ classroom_ready_teachers_accessible.pdf.

Weertx, D. J., & Sandman, L. R. (2010). Community engagement and boundary-spanning roles at research universities. *The Journal of Higher Education, 81*(6), 702–727.

Williams, J. (2014). Teacher educator professional learning in the third space: Implications for identity and practice. *Journal of Teacher Education, 65*(4), 315–326.

Wood, M. B., & Turner, E. E. (2015). Bringing the teacher into teacher preparation: Learning from mentor teachers in joint methods activities. *Journal of Mathematics Teacher Education, 18*(1), 27–51.

Zeichner, K. (1999). The new scholarship in teacher education. *Educational Researcher, 28*(9), 4–15.
Zeichner, K. (2010). Rethinking the connections between campus courses and field experiences in college-and university-based teacher education. *Journal of Teacher Education, 61*(1–2), 89–99.

Jennifer Clifton is a Senior Lecturer in the School of Education and Professional Studies at Griffith University. As an experienced school teacher and university educator, she teaches in teacher preparation programmes in the areas of professional experience, health education and professional issues in teaching. She researches within the area of work-integrated learning and partnerships between schools and universities.

Associate Professor Kathy Jordan is a researcher in the School of Education, RMIT University. Kathy has strong research interest in initial teacher education, including the changing policy context that is shaping practice and the importance of Work-Integrated-learning to preservice teacher development, with a focus on negotiating theory and practice and the development and implementation of innovative approaches using partnerships, shared responsibility and site-based learning. Kathy is also interested in changing notions of literacy, the use of ICT in school education and teacher decision-making particularly around ICT.

Chapter 5
Exploring What It Means to Be a Professional in Partnerships: Reflecting on Teacher Educator Narratives

Amanda Gutierrez, Kenneth Young and Kathy Jordan

Abstract School–university partnerships are complex and multivarious. Teacher educators working on the ground in this space traverse multiple settings and negotiate discourses in their attempt to meet the needs of all stakeholders spread across these settings. They are the implementers of the Teacher Education Ministerial Advisory Group (TEMAG) recommendations around partnerships, as they deal with the reality of trying to meet the Australian Institute of Teaching and School Leadership (AITSL) accreditation requirements around partnerships. Teacher educators negotiate university structures, school systems and often government and other organisational expectations of partnership outcomes. Through all of this, they also operationalise and often manage the partnership models around preservice teacher engagement with schools. This chapter utilises recently published material on partnership models (Chittleborough and Jones in *School-based partnerships in teacher education: A research informed model for universities, schools and beyond*. Springer Nature, Singapore, pp. 61–82, 2018; Hobbs et al. in STEPS interpretative framework. Science Teacher Education Program, 2015) to frame narrative reflections from teacher educators in the school–university space. Through narrative methodology, the stories of these teacher educators reflect the complex space they negotiate and broker, and their struggles to have their role valued, recognised and resourced. The commonality of professional relationships being developed between partnership participants, and their critical importance, was clearly reflected in each of the author's individual narrative writing.

A. Gutierrez (✉)
Australian Catholic University, Brisbane, QLD, Australia
e-mail: Amanda.gutierrez@acu.edu.au

K. Young
University of Sunshine Coast, Sippy Downs, QLD, Australia
e-mail: Kyoung@usc.edu.au

K. Jordan
RMIT, Melbourne, Australia
e-mail: kathy.jordan@rmit.edu.au

© Springer Nature Singapore Pte Ltd. 2019
A. Gutierrez et al. (eds.), *Professionalism and Teacher Education*,
https://doi.org/10.1007/978-981-13-7002-1_5

91

1   Introduction

School–university partnerships have received much attention in government policy over the last five years. The Teacher Education Ministerial Advisory Group (TEMAG) report (2014), the latest review in a long list of reviews and reports into teacher education (Louden, 2008; Mayer, 2014), argued that partnerships were vital to ensuring the interconnection of theory and practice, long lamented as an issue in Initial Teacher Education (ITE) (Mayer, 2014). The TEMAG report proposes that theory and practice, "must be inseparable and mutually reinforced in all program components" (TEMAG, 2014, p. x), ensuring that preservice teachers (PST) develop both content knowledge and pedagogical understanding to teach effectively. Placement or practicum is identified as providing a means for PSTs to practice this interconnection.

To accomplish this objective, the TEMAG report advocates ITE providers and schools form "structured and mutually beneficial partnerships" (TEMAG, 2014, p. x) and to document these arrangements via a partnership agreement. Partnerships between ITE providers and schools around professional experience are not a new phenomenon; however, the TEMAG recommendations and Australian Institute for Teaching and School Leadership (AITSL, 2015) accreditation requirements have changed even the simplest professional experience engagement, with a strong impetus for more systematic and documented connections between schools, universities and systems such as the Department of Education and Catholic Education. The TEMAG advisory group states "the single most important action to be pursued is the integrated delivery of initial teacher education. This can be achieved through close partnerships between providers, school systems and schools, and underpins improvement to all aspects of the preparation of teachers" (2014, p. xi). The TEMAG report recommends that these agreements should cover all aspects of professional experience and include, at a minimum,

> a structure to support placements, including flexibility of workplace arrangements; a description of shared roles and responsibilities, including expectations of school leaders; shared assessment of PSTs; identification and selection of supervising teachers; opportunity for additional professional development for supervising teachers; and better connection between staff, providers and schools (TEMAG, 2014, p. 32).

While informal partnerships have existed, new regulations have required those involved in partnerships to formalise and document all professional partnerships between ITE providers and school systems.

As is often the case with government mandates, the complexity of phenomena such as professional experience partnerships cannot always be captured or represented accurately. This chapter sets out to represent aspects of the complex nature of university–school partnership work, especially in relation to what this means for teacher educator professional identity, and for initial teacher education programmes as a whole. It utilises Hobbs' et al. (2015) and Jones et al. (2016) partnership framework, specifically their Principals of Partnership Practices, to frame individual narratives from three teacher educators across three university contexts. The narratives serve to represent the experiences of teacher educators, unpack the dimensions of their roles and the possible ramifications for teacher educator identity, as well as explore challenges and complexities embedded within school–university partnerships. It also analyses a metanarrative collaboratively developed by the authors from comments on each other's individual narratives. This constructs a dialogic collaborative discourse which represents shared exploration of what it means to be a professional teacher educator in the partnership space.

2 Literature Review

As outlined in the introduction, there are government policy and accreditation requirements to consider when formalising school–university partnership arrangements. How this translates into practice, and in particular what it means for those teacher educator professionals trying to develop and negotiate partnerships is much more complex than the representations in government policy and accreditation documentation. It has been extensively acknowledged in the literature that school–university partnerships tend to be under-resourced and run on the goodwill of inspired individual teacher educators, school leaders and teachers in schools (Grudnoff, Haigh & Mackisack, 2016; Herbert, Redman, & Speldewinde, 2018; Le Cornu, 2015; Ryan & Jones, 2014; White, Tindall-Ford, Heck, & Ledger, 2018). The teacher educator professional often acts as the "boundary broker," or "boundary crosser" (Gardiner & Lorch, 2015; Loughland & Nguyen, 2018; Sewell, Cody, Weir, & Hansen, 2018); the person who traverses and negotiates multiple university spaces, school spaces and often other organisations such as government, Catholic or Independent bodies, to find common goals and achievable outcomes. This includes negotiating what is at times a clash of priorities between systems relating to university expectations of graduates (Bloomfield & Nguyen, 2015), research agendas (Walsh & Backe, 2013), accreditation standards (Bloomfield & Nguyen, 2015) and perceived theory/practice dichotomies (Allen & Wright, 2014; Ryan & Jones, 2014; Zeichner, 2010).

Added to this complexity for the teacher educator professional is the negotiation of university classifications and role descriptions, which can create inner tension around defining and legitimising one's academic work in partnerships. Those working in partnerships, especially in professional experience/community engagement partnerships, often have their work categorised into the "third mission" or "service" category. This area "remains an ethereal component of what higher education actually does…third mission activity often covers everything besides traditional teaching and traditional research, this does little to help frame it as a task that can be shaped" (Jongbloed, Enders & Salerno, 2008, p. 312). In addition, "the role of community engagement is still obstructed by many institutional barriers, implying that the acceptance of a third mission is not a straightforward action" (Jongbloed et al., 2008, p. 317). The practical outcome of these obstructions is the need for academics in this space to continually legitimise their work and champion the outcomes and worth of partnerships to multiple stakeholders. Jongbloed et al. (2008) further argue that if universities were really committed to their stakeholders, they would engage dialogically to explore what is valued and what can be done better, including ways to sustain relationships. Sustainability of partnerships is an important concept in school–university partnership literature (see, e.g. Herbert et al., 2018; Le Cornu, 2015; White et al., 2018) and a serious concern for those individual academics who are left to manage these complex spaces with university pressure to create sustainable models. This pressure is amplified when universities, governments and systems appear to put much emphasis on ideals of partnerships on paper, however, "sub-optimally allocate[ing] their scarce human and physical capital" (Jongbloed et al., 2008, p. 304) to this space.

It is clear from the literature that successful operationalisation of partnerships relies on relational connections which Kruger, Davies, Eckersley, Newell, and Cherednichenko (2009) argue are "characterised by trust, mutuality and reciprocity among preservice teachers, teachers and other school colleagues and teacher educators" (p. 10). In addition, as just discussed, success and sustainability of partnerships "are contingent on provision of adequate resources" (Bloomfield & Nguyen, 2015, p. 27). The people in partnerships, and their communicative and negotiation skills are essential to success.

Considering the ethereal and multiple nature of partnerships, some authors have worked on developing models and frameworks for partnership practice. These are useful to consider when exploring and reflecting on teacher educator roles in partnerships. Seminal pieces of work conceptualising models of partnerships include Furlong et al. (1996), Kruger et al. (2009), Hobbs et al. (2015) and Hobbs, Campbell, and Jones (2018). The most recent framework from an Australian cross-institutional

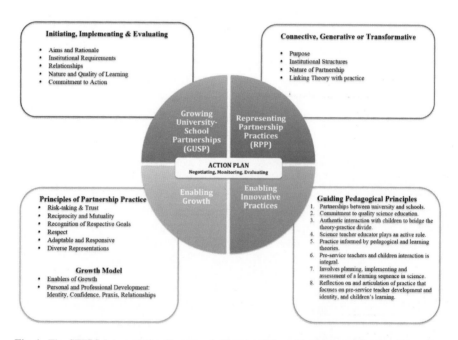

Fig. 1 The STEPS Interpretative Framework (Reprinted from Teaching and Teacher Education, Vol. 60, Jones, M., Hobbs, L., Kenny, J., Campbell, C., Chittleborough, G., Gilbert, A., Herbert, S., & Redman, C., Successful University–School Partnerships: An Interpretive Framework to Inform Partnership Practice, pp. 108–120, Copyright (2016, with permission from Elsevier)

STEM partnership project called STEPS, Science Teacher Education Partnerships with schools, draws on previous research and their own research into partnerships. The various members of the team have published their findings, including an evaluative report (Hobbs et al., 2015), a recently published book (Hobbs et al., 2018) and other publications (e.g. Jones et al., 2016). The evaluative report includes the conceptualisation of what they labelled the STEPS Interpretative Framework (see Fig. 1), which is further theorised in the Jones et al. (2016) publication. It provides a tool to discuss different levels of embeddedness in partnerships.

The main section of the Framework utilised for this chapter is the Principles of Partnership Practice (PPP) from the Enabling Growth domain. Enabling Growth considers the requirements for partnerships to grow and be sustainable. The PPP category includes "risk-taking and trust, reciprocity and mutuality, respect, recognition of respective goals, adaptability and responsiveness to changing needs, and diverse representations" (Hobbs et al., 2015, pp. 29–31) as summarised in Table 1.

Table 1 Gutierrez, Young and Jordan summarised version of the Principles of Partnership from Hobbs et al. (2015), pp. 29–31

Risk-taking and trust	– PST's capability and reliability – Quality of teaching and learning experience for PSTs – Organisation, commitment and contribution to the partnership – Honesty
Reciprocity and mutuality	– Mutual benefit – Nurturing the benefits—Schools contribute to PST learning – PSTs have authentic experiences – Teacher educators have school and classroom experiences
Respect	– Respect in the risk taking—Building trust over time – Respect needs and goals of each partner – Respect different stages of partnership work
Recognition of respective goals	– Recognise primary motivation of each partner – Cater for main goals – Schools want quality learning experiences for their students—Universities want authentic learning experiences for PSTs that brings together theory and practice
Adaptability and responsiveness to changing needs	– Willing to respond to emerging needs – Flexibility in structure and processes – Take account of time and resource limitations
Diverse representations	– Value all partnerships – Low-risk partnerships serve a purpose and can evolve

The authors of this chapter utilised the PPP to frame the individual reflective narratives about our teacher educator position in the partnership space.

The Representing of Partnership Practice (RPP) domain also influences the ways we reflect on the nature of our partnerships, and their purpose, however, is not specifically used to structure our narratives. Due to its influence on our thinking and what it contributes to partnership conceptualisation, it is useful to unpack this domain. The RPP is categorised into Connective, Generative and Transformative. Connective is defined as a "co-operative relationship in which there was a win-win outcome, or when one or other of the partners had a particular need that the other was able to service" (Jones et al., 2016, p. 115), which are often one-off or short term, but can seed future long-term relationships. Generative partnerships occur when "new or different practices ar[i]se in school/university programs as a result of the partnership…often requiring modifications to existing structures" (ibid., p. 115). Transformative partnerships reflect both Furlong et al. (1996) and Kruger et al.'s (2009) collaborative partnership description in that "transformative partnerships focus on the active involvement of all partner members in the planning and delivery of curriculum for the purpose of professional learning. They are on-going and embedded in the programs of the collaborating institutions" (ibid., p. 115).

Hobbs et al. (2015) argue that their RPP model is not intended to suggest one type of partnership has more value than the others. Evidence from Furlong et al. (1996) and Kruger et al. (2009), however, suggest collaborative partnerships produce better outcomes for teacher education and both teacher and PST professional learning. In addition, Ryan, Butler, Kostogri, and Nailer (2016) argue that "joint planning and execution of a teacher education initiative prevents universities from becoming narrowly focused on preoccupations like finding placements for PSTs. Instead it means that there is a joint articulation by both the schools and the university participants of what the desirable future teachers might be like" (p. 189). Walsh and Backe (2013) also argue that collaborative, systemic level partnerships, while requiring significant work from all stakeholders to negotiate shared understandings, "can pave the way for both systemic change in the school district and important developments in practice, theory, and research at the university" (p. 595). Hence, while collaborative/transformational partnerships can be consuming in relation to time and resources, the benefit to educational communities far outweighs these issues. This can and does, however, create pressure on the individuals working in these partnerships who aspire to partnerships of this kind.

3 Theoretical Framework and Research Methodology

This chapter utilises narrative inquiry in the form of individual narrative writing, in addition to a dialogic narrative between the authors. Narrative inquiry was deemed to be a particularly appropriate research methodology, as Connelly & Clandinin propose:

> Narrative inquiry, the study of experience as story, is first and foremost a way of thinking about experience. Narrative inquiry as a methodology entails a view of the phenomenon. To use narrative inquiry methodology is to adopt a particular narrative of experience as phenomena under study (Connelly and Clandinin, 2006, p. 477).

The authors each possess stories of their experiences with developing partnerships, and believe in the importance of sharing their exploration of the partnership phenomenon with other educators. Sociality is a central element in the development and continuance of partnerships. Connelly and Clandinin (2006) state, "we cannot subtract ourselves from relationship" (p. 480), and this recurring theme is clearly demonstrated in this chapter. To provide an additional framework within which to explore the shared experiences, the partnership narratives were viewed through the lens of Jones et al. (2016) Principles of Partnership Practice (PPP).

The research was undertaken in two distinct phases. Initially, the research involved the construction of individual written narratives from all three authors utilising key elements drawn from the STEPS Interpretive Framework (i.e. Risk Taking and Trust, Reciprocity, Mutuality and Respect, Recognition of Respective Goals, Adaptable and Responsive to Changing Needs and Diverse Representations). These key elements are drawn from the Principles of Partnership Practice (PPP) quadrant of the STEPS Framework. Additionally, the components of the Representing Partnership Practices (RPP) quadrant, were foregrounded in reflections and discussions held between the authors. The authors then commented in track changes on each other's narratives. Common threads in the track changes were used to develop the metanarrative.

In a second phase, the narratives were examined and coded to find patterns and themes relating to each author's experiences (complications, images and metaphors that represented the experiences). These were referenced against the PPP quadrant of the STEPS Framework (Jones et al., 2016). Additionally, the authors identified particular actors, settings or events that were represented in positive or negative ways, and included these elements into the coding process (McAlpine, 2016). This inclusion allowed the authors to explore the actions, connections and consequences of partnership events on their professional identity over time. Chase (2005) suggests these actions, connections and consequences are represented through "emotions, thoughts, and interpretations" and were "both enabled and constrained by a range of social resources and circumstances" (p. 657). Chase's sentiments are reflected in observations made by Connelly and Clandinin (2006) and Huber, Caine, Huber and Steeves (2013). Utilisation of a narrative enquiry methodology, where the individual narratives are organised around the PPP framework headings and then a brief summary is provided at the end of each section, allowed the authors to explore the dynamics of partnership work from the practitioner (that is, implementer's) perspective.

The discussion of narratives is structured to enable a flow of themes across both the individual narratives and the metanarrative. The metanarrative is organised into themes that emerged when exploring the emotions, thoughts and interpretations represented in the narratives and a discussion follows each metanarrative theme.

4 Partnership Contexts

The three teacher educators worked in partnerships across three different institutions and two states. Kathy's partnership has external funding from the Victorian Government and is part of the Teaching Academies of Professional Practice (TAPP) programme. Amanda and Ken's partnerships receive no external funding. In all partnership programmes, a university representative is key to managing and sustaining the partnership programme, including ongoing negotiation with the schools. The information below provides a context of the partnership time, place and space.

4.1 Amanda in Victoria

Amanda established a cluster partnership programme in response to the need to form strong professional experience partnerships with secondary schools in the East, South-East, South and North of Melbourne. Her university had two existing funded partnerships with clusters of Western and North Western schools. The new partnership was established in 2016, and by the commencement of 2017, there were 6 clusters with 3–5 schools in each cluster, placing approximately 200–300 PSTs. Each cluster has a university cluster lead who works with the PSTs and their supervisors, as well as liaising with lead staff in each school.

4.2 Kathy in Victoria

In 2014, the Department of Education and Training in Victoria called for expressions of interest for schools and universities to form partnerships, to better integrate theory and practice and improve professional experience. Some 12 Teaching Academies of Professional Practice were formed, that were initially funded for two years (2015–2016), but later extended for another two years (2017–2018). Kathy's university established an Academy with some 12 primary schools in the northern corridor of Melbourne, centred around a second year Bachelor of Education course, with an embedded four-week placement catering for approximately 200 PSTs.

4.3 Ken in Queensland

Ken's university has been engaged in rural PST supervised professional experience, to reflect the charter of his university as a regionally engaged university. In 2014, the Darling Downs/South West Region of the Queensland Department of Education and Ken's university formalised a partnership to improve the experience and capacity of PSTs in rural areas of Queensland. This ongoing partnership is named the Coast to Country project and includes on average 30 PSTs each year.

5 Narrative Reflections Using the Lens of the Principles of Partnership Practice

The first step in the narrative reflection by the teacher educator authors was to utilise the Principles of Partnership Practice (Jones et al., 2016) to develop structured reflections on our partnership experiences. For the purposes of this activity, the six steps of the Principles of Partnership Practice were amended to four steps. The authors amended the six steps to include Respect with Reciprocity and Mutuality, and to include Adaptable and Responsive with Recognition of Respective Goals. This amendment was undertaken after extensive reflection on the nature of the educational partnerships that were being investigated. Each author's reflection on the categories is represented below, followed by a brief summary after each category.

5.1 Risk Taking and Trust

5.1.1 Narratives

Amanda

As there was no external funding for the cluster partnership project, significant work went into negotiation with schools and the university Executive Dean by the lead academic staff member and the Head of School to design a workload model consistent with the university's existing workload model as agreed in its Enterprise Agreement. Initially cluster lead roles were ongoing academic staff and some long-term sessional staff each looking after one of six clusters. Over two years, ongoing staff in leadership roles could not sustain the level of commitment required including travel, partnership hours and PST supervision, so sessional staff took over five clusters. This change over in staff ran the risk of losing the trust of the schools. To minimise the risk, there was a carefully staged transition from the ongoing leadership staff member to the new sessional staff, which proved to be effective. As the lead academic, I also began to realise the significance of risk taking and trust, not just for the direct stakeholders in the partnership relationship, but also at the level of university leadership. Both the schools and the on-the-ground university staff had the expectation/hope that the university would support the cluster leads, and the delivery of mentoring training. The positive benefits for PSTs and practicing teachers were evident to school leadership, university staff and commented on by the PSTs. Sustainability of unfunded programs from a university perspective, however, is difficult in a political climate of economic rationalisation. Many of the levels of support and systems were something I continually negotiated. The main concern for me was that the trust and relationships I had developed with schools would be forever damaged if the partnership could not continue.

Kathy

Although we knew many of the schools that we approached to partner with us, as they had previously hosted our PSTs for placement, we knew from the outset that we wanted a new kind of relationship with schools, one that was based on mutual respect and a shared commitment to teacher education rather than administrative convenience. We approached schools with little more than this big vision, and invited them to join us for a more formal meeting to talk through what a possible partnership could achieve. True some of the schools came along with some doubts and misgivings, but others came along with an openness and willingness to collaborate. We organised a breakfast meeting to talk through some of the challenges in teacher education and some of the possibilities that we thought we could collectively realise. Core ideas or tenets of the partnership such as interconnected coursework and practice in school sites, began to emerge as more trust was built and understanding of "the other" grew. We then organised a Think Tank Day and invited teachers, nominated by school leadership, to do just this—to redesign a course within the parameters of what had been accredited—taking our collective needs and constraints into account.

Ken

Despite a 600-km geographical dislocation between stakeholders, the shared experiences of rural teaching from sides of this partnership provided the element of trust upon which the partnership could build. The teaching fraternity in Queensland tends to be highly interconnected, despite the number of teachers in dispersed schools across the state. Forming the initial partnership occurred over a 12-month period and was in part supported by shared professional contacts and dialogues between teaching colleagues in both school and university contexts. As both sides of the partnership increasingly recognised the commonalities they shared within the professional sphere, the level of professional trust between parties correspondingly expanded. It was clear that trusting, professional relationships were to be the foundation upon which this project would develop. Trust was required by university academics when entrusting preservice teachers to rural experiences under the guidance and supervision of school practitioners. Academics trusted that school practitioners understood the nature of the experience that was needed to ensure a supportive environment for preservice teachers, one which would encourage them to continue that experience as an early career teacher. In a similar manner, there was an element of risk taking in consideration of the message being delivered by the university team being different to the message delivered by school practitioners. These early concerns were quickly set aside, as both sides of the partnership identified common ground and shared beliefs.

5.1.2 Summary of Narratives

Across these narratives, the teacher educators identify stories around the ways they worked in their partnerships to build trust between stakeholders, some of whom were great distances apart. These stories tend to concentrate on the organisation, commitment and contribution element of the PPP category of risk taking and trust when enabling partnership growth. For example, Amanda identified the importance in maintaining commitment during times of staff changes, and all narratives identified the significant levels of organisation, commitment and contributions required by the various stakeholders. This reflects the importance of the "goodwill" (Grudnoff et al., 2016) to get the partnerships off the ground. In addition, Amanda and Kathy touched on the partnerships' potential to address quality teaching and learning such as through mentoring training/coaching and designing interconnected coursework.

5.2 Reciprocity, Mutuality and Respect

5.2.1 Narratives

Amanda

Across the clusters, there is a variety of success in relation to reciprocity, mutuality and respect. In the more developed clusters, there is mutual respect and dialogic discussion between school leaders and the university cluster leads around the shared goal of partnerships contributing to PSTs having effective professional experiences, and mentors being trained and supported. For example, the support demonstrated by the schools in sending large groups of staff to mentoring training days and their schools hosting the training events. In other clusters, this reciprocity is not as evident which impacts on the success of the cluster. There were cases reported where schools asked "what is the university giving us," the school leadership team members did not prioritise the partnership, cluster leads were unable to meet with them, and some school leaders stalled the partnership unless there was a signed MOU. Partnership development requires respectful negotiation to find common ground across the agendas of school and university contexts. For example, when negotiating differences between unit requirements that have been through accreditation processes and school expectations of PST's learning. While all clusters have challenges, it is promising to see some of the clusters are more generative in relation to engaging in dialogic discussion around mentoring support structures, contribution to ITE and forward planning.

Kathy

Being open to co-designing a course is one thing, but relinquishing the power Higher Education Providers traditionally have is another. Keeping the bigger vision in mind helped, so too the increased respect that we developed between university colleagues and school colleagues as we collectively scoped and mapped out a new way to deliver the second year BEd course to include interconnected site based learning. We learned a lot from one another with a few surprises along the way. We were surprised for example that our school-based colleagues thought we could include any content we liked and had very little understanding of the accreditation requirements that governed our course design. When we began to scope out what was realistic and achievable in a course they developed a much greater understanding of our work. Over several months we developed course content, that we then mutually owned, then built a Google Site so that we could all access it and adapt it to our needs.

Ken

Initially, meetings with Department of Education members were conducted via conference phone calls and Zoom. Reciprocal face-to-face meetings at the university campus and partner schools were then undertaken, as it quickly was recognised by both parties that trust and mutual commitment to the partnership was strengthened by face-to-face meetings. Similarly, face-to-face meetings with teaching staff on site at the various partner schools were essential. It was noted by the university staff that the partner school staff had a great deal of pride in their schools, and every visit required a school tour to showcase facilities, classrooms and student work. Often these visits included lunch or morning tea; a simple act of sharing which reinforced the mutuality of the partnership arrangement. Anecdotally, it was also noted that the simple act of visiting a school site provided a type of informal validation to the teaching staff. As the project developed and the professional relationships between individual members matured, the mutually determined goals of the project became more apparent. The altruistic nature of teachers was evident, as teaching staff gave very freely of their own time to assist preservice teachers to gain a better understanding of the profession. There was a profound sense of "paying it forward" to support the new members of the teaching profession, against the backdrop of the life worlds of the teachers in the partnership schools. Additionally, university staff recognised the absolute necessity to respect the role of classroom practitioners, and to validate the valuable work undertaken by these teachers. There was a sense of mutual care for preservice teachers from both sides of the partnership.

5.2.2 Summary of the Narratives

The importance of finding common ground, or mutual benefits, and nurturing the benefits as identified in this category of the PPP is particularly evident in these narratives. The complexity of negotiation and the effort required for "boundary brokers" (Loughland & Nguyen, 2018) to bridge systems reflects Bloomfield and Nguyen's

(2015) discussion around the challenges that arise in partnerships due to differing priorities and requirements across educational systems. For example, Amanda raised the issue of the variability in the value placed on mentoring training for supervising teachers across the clusters, and Kathy identified the importance of explaining accreditation processes. Ken illustrated the ways partnerships deliver benefits for PSTs as they have greater access to teacher advice and more authentic experiences. The narratives illustrate the underlying theme of the centrality of relational connections as emphasised by Kruger et al. (2009) and the STEPS team of researchers.

5.3 Recognition of Respective Goals, Adaptable and Responsive to Changing Needs

5.3.1 Narratives

Amanda

The university goals of the cluster schools partnership are to increase placements in particular geographical areas and provide stronger support to schools. There is also the shared goal between the university and schools to improve the quality of professional experience for PSTs, and also for school students in PST classes. Many school leaders are explicit about their goal of improving mentoring capability in their schools. As the academic lead, I felt there needed to be structures in place that would allow cluster leads to share and reflect on their experiences of respective goals and on partnership scholarship. I ran half day professional development events at the beginning and end of the year, and two-hour meetings in the other two terms of the school year. This structure enabled reflective discussion on partnership theories, research, practical implementation, university structures and brainstorming of strategies to develop stronger connections within the restrictions of university and system accreditation requirements. It was a creative space in which the cluster leads could develop an understanding of tertiary contexts and bring their understanding of school needs to negotiate partnership solutions. Late in 2017, I transferred to another campus, meaning the partnership model had to adjust to the loss of the academic lead. The ability of the cluster leads and schools to adapt to these changes and stay committed to a common goal has enabled the continuation of partnerships.

Kathy

Both the university and our partners had goals, including several partners who saw the benefits that a coaching model could have in increasing the leadership capacity of staff. Others also saw how their commitment could help prepare the next generation of teachers. That first year, our goal to transform teacher education receded somewhat as we dealt with the practicalities of organising placements for some 200 PSTs, preparing PSTs for a "new" model which incorporated more school-based learning, hiring coaches to support groups of PSTs in each partner school (sometimes 4 at each school) and running a three-day professional learning day to ensure that all coaches were ready to teach the newly designed program. This was a testing time, and we did have doubts. During the placement block, my university colleagues and I visited all 12 schools, usually more than once, and we set up some webinars for coaches to check in with us. It was important to further build these relationships, and schools saw by our actions that we were committed to honouring the partnership and making it work. At the end of that year, we held another professional learning day so that coaches could share their experiences with others and foster cross-school relationships and shared practice.

Ken

The goals of both partners involved in the Coast to Country project were clearly identified and clearly articulated during discussions and planning sessions. The overarching goal for both partners was to attract an increased number of teachers to support the workforce needs of rural, remote and regional schools. For the university partner, this provided an avenue to expand experiences for our students, which would potentially lead to a supervised professional experience placement and ongoing employment. For the school partner, the goals were skewed more towards future workforce needs, including the identification and support of aspirant leaders at an early point in their professional pathway. As the partnership and the project matured, discussion and reflection by both partners began to identify adaptations that could enhance the experience. For example, additional attention was placed towards dispelling myths associated with rural or remote areas/communities and living, learning and working in these areas. The school partner, supported by the university academics, introduced some additional experienced staff who were able to demonstrate the many positive aspects of rural work and life, which enhanced the student experience enormously. This resulted in increased number of students wishing to attend the following Coast to Country experience.

5.3.2   Summary of Narratives

While university and schools in the partnerships had some differences in motivations, common goals such as improving PST experiences and strengthening mentoring/coaching are evident across the narratives. Mentoring is a key topic of discussion in professional experience literature (Kruger et al., 2009; Le Cornu, 2015). Another aspect of this component of the PPP evident across the narratives is the brokering methods used to respond to emerging needs. This included meetings and professional development with cluster leads/coaches and bringing together university and school stakeholders. This ensured the partnerships had the capacity to develop shared goals and adapt.

5.4 Diverse Representations

5.4.1 Narratives

Amanda

The cluster partnership project highlighted for me the diverse range of partnerships that can exist. At this early stage, none of the partnerships have reached a transformative stage. During the meetings with the cluster leads many spoke of the positive outcomes for schools and our PSTs, and some expressed their frustration about their perceived lack of progress compared to other clusters due to a lack of reciprocity or respect. External factors such as delays in the MOU processes, change of lead staff, and school and university pressures such as marking, unit development, research outcomes, overloaded curriculum and managing multiple partnerships impact the stakeholders' ability to create negotiation space. In addition, without external funding, both university and school staff worked with a small allocation of time and no additional resources which limited their ability to innovate. Those clusters that were able to find common ground and create these spaces, which included the one I managed, were inspiring, engaging, creative and collegial. However, during the first year, the focus was mostly on building trust and relationships rather than aiming for transformational changes. They did demonstrate to me the future potential for these partnerships to make significant impact on university staff, school staff and PST's critical capacity to reflect on the teaching profession and ITE.

Kathy

While the first year operated on the agreed belief that the new partnership model was a good idea, by the second year, the benefits of working together were more tangible and having transformative effects. PSTs knew about the Academy from their colleagues and were familiar with its key tenets and excited by the prospect of working closely with a coach. They saw the benefits of being able to connect their coursework to practice on site in schools, and felt that this made it more authentic. They really liked having a coach to support them. Schools had seen the benefits of the course that underpinned this partnership. For example, they knew what PSTs learned at the university and what they were expected to learn on site in schools. Coaches felt valued, not only by PSTs but by their school leaders who saw them undertaking an important role. We felt much more connected to schools, and knew a lot more about their programmes and their priorities. After four years of the partnership, we know that partnerships take ongoing commitment, as the relationships that underpin them require constant attention. Partnerships also have a lifecycle, and it is perhaps an opportune time now for us to renew them and begin a new lifecycle.

Ken

Due to the highly decentralised nature of the Queensland population (and, by extension, schools), the employment realities of early career teachers seeking employment with the Queensland Department of Education can be daunting. The vast proportion of our preservice teachers has little to no experience of Queensland outside of the south-east corner of the state. Introducing preservice teachers to new environments has been challenging, yet rewarding for all involved in the project. The high proportion of our graduates currently employed by the state government in rural or remote Queensland schools both validates the work undertaken by the partnership to date, while providing an imperative for the continuing partnership between the university, and the Darling Downs/South West Region of the Queensland Department of Education.

5.4.2 Summary of Narratives

The teacher educators' passion to develop and sustain partnerships that can make a contribution to improving PST experiences and ITE weave across the stories. The stories highlight the evolving nature of partnerships that is a feature of this element of the PPP and the positive reciprocal outcomes such as those identified by Kathy and Ken. Also apparent are the challenges that teacher educators can face when creating partnerships that are diverse, complex, often do not conform to traditional university structures, and require regular renewal. For example, Amanda identified some of the cluster lead's frustrations in moving their partnerships forward. While Jones et al. (2016) suggest it is important to value diverse partnerships, and connective partnerships serve a purpose, in a model where some partnerships are growing and others are not at the same rate, there can be pressure on the university representative to be accountable for the lack of growth.

6 Creating a Metanarrative—Intersection of Voices on Teacher Educators' Roles in Partnerships

The metanarrative presented below may be approached via the narrative lens described by McAlpine (2016). In this instance, the authors aim to understand the "arc of meaning in an individual's experience" (McAlpine, 2016, p. 36). Further, McAlpine (2016) proposes that "narratives incorporate temporality, a social context, complicating events, and an evaluative conclusion that together make a coherent story" (p. 33). Within this metanarrative, the authors have utilised narrative inquiry to consider each other's individual narratives and experiences about significant partnership issues, and to focus on the discourse that emerged from these stories (McAlpine, 2016). These naturalistic and literary approaches allowed the authors to contemplate "images and metaphors" within their and each other's narratives, and consider the "actors, settings and plotlines" that emerged (McAlpine, 2016, p. 35). The authors ultimately identified two major themes within the metanarrative. These themes emerged from analysis of annotations made to the narratives of each author.

These are discussed after each metanarrative, and broad reference is again drawn to Jones et al.'s Principles of Partnership Practice (2016) in order to anchor the themes to a previously identified theoretical framework.

6.1 Theme 1: Our Role as Teacher Educators in Partnerships

6.1.1 Metanarrative

Kathy   Amanda, after reading your discussion on workload negotiations, what I find really interesting here is that I still don't have a workplace model. Perhaps this is because my role is evolving, meaning I find it challenging to articulate, and sometimes justify, what I am doing. Many of my colleagues do not fully understand what is involved in forming partnerships and maintaining positive relationships with schools. I think we have to start articulating what these new roles are and what is involved and why they are so important. A lot of our work becomes invisible.

Amanda I feel the same way Kathy and struggle with rationalising my work and arguing for the value of partnerships. When trying to think about where I fit in the priority areas of the university, I struggle to see whether my partnership work is teaching (in the traditional sense), research (including evaluation of the partnership to make improvements), or service (which seems to be the place partnerships are usually located). I know my work is valuable, I know it produces good outcomes, but it does become exhausting trying to justify your work, and what that work encompasses.

Ken   Completely concur. My institution values reporting on the success stories that flow out of partnership; however, the time and effort is not reflected internally in workload allocations. I generally include all of this work under the engagement/service component of my workload. Ultimately it is done for the benefit of our preservice teachers.

Kathy   I think one of the key implications from our narratives is how do we re-write our job descriptions that clearly articulate our roles? How do we shift this space—from one that has a rather fixed view of the academic role, the PX office role, and so on to one that is much more accepting of new roles.

Ken   This is exactly my experience, and a common talking point with colleagues informally and at staff meetings. As a program coordinator who deals with hundreds of students, I would add the roles of counsellor, mentor, travel agent and, sometimes, disciplinarian to my role description.

Amanda And there is also the skills needed in those initial negotiation stages of partnerships.

Kathy   I think our role is really changing. There is now an increasing expectation for us to be much more connected with our schools—so as to have that interconnection of theory and practice. I think many of my colleagues are struggling with this. As Zeichner has argued, there is an academic snobbery at play here. I also think there is a real fear emerging, that the more we work with schools, the more our role is changing—and perhaps, what was once our role will no longer exist in future. Are we beginning to see the emergence of the hybrid teacher educator?

Ken   I completely agree with this statement. Particularly since TEMAG, I have noticed a divide opening within my School of Education. There are the "research focussed" folk, and there are the folk who work very hard in the nexus between craft and scholarship. In part this may be driven by the university requirements to grow their academic rankings. I also suspect that at some point, research focussed academics may lose "street cred" because they have not engaged with schools and teachers in a reciprocal manner.

Amanda While I can see this trend, I think there are so many missed opportunities for research to occur in our partnerships in a reciprocal way, and it would be fantastic if there were more support for teacher educators to seize these opportunities. I reflect on the idea of a hybrid or third space and particularly Walsh and Backe (2013) and Bloomfield and Nguyen's (2015) comments about the co-construction and renegotiation of knowledge bringing together theory, research and practice

6.1.2   Discussion

Across the narratives we, as the authors, represented our past and present experiences, and our hopes for future experiences as teacher educator professionals in the higher education partnership space. Particularly evident in the individual and metanarratives was the representation of our role as actors in this space. The metaphor of actor is apt, considering the slippages in character as the actors move from one setting to another, trying to navigate the hybridity of their roles, at times feeling like "imposters" in schools, or struggling with inconclusive roles and their professional status in university defined borders of teaching, research and service.

The narratives also identify the actors' interpretations and representations of their settings in this ethereal component (Jongbloed et al., 2008) of partnership work. They represent the struggles and tensions as they try to validate their work to their colleagues, leadership teams and the wider university. The narratives provide practical examples of the issues raised in both historical and recent literature by authors such as Zeichner (1992), Furlong et al (1996) and recent examples such as Grudnoff et al. (2016), Herbert et al. (2018) and Le Cornu (2015). Examples such as feeling the need to rationalise partnership work, undertaking much of the work without adequate resourcing and difficulties justifying one's border identities in workplan models that do not accurately reflect what the actors do, nor the time and effort they put into doing them. Despite the twenty-five years of research represented in the papers just listed, we, as the teacher educators, represent stories reflecting similar themes and tensions. Zeichner identified as early as 1992 that universities place practicum as a low priority and called for the "creation of new structural arrangements for the practicum that allow the expertise of cooperating teachers, and university supervisors to be better used, recognized and rewarded" (p. 301). While much has been done in the Australian context, for example the Teaching Academies reported on in Kathy's narrative and other government funded programmes across the states and territories, these issues are clearly apparent across all narratives in this chapter and the recent literature.

We feel that our roles as teacher educators are evolving including an increased expectation to be more connected with schools so as to have a greater connection between university ITE expectations and practice. The narratives represent the feeling that there is a lack of understanding around the multiple dimensions of these boundary brokering roles (Gardiner & Lorch, 2015; Loughland & Nguyen 2018; Sewell et al., 2018), and universities do not know what the role involves, or how to value them. We, as the actors, expressed concern around narrow definitions of our work and felt there was a need to articulate these new roles and what that work encompasses, particularly when there is no funding to support this work. This includes making this brokering work visible in university systems, as emphasised by Kathy when she comments about the "invisible" aspects of partnership work. A common theme around the desire to foster a connection between the teaching, research and service roles was voiced, to encourage the facilitation of a hybrid or third space. The kind of hybrid space as suggested by Walsh and Backe (2013) and Bloomfield and Nguyen's (2015) that can enable the co-construction and renegotiation of knowledge bringing together theory, research and practice. Overall the synergies between the narratives suggested we, as teacher educators in partnerships, were proud of our diverse role in the partnerships and could articulate many of our actions across settings. There are multiple struggles, however, as a result of existing in a third or boundary space.

6.2 Theme 2: Sustaining Our Role as Relationship Managers

6.2.1 Metanarrative

Kathy   How to sustain partnerships that are dependent on relationships is a big issue. I have quite a lot of guilt about the Teaching Academy. When my colleague and I set it up we really were not thinking that much about the partners and sustaining them. When she left we spoke a bit about how she felt. She spoke to me about how she had said her goodbyes and was feeling comfortable. However, I was still here and felt a real burden, how could I honour these partnerships on my own? Colleagues say to me, just move on, but I cannot. These are real people here, people that I have worked with, laughed with and shared coffee with. It is not that easy to just let go. And I do think about the consequences. Will these schools trust us again, if we just walk away?

Amanda Yes, this is really important. We had a few situations in the past where partnerships had broken down and it made negotiation with these partic- ular schools for the cluster partnership difficult. Some principals stated outright that they will not take our PSTs because we could not deliver on our promises, and that when university staff left, no-one took over. We need to be careful about what we promise in partnerships, and there needs to be a commitment to dialogic reciprocity and maintenance of staffing.

Ken Nice insight Amanda….and also a very brave statement Kathy! One of the central traits of teachers is that of being caring and demonstrating a level of humanity. It is extremely hard to walk away from partnerships where both parties have shared a common humanity. I often feel that the economic-rationalist view that universities take, where project outcomes are often measured in dollars, or at least in highly tangible assets, does not include this more humanistic perspective.

Kathy And something that really stands out to me when reading your narrative Ken is what a complex undertaking forming these partnerships is. All of the schools I imagine have their own programs and priorities, therefore getting them to the table would require considerable negotiation and I dare say a lot of good will. The schools are also geographically distant from each other, so just the pragmatics of getting together would be so difficult. And it is all very well to have Skype meetings, but these can be challenging when you do not know the people involved—it is very hard to build relationships, and partnerships because of this. Did you consciously look for commonalities in order to build these relationships? How else did you navigate the diverse school settings? Were schools comfortable with this approach?

Ken The commonalities were that these schools were all State Government schools, all shared that same common "DNA" of how the organisa- tion worked. As I have been a state school teacher for 23 years before moving to tertiary education 13 years ago, I shared much of the same "DNA"—(sounds a bit weird, but it is a pretty accurate description). Because we could use the same organisational discourse, we built our relationship from these shared understandings and experiences, and then looked at how the goals of the project would be developed: once our relationship was developed.

Amanda I think that relational aspect is a key part of the teaching profession no matter what system you are in. It is also important for academics to get out of their offices and see what is happening in schools. I am reflecting now on an earlier comment in which Kathy mentioned "invisible skills" required to negotiate and maintain partnerships, I wonder if this comes into play? We should also consider comfort zones and of course boundaries that we, as academics, put on our work, and sometimes through necessity need to put on our work. Can everyone really get out to schools, think of a teaching focussed academic who has a full-time teaching load, they may dream of getting opportunities for their PST's to see what they are teaching in practice, but setting up partnerships might be too time consuming and daunting.

6.2.2   Discussion

Across the individual and metanarratives that have been presented in this study, the representation of the teacher education professional as a manager of relationships is an underlying constant. Relationships are dynamic and require ongoing review and reflection to flourish. The work of Jones et al. (2016), as shown in the STEPS Interpretive Framework in Fig. 1, and the Principles of Partnership Practice summarized in Table 1, echo the essential components of healthy relationships in general—trust, reciprocity and mutuality, respect, recognition of respective goals and responsiveness to changing needs. The narratives illustrate the authors' common beliefs that relationships between schools and ITE institutions need to move away from traditional models based on legacy issues of top-down compliance, as agreements or administrative arrangements. Rather, professional partnership relationships should aim to facilitate placement, support the payment of supervising teachers and work to alleviate the tensions between the scholarship aspect of preservice teaching and the craft of teaching at school sites.

The narratives represent the belief that ITE providers need to define a new relationship with schools and recognise that this new relational aspect of our emerging role is vital to connecting with schools in meaningful, new ways. This process, like any developing relationship, will take time, sensitivity and respect. Forming partnerships is complex and involves overcoming the hurdles of distance in order to get together, as well as learning to navigate diverse school programmes and priorities. Relationships require communication and negotiation and understanding of enablers and constraints. As discussed earlier in this chapter, these constraints can include national accreditation requirements, which directly impact on programmes and course design as well as negotiation with university leadership.

Partnerships require trust and dialogic reciprocity. The authors recognise that it is difficult to both honour partnerships (by delivering on promises, and resourcing them), and acknowledge they have a lifecycle, that both parties need to refresh priorities, and need to be brave enough to walk away from partnerships where both parties have shared a common humanity. The emotional connection to partnerships is illustrated by the authors use of highly emotive words such as "guilt" and "humanity," illustrating the personal investment teacher educators contribute to their partnerships. This highly emotive connection can assist in understanding the discursive tension with administrative and university structure systems represented in some of the narrative extracts. Partnerships have many benefits, including working collaboratively, and other intangible benefits such as being part of a school community, improving future teachers and ITE programmes. Partnerships produce good outcomes for preservice teachers in schools, supporting their future growth as professionals in education and reinforcing links between schools and ITE providers.

7 Conclusion and Implications

In November 2018, the most recent inquiry into teaching was announced by the federal Minister for Education ("Status of the Teaching Profession," 2018). In addition, the Australian Institute for Teaching and School Leadership (AITSL) are scrutinizing universities to ensure they are meeting TEMAG recommendations as reflected in accreditation requirements. In this political climate, it is essential that school–university partnerships, a significant focus of TEMAG reforms, are taken seriously. These types of professional partnerships require an understanding the role of the academic teacher educators who ultimately control the success or otherwise of these partnerships. Additionally, these professional partnerships also include an understanding of the resources needed for these professionals negotiating and brokering the multiple borders in partnership development and maintenance.

The narratives in this chapter illustrate the complexities partnership teacher educators face, their struggles to work through barriers, their quests to find their place in dichotomous university workload classifications and their determination to have their partnerships and work recognised, valued and resourced. These actions are difficult to sustain in funded partnerships let alone in unfunded partnerships. Should we remain complicit and be happy with connective level partnerships? It seems schools want more, as the narratives illustrate, and they are more likely to engage in the process of Initial Teacher Education if teacher educators can be more present in school settings. The narratives illustrate that many stakeholders benefit from generative and transformative style partnerships. The collaborative relationship creates opportunities for schools to engage in research and professional learning, as well as influence content decisions around initial teacher education programmes. Preservice teachers have greater access to school experiences and voices that embed theoretical perspectives in practical contexts. University staff develop stronger bonds with schools and enhance their understandings of practical settings. The strengthened relationship between universities, schools and school districts can also "value add" to tertiary institutions through a flow on effect of student enrolment in a "known" university, which is a consideration that is particularly relevant to institutions involved in partnerships in rural and regional areas.

There is no doubt that teacher educators are invested in the development and maintenance of multivarious partnerships across Australia. These partnerships must be appropriately recognised and supported within the economic constraints of current university and government boundaries. The narratives presented in this chapter illustrate the passion and commitment some teacher educators and schools have towards building links between schools, universities (and systems). They also illustrate the exhaustion and sustainability risks if the role teacher educators play is not adequately recognised or resourced. Partnerships, their value, their complexity and the importance of all stakeholders, including teacher educators, must become visible.

References

Australian Institute for Teaching and School Leadership. (2015). *Accreditation of initial teacher education programs in Australia, Standards and Procedures*. Melbourne: AITSL.

Allen, J., & Wright, S. (2014). Integrating theory and practice in the pre-service teacher education practicum. *Teachers and Teaching: Theory and Practice, 20*(2), 136–151.

Bloomfield, D., & Nguyen, H. T. (2015). Creating and sustaining professional learning partnerships: Activity theory as an analytic tool. *Australian Journal of Teacher Education, 40*(11). http://dx. doi.org/10.14221/ajte.2015v40n11.2.

Chase, S. E. (2005). Narrative inquiry: Multiple lenses, approaches, voices. In N. K. Denzin & Y. S. Lincoln (Eds.), *Handbook of qualitative research* (3rd ed., pp. 651–679). Thousand Oaks, CA: Sage.

Chittleborough, G., & Jones, M. (2018). Linking theory and practice through partnerships. In L. Hobbs, C. Campbell, & M. Jones (Eds.), *School-based partnerships in teacher education: A research informed model for universities, schools and beyond* (pp. 61–82). Singapore: Springer Nature.

Connelly, M., & Clandinin, J. (2006). Narrative Enquiry. In J. Green, G. Camilli, & P. Elmore (Eds.), *Handbook of complimentary methods in education research* (3rd ed., pp. 477–487). Mahwah, NJ: Lawrence Erlbaum.

Furlong, J., Whitty, G., Whiting, C., Miles, S., Barton, L., & Barret, E. (1996). Redefining partnership: Revolution or reform in initial teacher education? *Journal of Education for Teaching: International Research and Pedagogy, 22*(1), 39–56.

Gardiner, W., & Lorch, J. (2015). From outsider to bridge: The changing role of University supervision in an urban teacher residency program. *Action in Teacher Education, 37,* 172–189.

Grudnoff, L., Haigh, M., & Mackisack, V. (2016). Re-envisaging and reinvigorating school-university practicum partnerships. *Asia-Pacific Journal of Teacher Education,* 1–14.

Herbert, S., Redman, C., & Speldewinde, C. (2018). Sustaining school-university partnerships: Threats, challenges and critical success factors. In L. Hobbs, C. Campbell, & M. Jones (Eds.), *School-based partnerships in teacher education: A research informed model for universities, schools and beyond* (pp. 169–192). Singapore: Springer.

Hobbs, L., Campbell, C., Chittleborough, G. Herbert, S., Jones, M., Redman, C., ... Gilbert, A. (2015). STEPS interpretative framework. Science Teacher Education Program. http://www.stepsproject.org.au/__data/assets/pdf_file/0009/341010/STEPS-Interpretive-Framework-Final-May-2015.pdf.

Hobbs, L., Campbell, C., & Jones, M. (Eds.). (2018). *School-based partnerships in teacher education: A research informed model for universities, schools and beyond*. Singapore: Springer Nature.

Huber, J., Caine, V., Huber, M., & Steeves, P. (2013). Narrative inquiry as pedagogy in education: The extraordinary potential of living, telling, retelling, and reliving stories of experience. *Review of Research in Education, 37*(1), 212–242.

Jones, M., Hobbs, L., Kenny, J., Campbell, C., Chittleborough, ... Redman, C. (2016). Successful university-school partnerships: An interpretative framework to inform partnership practice. *Teaching and Teacher Education, 60,* 108–120.

Jongbloed, B., Enders, J., & Salerno, C. (2008). Higher education and its communities: Interconnections, interdependencies and a research agenda. *Higher education, 56*(3), 303–324. https:// doi.org/10.1007/s10734-008-9128-2.

Kruger, T., Davies, A., Eckersley, B., Newell, F., & Cherednichenko, B. (2009). *Effective and sustainable university-school partnerships. Beyond determined efforts of inspired individuals*. Canberra: Teaching Australia [Electronic version]. Retrieved from http://hdl.voced.edu.au/10707/144200.

Le Cornu, R. (2015). *Key components of effective professional experience in initial teacher education in Australia*. Melbourne: Australian Institute for Teaching and School Leadership.

Louden, W. (2008). 101 Damnations: The persistence of criticism and the absence of evidence about teacher education in Australia. *Teachers and Teaching: Theory and Practice, 14*(4), 357–368.

Loughland, T., & Nguyen, H. (2018). Boundary objects and brokers in professional experience: An activity theory analysis. In J. Kriewaldt, A. Ambrosetti, D. Rorrison, & R. Capeness (Eds.), *Educating future teachers: Innovative perspectives in professional experience* (pp. 71–90). Singapore: Springer.

Mayer, D. (2014). Forty years of teacher education in Australia: 1974–2014. *Journal of Education for Teaching, 40*(5), 461–473. https://doi.org/10.1080/02607476.2014.956536.

McAlpine, L. (2016). Why might you use narrative methodology? A story about narrative. *Eesti Haridusteaduste Ajakiri, 4*(1), 32–57.

Ryan, J., & Jones, M. (2014). Communication in the Practicum: Fostering relationships between universities and schools. In M. Jones & J. Ryan (Eds.), *Successful Teacher Education: Partnerships, reflective practice and the place of technology* (pp. 103–120). The Netherlands: Sense Publishers.

Ryan, J., Butler, H., Kostogriz, A., & Nailer, S. (2016). Advancing partnership research: A spatial analysis of a jointly-planned teacher education partnership. In R. Brandenburg, S. McDonough, J. Burke, & S. White (Eds.), *Teacher Education: Innovation, interventions and impact* (pp. 175–192). Singapore: Springer.

Sewell, A., Cody, T.-L., Weir, K., & Hansen, S. (2018). Innovations at the boundary: an exploratory case study of a New Zealand school-university partnership in initial teacher education. *Asia Pacific Journal of Teacher Education, 46*(4), 321–339.

Status of the Teaching Profession. (2018). Retrieved from https://www.aph.gov.au/Parliamentary_Business/Committees/House/Employment_Education_and_Training/TeachingProfession.

Teacher Education Ministerial Advisory Group (TEMAG). (2014). *Action now: Classroom ready teachers*. Retrieved from http://www.studentsfirst.gov.au/teacher-education-ministerial-advisory-group.

Walsh, M., & Backe, S. (2013). School-university partnerships: Reflections and opportunities. *Peabody Journal of Education, 88*(5), 594–607.

White, S., Tindall-Ford, S., Heck, D., & Ledger, S. (2018). Exploring the Australian teacher education 'partnership' policy landscape: Four case studies. In J. Kriewaldt, A. Ambrosetti, D. Rorrison, & R. Capeness (Eds.), *Educating future teachers: Innovative perspectives in professional experience* (pp. 13–32). Singapore: Springer.

Zeichner, K. (1992). Rethinking the practicum in professional development school partnership. *Journal of Teacher Education, 43*(4), 296–307.

Zeichner, K. (2010). Rethinking the connections between campus courses and field experiences in college- and university-based teacher education. *Journal of Teacher Education, 61*(1/2), 89–99.

Dr. Amanda Gutierrez is a senior lecturer and Professional Experience Coordinator (Secondary Postgrad Courses) in the QLD School of Education at the Australian Catholic University. She is an experienced teacher educator who works in the fields of literacy, professional experience and partnerships. Her major research interest is professional becoming of preservice and practicing teachers and partnerships, with a minor research interest in critical literacy. She has developed and coordinated multiple partnership programmes in Victoria and Queensland.

Dr. Kenneth Young has been a lecturer at the University of the Sunshine Coast since 2007. Prior to taking up a Lecturer B position at USC, Kenneth worked for the Queensland Department of Education and Training (DET) as an Industrial Technology and Design teacher from 1985 until 2006. During this time, he taught in rural, remote and provincial secondary and primary schools throughout Queensland. At USC, Kenneth's first leadership role was the positon of Program Coordinator for the secondary combined degree programs between 2009 and 2011. He then undertook the leadership position of Program Coordinator for the Graduate Diploma in Education, a position he held between 2012 and 2018. Kenneth's current leadership role is the position of Program Coordinator for the Master of Teaching (Secondary) program pathways for preservice teachers into rural schools in Queensland. Kenneth's doctoral research focused on preservice teacher education—in particular, the perspectives of preservice teachers on the roles and identities of secondary teachers within Queensland state schools. This qualitative research focus on preservice teacher experiences and perspectives is continuing with current research agendas which investigate preservice teacher perspectives of rural schools and teaching experiences.

Associate Professor Kathy Jordan is a lecturer and researcher in the School of Education, RMIT University. Kathy has strong research interest in initial teacher education, including the changing policy context that is shaping practice and the importance of Work-Integrated-learning to preservice teacher development, with a focus on negotiating theory and practice and the development and implementation of innovative approaches using partnerships, shared responsibility and site-based learning. Kathy is also interested in changing notions of literacy, the use of ICT in school education and teacher decision-making particularly around ICT.

Chapter 6
Learning to Be a Professional: Bridging the Gap in Teacher Education Practice

Rebecca H. Miles, Stephanie Garoni and Sally Knipe

Abstract The aim of this chapter was to discuss the findings of a research project that examines the perspectives of graduate teachers, and their school principals/supervisors, regarding the benefits of the professional attachment as an effective model for bridging the gap between preservice teacher preparation and beginning teaching. This professional experience model for postgraduate initial teacher education provides for 60 days of mandatory professional experience across the first 18 months (equivalent) of the course, while the final 6 months of the course is undertaken through a professional attachment of 45 days in school, while implementing a participatory action research project investigating teaching impact on student learning. The teaching candidate assumes responsibility as a classroom teacher with a reduced teaching load, supported by the school as well as the University. The findings from this study indicate that the professional attachment is a very effective model to support graduate teachers as they transition to the profession.

1 Introduction

Graduates of initial teacher education courses are expected to enter the teaching profession with a level of professional knowledge and practice that flags them as "ready" to take up the challenges of their new profession. School environments, however, have manifold, varied and complex cultures which contribute in unique ways to the specific learning needs of students, staff practices and leadership cultures (Ball & Forzani, 2009; Grundy, 1998; Schwab, 2013). Despite this, graduate teachers are expected to be "ready" to teach in schools across a variety of contexts and situations, ranging from remote Indigenous settlements to inner metropolitan schools

R. H. Miles (✉) · S. Garoni · S. Knipe
La Trobe University, Albury-Wodonga, VIC, Australia
e-mail: r.miles@latrobe.edu.au

S. Garoni
e-mail: s.garoni@latrobe.edu.au

S. Knipe
e-mail: s.knipe@latrobe.edu.au

© Springer Nature Singapore Pte Ltd. 2019
A. Gutierrez et al. (eds.), *Professionalism and Teacher Education*,
https://doi.org/10.1007/978-981-13-7002-1_6

catering to students from refugee backgrounds (Rowan, Mayer, Kline, Kostogriz, & Walker-Gibbs, 2015). Universities, in both Australia and overseas, must contend with the predicament of ensuring that graduates of their teacher education courses enter the profession of teaching "classroom ready" upon graduation.

While employers and policy makers have shown increased commitment to mentoring new graduates in their first year of teaching (Ballantyne, Hansford, & Packer, 1995; Hudson, 2012), often this focus has been on socialisation into the current system and is managed through employer and education departments (Achinstein & Athanases, 2005). The current model allows for a divide that graduate teachers must navigate between their experiences of learning about teaching (preservice teaching) and practicing as a professional (in-service teaching). In this paper, we present a model for learning to be a professional, providing research supporting the professional attachment as an effective and innovative model for bridging preservice and in-service teaching. In doing so, we draw from a multi-year study of recent graduate teachers, and their school principals/work supervisors, to investigate how participation in a professional attachment has enabled an ease of transition between preservice and in-service teaching in learning as a graduate teacher. Through this, we contend that the additional support for graduate teachers, provided in partnership between university and school, shows the professional attachment as an effective model for bridging the gap between preservice teacher education and beginning teaching.

2 Literature Review

Learning to become a teacher requires complex understanding and knowledge in practice. Impacting the growth, professional development and practices of new teachers is a range of diverse challenges. This section examines current research that addresses the transition of graduate teachers to enter the classroom initially through a discussion of the factors impacting the readiness of graduate teachers, with a particular focus on preparation to cater for the individual and collective needs of diverse students; a core issue for graduate teachers. A discussion of the connection between university and school through the preparation for teaching from professional experience follows, concluding with an investigation into the transition to teaching models that are adopted in Australia. Given the latest review into teacher education in Australia (Craven et al., 2014) such an evaluation is warranted and contributes to the ongoing debates about teacher education policy and the way in which teacher education programs are structured and worked in relation to the school sector (Knipe & Fitzgerald, 2017; Fitzgerald & Knipe, 2016).

2.1 Preparedness of Graduate Teachers for Diverse and Inclusive Classrooms

The professional expectations that guide the structure and content of initial teacher education courses through accreditation are designed to prepare preservice teachers for everyday classroom practice. It is anticipated that graduate teachers transition into the classroom ready to teach and ready to have a positive impact on student learning. Despite this, national and international research has shown that graduate teachers face numerous challenges in the first five years of entering the profession, which can lead to distress, burnout and a decision to leave the profession (Mansfield, Beltman, Weatherby-Fell, & Broadley, 2016).

Findings of the Australian four-year long *Studying the Effectiveness of Teacher Education* research project have highlighted the challenges associated with preparing preservice teachers for such a broad range of socio-economic, geographic, culturally and linguistically diverse school settings. By tracking 2010 and 2011 graduate teachers across two states (Victoria and Queensland), the study reveals that many graduate teachers felt unprepared to work confidently within these diverse contexts, especially when teaching "culturally, linguistically and socio-economically diverse learners" (Mayer et al., 2017, p. 124). Further, graduates reported suffering "reality shock" during their transition from university to the profession (Friedman, 2004). This is supported by Hemmings and Woodcock (2011) who found that significant numbers of preservice teachers stated they were poorly prepared to teach students with diverse needs. Preservice teachers' responses concentrated on how challenging it was to manage time and energy when aiming to meet the needs of all their students (Hemmings & Woodcock, 2011). Regardless, Perry and McConney (2010) report that there are more less-experienced teachers (mostly non-Indigenous, female and middle class) in schools with high concentrations of culturally and linguistically diverse students.

A significant educational challenge for communities in rural and remote Australia has been their ability to attract and retain graduate teachers (Hudson & Millwater, 2010). Research by Herrington and Herrington (2001) found that many teachers leave the profession within the first five years of rural and regional practice due to the geographic isolation and lack of access to professional development. Sharplin's (2002) study of preservice teacher's perceptions of rural life reflects a lack of clear understanding by them about what it is like to teach and live in rural communities. She found that preservice teachers were under-informed about rural and remote teaching, relying just on narrow, stereotypical images of the rural and remote teaching experience. Preservice teachers identified concerns about isolation, lack of resources, lack of access to professional and personal support, standards of housing and cultural differences of students (Sharplin, 2002). Kline and Walker-Gibbs (2015) further maintain that graduate teachers' preparedness for working in remote settings is mediated by the development of pedagogical expertise, professional engagement with parents and the community, and broader notions of preparation to teach in such contexts.

Other findings from the *Studying the Effectiveness of Teacher Education* research project further support the notion that not all of the learning in these areas can be developed during teacher education, and that expertise must mature in the specific setting of an individual teacher's workplace. Graduate teachers, when self-reporting their challenges, often acknowledged that these were areas of teaching that could only be learned "on the job" (Mayer et al., 2017, p. 93). This implies that the workplace setting and learning support available during induction is particularly influential on how knowledge and skills in these areas develop (Mayer et al., 2017). Forlin and Chambers (2011) also call for a more collaborative and systematic effort between universities and educational systems to ensure a cohesive transition from undergraduate teacher preparation to becoming a competent and effectively trained inclusive teacher. Mayer et al. (2017) recommend that if graduate teachers are to succeed in diverse contexts, schools of education must design programmes that transform the kinds of settings in which novices learn to teach and later become teachers. This means that initial teacher education programmes must venture out further and further from the university and engage ever more closely with schools in a mutual agenda of transformation.

2.2   (Dis)Connection with Schools Through Professional Experience

Given the issues in preservice preparation and beginning teaching identified in the previous section, the role of partnerships in connecting schools and universities through professional experience is highly relevant. Despite this, the prevailing model for teacher education is founded on a structure that reflects the historical development of teacher preparation, that is, a mix of theoretical studies with pockets of professional practice scattered throughout a course. This model has attracted criticism and condemnation due to there being "often a huge disparity between the types of skills and knowledge taught in preservice programmes and the realities of workplace practice" (Allen & Wright, 2014, p. 136; Yayli, 2008).

The professional experience model in teacher education encompasses the proficiencies of preservice teachers in the practices of the profession, including placement, professional attachment, practicum and fieldwork. This is consistently considered by preservice teachers and those working in the profession as highly valuable for learning to become a professional. However, Pridham, Deed, and Cox (2013) highlight the complexities of professional experience where "the primary focus of pre-service teachers immediately prior to and then during their first practicum may not strictly concern pedagogy (although this is the focus of much university and school attention), but emphasise coping with the anxiety and stress of being placed into a complex, dynamic and combative workplace environment" (p. 30).

While there is much focus on professional experience and how it can be better situated in teacher education courses (AITSL, 2016; Craven et al, 2014), there is a disconnection between university teacher education and school-based professional experiences which is an ongoing and central problem in preservice teacher education. As Zeichner (2010); see also Grossman, Hammerness & McDonald, 2009) explains, the problem of this disconnect carries through into the practice of the graduate teacher;

> in the historically dominated "application of theory" model of preservice teacher education … prospective teachers are supposed to learn theories at the university and then go to schools to practice or apply what they learned on campus… there is very little preservice preparation before candidates assume full responsibility for a classroom, [and] it is assumed that most of what novice teachers need to learn about teaching can be learned on the job in the midst of practice. (pp. 90–91)

Zeichner (2010) suggests instead that the creation of hybrid spaces for teacher education which allow teacher education graduates "to enact desired practices in complex school settings" (p. 89) is necessary to counter this disconnect. Likewise, there is a growing body of research supporting an understanding of professional experience in teacher education courses as third space (Zeichner, 2010), where the practices of teacher educators and those of teachers interact recursively in the professional preparation and learning of preservice teachers (Miles, Lemon, Mathewson Mitchell, & Reid, 2016; Soja, 1996; Somerville, 2007; Zeichner, 2010). The research project discussed in this chapter provides a model of professional experience where university and school's work together in bridging the gap between preservice teacher education and in-service teaching.

3 Learning to Be a Professional: The Professional Attachment

The review of literature above has provided an overview of some of the key issues impacting the transition to teaching that graduate teachers face. In particular, we discussed the effect that the increasingly diverse needs of students in schools have on preservice teachers not adequately prepared for the profession, as well as the impact on those students they are charged with. In turn, we have discussed the importance of the professional experience through teacher education courses in preparing graduate teachers for the classroom, suggesting the possibilities of these experiences when there is connection between school and university. The research project discussed in this chapter is centred on the experiences of beginning teaching of graduates from a teacher education course where students undertook a professional attachment—an additional 45 days in schools designed as a way of bridging the gap between preservice and in-service teaching. The professional attachment model is discussed below, prior to the overview of the research project and discussion of key findings.

Learning to become a professional and developing pedagogical expertise sees novice teachers moving from largely decontextualised and rules-based understandings to more complex, nuanced and context dependent practices in the first years of teaching (Miles & Knipe, 2018; Flybjerg, 2001). The developmental "mastery" required for teacher proficiency and teaching practice is a complex process involving ways of knowing, discipline knowledge and specialised expertise (Turner-Bisset, 2001). Graduate teachers suffer from "transition shock" as they move from teaching programs into employment as a teacher. This can lead to conformity and dismissing or reducing the opportunities to try reform-based strategies in their practices (Korthagen, Kessels, Koster, Lagerwerf, & Wubbels, 2001). Despite the extensive amount of research into the career readiness of early career teachers, the introduction of support and mentoring programmes, and now professional standards that determine the content of teacher education programmes, issues persist for graduate teachers as they make the transition into the teaching profession (Strangeways & Papatraianou, 2016; Schuck, Aubusson, Buchanan, Varadharajan, & Burke, 2017).

Professional experience is a core component of initial teacher education programmes where preservice teachers are provided with structured opportunities to develop and demonstrate classroom skills. The number of mandatory professional experience days in Australian teacher education programmes varies from 80 days for Bachelor programmes to 60 days in Master of Teaching degrees. A random audit of professional experience days undertaken in teacher education programmes at Australian Universities reflect the number of mandatory days required. However, some universities support additional days and in some cases offer alternative models of workplace learning such as internships, as indicated in Table 1.

Professional experience days are divided into blocks of time of varying length. While this is an important aspect of initial teacher education programmes, access to high-quality mentoring is crucial in developing preservice teaching success. However, often mentor teachers do not have the time to provide preservice teachers with the type of effective feedback that allows for reflection and growth in practice (AITSL, 2013). Added to this is the further complication of the Federal Governments' financial contribution for practicums (DEEWR & Gonski, 2011). This does not adequately cover the cost of delivery of rich placement experiences. Providers are constrained in their use of this funding due to payment requirements to supervisory teacher payments.

The benefit of a *"professional attachment"* is where a preservice teacher is attached to the whole school professional community, to become a contributing member of that community and allowing the preservice teacher to learn, in part, by immersion in that community. The attachment in the course that was the basis of this project was 45 days long and usually completed over nine weeks full time, positioned in the final semester of the course. Prior to the attachment, students completed 60 days of mandatory placement during three 20-day placements. Students could elect to exit with a Graduate Diploma prior to the final semester; however, by continuing they gained a Masters level qualification, as well as a further experience in school before beginning teaching.

The attachment model provides contemporary understandings of the place of professional practice in the concept of learning to teach and offers an extended, supported, transition between the experiences of being a student teacher through to membership of the teaching profession. This model enables preservice teachers to

Table 1 Placement days in postgraduate ITE courses

University	Sector	Placement days	
University F	Primary and secondary	60 days placement + 45 days attachment	Victoria
University A	Secondary	80 days	Queensland
University E	Primary and secondary	40 days placement + 45 days internship	New South Wales
University E	Primary	40 days placement + 45 days internship	New South Wales
University G	Secondary	65 days	South Australia
University A	Primary	60 days	Queensland
University B	Primary	60 days	Victoria
University B	Secondary	60 days	Victoria
University C	Primary and secondary	60 days	Tasmania
University D	Primary	60 days	New South Wales
University D	Secondary	60 days	New South Wales
University F	Secondary	60 days	Victoria
University H	Primary	60 days	Queensland
University I	Primary	60 days	Victoria
University I	Secondary	60 days	Victoria
University J	Primary	60 days	New South Wales
University J	Secondary	60 days	New South Wales

experience all aspects of teachers' work under increasingly autonomous conditions and as the attachment is not classified as practicum, there are no financial requirements. To further consolidate professional learning and engagement, in conjunction with the professional attachment, preservice teachers undertake a small-scale action research project focused on improving an aspect of their teaching or student learning. This project is a way of undertaking a professional learning activity that can benefit both the school and the preservice teacher.

4 Research Design

The research reported in this chapter is drawn from a project tracking graduate teachers' preparedness, readiness and transition to the classroom. This research examined classroom readiness and the transition from preservice to graduate teacher. Graduate teachers were interviewed using a schedule of questions intended to establish their perceptions of programme experience, classroom preparedness and transition to teaching. Further, to develop credibility and authenticity in the research design, the work supervisors of the graduate teachers were interviewed to ascertain their perceptions of the graduate teachers' transition to teaching. This saw the development of two semi-structured interview schedules used to ascertain (1) the graduate teachers' perceptions on their readiness to teach and perceptions of their transition to teaching, and (2) each graduate teachers work supervisors' perceptions of the graduate teachers' transition to teaching, classroom readiness and how well they had been prepared for teaching. Interview participants were graduates within six months of completing their initial teacher education and who were employed in government or Catholic schools across Victoria, as well as their work supervisor—mostly senior teachers or school principals. In total, 61 graduates and 32 work supervisors participated. Of these, 22 graduates had undertaken the professional attachment with 13 corresponding supervisors, and it is this group of participants that the research discussed here focuses on.

A qualitative interpretivist methodology enabled the researchers to approach the research design and data collection with a focus on the empathetic understanding "of the everyday lived experience of people in specific … settings" (Neuman, 2000, p. 70), resulting in detailed descriptions and limited abstraction in the reporting of the data. The use of interviews to collect data through a set of guiding questions asked of all participants, allowed for consistency in comparison with participant responses while also enabling scope to develop a depth of understanding of participants' experiences. In this case, the interpretive methodology enabled the goal of the research, which was to explore the perceptions of participants' transition to teaching (or supervision of a graduate teacher) from their own perspective. Further, an interpretive approach in the analysis of the data was utilised through coding data into themes and categories by multiple researchers involved in the project. This resulted in richer interpretations of the participants' experiences of transition to teaching, highlighting common threads of experience across and within the groups of participants (Neuman, 2000).

4.1 Participants

The participants involved in this project were drawn from a purposive and convenient sample of graduate teachers, with all having graduated within 6–12 months from teacher education programmes that qualified candidates to teach in Primary, Secondary or F-12 contexts. The participants in this study were drawn from schools in a range of geographical locations and across Victorian public and Catholic school sectors. After the graduate teachers were recruited, their work supervisors were approached and invited to participate in the research project. The work supervisors were senior staff such as the school principal, deputy principal, head of department or worked in a coordinator or lead teacher capacity. This provided credibility and triangulation to the research through scoping a broader range of perceptions and experiences from the work supervisors, which then complemented those of the graduate teachers. The inclusion of work supervisors was an important aspect of the research design given their roles as experienced and lead teachers. We found that the perceptions of the graduate teachers, while valid and worthwhile, were mediated through their limited experience in the classroom. In contrast, the perceptions given by proficient and expert level teachers provided a more nuanced understanding, based on their experiences of mentoring and supervising the graduate teachers. Also contributing to this, we found that the supervising teachers drew on their previous experiences of classroom practice and of mentoring and supporting early career teachers, which informed their perceptions of the graduate teachers involved in this study.

Approval to conduct this research came from the presiding university, the Department of Education in Victoria, and the four Catholic Education Office dioceses in Victoria, Australia. In total, 51 graduate teachers and 28 supervisors were interviewed; some of the graduate teachers interviewed had the same supervisor, as they were located in the same school, while other graduate teachers were working as Casual Relief Teachers and therefore did not have an allocated supervisor.

4.2   Data Collection and Analysis

The authors had been involved in teaching the graduate teacher participants; therefore, a project officer was employed to recruit and interview participants. The project officer was not known to the graduate teacher or supervising teacher participants. Interviews were typically one hour in duration and conducted in person at the school. For interviews with supervisors that were not possible in person, telephone interviews were arranged. Participants gave permission for interviews to be recorded for transcribing. A research assistant was also employed to transcribe and undertake an initial coding of data. NVivo was used to identify themes and patterns in the data. At this initial coding stage, the themes were a priori and drawn from key literature as well as the interview schedule, an important element in establishing consistency in data analysis. Following initial coding, the researchers involved in the project utilised the data for more nuanced analysis and posteriori coding of the data that drew on themes and ideas which evolved through close reading. At this stage of the research, there were five members of the research team, including the research officer and research assistant. As such, multiple analysts as well as multiple sources allowed the data to be triangulated and provided the results of the study with credibility. The research officer followed a semi-structured interview schedule for all interviews, giving the study further credibility.

5   Analysis and Discussion

A number of themes have emerged from the data relevant to the value of the professional attachment as a model for bridging preservice and in-service teaching. Specifically, much of the focus of the discussion centred on the value of the professional attachment model towards the graduate teachers' feeling of readiness to teach. Other themes emerging from the data included the value of the professional attachment model from supervisor teachers' perspectives, and the contribution such a model made to the graduate teachers' professional learning and practice. These themes are discussed in the following sections.

5.1   Value of the Professional Attachment Model and Graduate Teachers' Readiness to Teach

There was strong agreement amongst graduates on the value of the professional attachment model to their readiness for teaching. Graduate MA acknowledged that the professional attachment was *"really important in making me feel ready"* and *"a great part of the course"* (Graduate GG).

All graduate teachers highlighted the professional attachment model's importance within their course structure, agreeing that it was pivotal in their preparedness to teach. As Graduate MR commented, *"Without the attachment, I definitely wouldn't have felt as prepared"*.

While establishing the value of the attachment for preparation for beginning teaching, there was also recognition that the participants found it professionally fulfilling and valuable *"I enjoyed that 6 months. Immensely"* (Graduate SC) and *"I really can't put a price on what I learnt"* (Graduate MR). Likewise, Graduate GG highlighted their changing role and identity that played out during the attachment:

> that whole term gave me a good understanding of how a school works, not just from one subject, but from a longer stay and understanding how it all works … you were more of a teacher than a trainee. (Graduate GG)

When compared to the circumstances of a "normal placement," one particular aspect of the model that was appealing to graduates was the opportunity to *"spend more time in the classroom"* (Graduate JR). This made them feel more autonomous, and their supervisors, they claimed, considered them *"more of a co-teacher"* (Graduate MA). Graduate GG further commented that he felt *"responsibility was mine, rather than under the close watch of a supervisor in the 4-week blocks"*. Other responses supporting this view included participants articulating how the 20 days placement blocks ended when they were *"just kind of getting to the point where I'm going alright…So you'd just get your rhythm and that's the end"* (Graduate MW). Alternatively, participants found the attachment prepared them substantially more for the day to day work of teaching across a school term, with benefit perceived for their capacity for building relationships, curriculum planning and developing routines, as the following Graduates note:

> The final professional attachment as well was just really fantastic because it was long enough to actually get a feel for what we were doing. Some of the other [placements], like four weeks, you only feel like you're just getting the hang of it. And then it's over. So having one where we were there for the whole term and got to like really know the students. (Graduate MA)

> It was just the coming in, just getting that whole routine from the start, with the planning of a term and working out curriculum, you know weeks of work and things like that. And seeing it right through to the end. (Graduate SC)

As identified in the literature review, Hemmings and Woodcock (2011) found that preservice teachers felt poorly prepared for beginning teaching, particularly with students with diverse needs. Given the findings from our research, with participants discussing the value and benefit of the professional attachment, we suggest that the professional attachment model is highly beneficial in teacher education. Particularly where preservice teachers are exposed to diverse learning contexts, the attachment was found to provide greater preparation for beginning teachers for the complex daily practices of teaching, as well as negate some of the difficulties faced through the transition to teaching.

5.2 Value of the Professional Attachment Model from Supervisor Teachers' Perspectives

Overall, supervisors agreed on the value of the attachment model for graduate teachers' readiness to teach in the classroom and "*hit the ground running*" (Supervisor JK). They stated that, as preservice teachers, students sometimes miss out on developing important skills due to the time restrictions of "normal" placements. As such, while there was recognition that preservice teachers cannot be present for all key events in schools, it was also noted that this was a challenge. Consistent with research on practice shock and beginning teaching (Friedman, 2004; Korthagen et al., 2001), many supervisors noted that these challenges led to preservice teachers feeling overwhelmed and unsure, losing sight of what is central, as they moved to beginning teaching. Supervisor SN articulated it as:

> Lots of other new graduates come out; it's hard because they get so overwhelmed with all the paperwork they have to do that they forget it's all about the relationships. And managing those behaviours. But I think that comes with more time practicing and being in the classroom. (Graduate SN)

In contrast, several supervisors commented on improved readiness to teach from those graduates who had participated in the professional attachment program, with Supervisor AS commenting "*[h]e definitely comes across as though he's been teaching for quite a while*" and another stating "*[s]o at the moment you wouldn't know that he was a first year teacher*" (Supervisor JK). Comments here tended to focus on the increased ease of transition into teaching, the more substantial understanding that they had of the profession, and the initiative, resilience and contribution that they had as beginning teachers. These are typified by the following comments:

> That's sort of helped him to be able to feel like, oh well I have experience and I have something to give. You know he's not afraid. He just doesn't sit back idly absorbing information from us. He'll also be able to contribute. And maybe with something we haven't thought of (Supervisor AS).

He didn't come with any huge gaps. He seems quite confident and if he isn't sure of something, he's quite capable of asking. (Supervisor SG)

I think she seemed to be well prepared…She's just very unflappable. Whatever you throw at her, it's all good. (Supervisor JK)

5.3   Value of the Professional Attachment Model to Professional Learning and Practice

In contrast to Allen and Wright's (2014) articulation of professional experience as often disconnected to the realities of teaching and workplace practice, many graduates found the professional attachment model supported their developing professional learning and practice in preparation for teaching. As Graduate GG explained, "*[t]he attachment…, it helped consolidate the learning I had. It was more self-directed learning*". Graduate CD added, "*I think the attachment was really good. I can see the impact that it's had on my approach to practice and I'll carry that on … it definitely adds a lot of value*".

Some graduates found the professional attachment model helpful in bringing together the "*theory side of things*" (Graduate RC) accomplished at University and "*putting it into practice; that's where you really learn how to teach*" (Graduate RC) during the professional attachment. Graduate CP described the relationship between University based theory and the professional attachment experience as:

> You can learn a lot of theoretical stuff, but so much of it you just pick up when you're actually in front of the class. And you quickly start to realise what's not working and what is working. (Graduate CP)

They discussed the importance of making tangible links between the final research project, a participatory action research project undertaken while completing the professional attachment, and their practice, as something they would not have achieved in the shorter placement blocks. Graduate SC acknowledged it as "*a game changer for me. It allowed me, as a teacher, to be true learner again*". Other comments highlighted the value of the research project to improving their practice in tangible ways:

> Probably, if I hadn't done the [attachment and research project] … I wouldn't have had all the theoretical understanding behind me. I probably wouldn't have gone through and read all the research articles because I wouldn't find the time to do it – but somehow you do when you've got to write a thesis about it. (Graduate CP)

> I was able to implement some of the ideas from the course and combining that with my research was able to implement that and discuss it with my colleagues and develop strategies and teaching ideas they might not have been aware of or thought of. That was good. (Graduate GG)

> Well the research, the final research project, was really beneficial in terms of getting me prepared for like the data collection side of things. Cause that's the thing you know. That's huge. (Graduate MA)

Many beginning teachers also indicated an ongoing commitment to pursuing an evidence-based approach to practice once graduated, with Graduate CD commenting, *"I think the final part is really important because it has that focus on evidence-based practice…and I think it set me up really well for having that approach as ongoing"* (Graduate CD). Other graduates discussed how they will now use research when they encounter a problem, identifying the usefulness of the participatory action research framework:

> I've found myself even since then, some of the things I've been encountering in the classroom, I'll go back and do my own little bit of background research and see what I can find in literature and things like that. So I think the attachment was really good. I can see the impact that it's had on my approach to practice and I'll carry that on so I definitely, I think it definitely adds a lot of value. (Graduate CD)

5.4 Diversity of Workplace Circumstances

The final theme emerging from the interview data revealed the changing and diverse circumstances around employment opportunities for graduates in their first year of teaching. Graduates recognised the utility of the F-12 degree in firstly securing employment, and then secondly in meeting the demands of a diverse workplace. They acknowledged that the degree provided *"much more flexibility in what you can aim towards"* (Graduate CD), reporting that they *"really enjoyed the diversity"* (Graduate CP) of the course. Other comments included:

> When it comes to obviously job prospects it gives you so many more job opportunities… There's pretty tough competition for teaching jobs so it just gives you a point of difference. (Graduate CD)

> Because we did cover so many different age groups. So when something hasn't been working, I've been able to try something else. (Graduate MR)

> So for the Special Ed stuff that I'm currently doing, it's been really beneficial because…some students have really age appropriate interests and behaviours and things like that. So having that background in the high school curriculum and things is really beneficial…But some of the others in the class have interests that are much much more common for younger kids. They might have a language capacity that's much lower so I've had at least some experience with quite a wide range of age groups on all of my placements. (Graduate MA)

> I've found myself teaching in prep and then teaching in Year 9, and my classroom management was sort of quite similar across both groups. Of course, my language was different. But the consequences and things like that were not too dissimilar. (Graduate RC)

Despite the overall feeling of satisfaction with the course, graduates did identify some areas for improvement to better equip them for the diverse range of teaching environments awaiting them. The graduates worked in primary, secondary and special education schools in both rural and urban contexts, with three graduates working casually as emergency teachers across sectors. Consistent with the findings of Mayer et al. (2017), there were a range of teaching practices and challenges, which were learnt on the job. An example of this is Graduate MA description of her current teaching load:

So in hearing support, my youngest students are in kindy and then at the high school my oldest student is in year 11. So it's quite varied in terms of age. And then in the Special Ed High School, like there's a really big focus on behaviour management…neither of them are mainstream and neither of them are teaching according to the curriculum. (Graduate MA)

Graduate CD, who worked in a small rural community had a very different experience for her first year of teaching than Graduate MA. Consistent with the findings of Herrington and Herrington (2001) she struggled in her first year of teaching with feelings of isolation as she "*didn't have a lot of that collegial support or a mentor and things like that*". She recommended "*[e]ncouraging rural placements*" as "*something obviously really practical*" for universities to consider.

Another area identified by graduates was further guidance in the area of "*challenging behaviours and learning difficulties*" (Graduate CD). Graduate CP explained: "*I'm just not sure if it's just the particular students who are at my school or, but it seems like there are a lot of students with auditory processing delays or dyslexia*". Graduate CD, in her description of dealing with challenging behaviours and learning difficulties, suggested:

We do in the classroom encounter a huge range of challenging behaviours and learning difficulties. And I think there's only a certain extent to which you can teach that and the rest you have to approach on a case by case process but the significance of that and, I don't know if it's just the context I am working in but it's, it's really huge and it affects the day to day teaching just so significantly. Yeah, so maybe a little more content on that. (Graduate CD)

In presenting the above analysis and discussion of the research on the professional attachment, we present it as a model of professional experience that is collaborative and systematic in preparing a cohesive transition to the profession for beginning teachers (Forlin & Chambers, 2011). The value of the professional attachment as a model for professional experience in teacher education cannot be overstated. In particular, is its contribution to the graduates' contextual knowledge in practice. Likewise, the professional attachment allowed for a third space of learning to become a teacher and professional. In this third space, the nexus between university and school, research and practice occurs through co-collaboration and co-mentoring of preservice teachers to beginning teaching.

6   Implications of the Research Findings

The findings from this study confirm that professional experience is highly valued by graduate teachers and schools in supporting teaching candidates. The experience gained through the professional attachment that provided the opportunity to "put into practice" what the graduate teachers have learnt in a way that develops a strong connection to feelings of "readiness". Likewise, the supervising teachers supported that these graduate teachers, through both the additional time spent in school, as well as the depth of the experience, were subsequently more prepared, confident and ready for teaching diverse and inclusive needs students. These are attributes identified in research literature as areas that teachers are often less prepared for upon beginning teaching (Forlin & Chambers, 2011; Mayer et al., 2017).

The professional attachment provided the participants an opportunity to engage deeply and authentically in the everyday practices of teaching, easing the transition experience. The participants, although still facing some challenges as they began teaching, experienced wider-ranging mentoring. As for Kline and Walker-Gibbs (2015), we found that the professional attachment model provided an external and pedagogic support and preparation to teach in a range of contexts. Pivotal to this was the oversight of the university in the process, including guiding preservice teachers in completing participatory action research projects. The research projects that were undertaken during the professional attachment provided an opportunity for preservice teachers to "give back" to their attachment schools. Through this process, they provided staff professional development on the research that they had undertaken, providing the normal partnerships of professional experience to a deeper level. Further, given the complexity of funding for professional experience placements and the time-poor nature of teaching, where feedback and supervision is an identified issue, the professional attachment model provides a new way of conceptualising workplace experiences and learning to be a professional (Allen & Wright 2014; Zeichner, 2010).

In the light of the ongoing debate regarding the nature of teacher professionalism (Sachs, 2016), there is a need for re-conceptualising and re-developing teacher education in line with other professional degrees, providing a greater transition and support for those entering teaching (Ball & Forzani, 2009; Flyvbjerg, 2001; Grossman, 2011; Shulman & Shulman, 2004). Through the research reported in this chapter, we provide evidence of a re-considered design of professional experience. The evidence from this research advocates the value of a professional attachment model that supports and develops greater professional practice and classroom readiness for graduate teachers.

References

Achinstein, B., & Athanases, S. (2005). Focusing new teachers on diversity and equity: Toward a knowledge base for mentors. *Teaching and Teacher Education, 21*(7), 843–862.

Allen, J. M., & Wright, S. E. (2014). Integrating theory and practice in the pre-service teacher education practicum. *Teachers and Teaching, 20*(2), 136–151.

Australian Department of Education, Employment and Workplace Relations (DEEWR), & Gonski, D. M. (2011). *Review of funding for schooling.* Australia. Department of Education, Employment and Workplace Relations. Review of Funding for Schooling.

Australian Institute for Teaching and School Leadership (AITSL). (2013). *Initial teacher education: Data report.* Retrieved from http://www.aitsl.edu.au/docs/default-source/initial-teacher-educationresources/2013_aitsl_ite_data_report.pdf.

Australian Institute for Teaching and School Leadership (AITSL). (2016). *Initial teacher education: Data report.* Retrieved from https://www.aitsl.edu.au/docs/default-source/research-evidence/ite-data-report/ite-data-report-2016.

Ball, D. L., & Forzani, F. M. (2009). The Work of Teaching and the Challenge for Teacher Education. *Journal of Teacher Education, 60*(5), 497–511.

Ballantyne, R., Hansford, B., & Packer, J. (1995). Mentoring beginning teachers: A qualitative analysis of process and outcomes. *Educational Review, 47*(3), 297–307.

Craven, G., Beswick, K., Fleming, J., Fletcher, T., Green, M., Jensen, ... Rickards, F. (2014). *Action now: Classroom ready teachers.* Teacher Education Ministerial Advisory Group.

Fitzgerald, T., & Knipe, S. (2016). Policy reform: Testing times for teacher education in Australia. *Journal of Educational Administration and History, 48*(4), 1–12. https://doi.org/10.1080/00220620.2016.1210588.

Flyvbjerg, B. (2001). *Making social science matter.* Cambridge: Cambridge University Press.

Forlin, C., & Chambers, D. (2011). Teacher preparation for inclusive education: Increasing knowledge but raising concerns. *Asia-Pacific Journal of Teacher Education, 39*(1), 17–32.

Friedman, I. A. (2004). Directions in teacher training for low-burnout teaching. In E. Frydenberg (Ed.), *Thriving, surviving, or going under: Coping with everyday lives* (pp. 305–326). Greenwich, CT: Information Age Publications.

Grossman, P. L. (2011). Framework for teaching practice: A brief history of an idea. *Teachers College Record, 113*(12), 2836–2843.

Grossman, P., Hammerness, K., & McDonald, M. (2009). Redefining teaching, re-imagining teacher education. *Teachers and Teaching: theory and practice, 15*(2), 273–289.

Grundy, S. (1998). The curriculum and teaching. In E. Hatton (Ed.), *Understanding teaching* (2nd ed., pp. 27–37). Orlando: Harcourt & Brace.

Hemmings, B., & Woodcock, S. (2011). Preservice teachers' views of inclusive education: A content analysis. *Australasian Journal of Special Education, 35*(2), 103–116.

Herrington, A., & Herrington, J. (2001). Web-based strategies for professional induction in rural, regional and remote areas. In P. L. Jeffery (Ed.), *Proceedings of the Australian Association for Research in Education (AARE) International Educational Research Conference.* Fremantle.

Hudson, P. (2012). How can schools support beginning teachers? A call for timely induction and mentoring for effective teaching. *Australian Journal of Teacher Education, 37*(7), 70–84.

Hudson, S., & Millwater, J. (2010). Rural teaching: Over the hill is not so far away. *Curriculum Leadership, 8*(13).

Kline, J., & Walker-Gibbs, B. (2015). Graduate teacher preparation for rural schools in Victoria and Queensland. *Australian Journal of Teacher Education, 40*(3), 68–88.

Knipe, S., & Fitzgerald, T. (2017). Caught between competing worlds: Teacher education in Australia. In J. Nuttal, A. Kostogriz, M. Jones, & J. Martin (Eds.), *Teacher education policy and practice: Evidence of impact, impact of evidence* (pp. 129–142). Singapore: Springer.

Korthagen, F. A., Kessels, J., Koster, B., Lagerwerf, B., & Wubbels, T. (2001). *Linking practice and theory: The pedagogy of realistic teacher education.* Marhwah, NJ: Routledge.

Mansfield, C., Beltman, S., Weatherby-Fell, N., & Broadley, T. (2016). Classroom Ready? Building Resilience in Teacher Education. In R. Brandenburg, S. McDonough, J. Burke, & S. White (Eds.), *Teacher education: Innovation, intervention and impact* (pp. 211–230). Singapore: Springer.

Mayer, D., Dixon, M., Kline, J., Kostogriz, A., Moss, J., Rowan, L., ... White, S. (2017). *Studying the effectiveness of Teacher Education: Early career teachers in diverse settings.* Singapore: Springer.

Miles, R., & Knipe, S. (2018). "I Sorta Felt Like I was out in the Middle of the Ocean": Novice Teachers' Transition to the Classroom. *Australian Journal of Teacher Education, 43*(6), 105–121. http://dx.doi.org/10.14221/ajte.2018v43n6.7.

Miles, R., Lemon, N., Mathewson Mitchell, D., & Reid, J.-A. (2016). The recursive practice of research and teaching: Reframing teacher education. *Asia-Pacific Journal of Teacher Education, 44*(4), 401–414. https://doi.org/10.1080/1359866X.2016.1169502.

Neuman, W. L. (2000). *Social research methods: qualitative and quantitative approaches.* London: Allyn and Bacon.

Perry, L., & McConney, A. (2010). School socioeconomic composition and student outcomes in Australia: Implications for educational policy. *Australian Journal of Education, 54*(1), 72–85.

Pridham, B. A., Deed, C., & Cox, P. (2013). Workplace-based practicum: Enabling expansive practices. *Australian Journal of Teacher Education, 38*(4), 49–65.

Rowan, L., Mayer, D., Kline, J., Kostogriz, A., & Walker-Gibbs, B. (2015). Investigating the effectiveness of teacher education for early career teachers in diverse settings: The longitudinal research we have to have. *The Australian Educational Researcher, 42*(3), 273–298.

Sachs, J. (2016). Teacher professionalism: why are we still talking about it? *Teachers and teaching: Theory and Practice, 22*(4), 413–425.

Schuck, S., Aubusson, P., Buchanan, J., Varadharajan, M. & Burke, F. P. (2017). The experiences of early career teachers: new initiatives and old problems, *Professional Development in Education*, 209–221. https://doi.org/10.1080/19415257.2016.1274268.

Schwab, J. J. (2013). The practical: A language for curriculum. *Journal of Curriculum Studies, 45*(5), 591–621. https://doi.org/10.1080/00220272.2013.809152.

Sharplin, E. (2002). Rural retreat or outback hell: Expectations of rural and remote teaching. *Issues in Educational Research, 12*, 49–63.

Shulman, L. S., & Shulman, J. H. (2004). How and what teachers learn: A shifting perspective. *Journal of curriculum studies, 36*(2), 257–271.

Soja, E. W. (1996). *Thirdspace: Journeys to Los Angeles and other real-and-imagined places.* Oxford: Blackwell.

Somerville, M. (2007). Postmodern emergence. *International Journal of Qualitative Studies in Education, 20*(2), 225–243. https://doi.org/10.1080/09518390601159750.

Strangeways, A., & Papatraianou, L. H. (2016). Case-based learning for classroom ready teachers: Addressing the theory practice disjunction through narrative pedagogy. *Australian Journal of Teacher Education, 41*(9), 117–134. http://dx.doi.org/10.14221/ajte.2016v41n9.7.

Turner-Bisset, R. (2001). *Expert teaching: Knowledge and teaching to lead the profession.* London: Fulton.

Yayli, D. (2008). Theory-practice dichotomy in inquiry: Meanings and preservice teacher-mentor teacher tension in Turkish literacy classrooms. *Teaching and Teacher Education, 24*, 889–900.

Zeichner, K. (2010). Rethinking the connections between campus courses and field experiences in college-and university-based teacher education. *Journal of Teacher Education, 61*(1–2), 89–99.

Dr. Rebecca Miles is a lecturer in curriculum theory and course coordinator of the Master of Teaching courses at La Trobe University. Rebecca's research is focused on curriculum inquiry and preservice teacher education, with a particular interest in the interplay between teacher professional practice and pedagogy in online teaching and learning. Through her teaching, she facilitates preservice teacher understanding of the impact that research can have when it informs teaching.

Stephanie Garoni has many years experience as a classroom teacher, teacher librarian, learning support teacher, enrichment coordinator, literacy and numeracy advisor and deputy principal in both Australian and overseas schools. From 2001, she has lectured in the field of education at Central Queensland, Charles Sturt and La Trobe universities. Her Ph.D. studies were in classroom interaction, and her current areas of expertise include child development, classroom management and professional transitions.

Sally Knipe is Associate Professor (Teacher Education) at La Trobe University, Faculty of Education. Sally is an experienced teacher and academic with an extensive background in the leadership and development of teacher education programmes, which includes working as a national assessor of initial teacher education programs. Sally has published in the area of teacher education, is on the executive of the Australian Teacher Education Association (ATEA). Sally draws on existing data and data mining techniques in a range of research projects.

Part III
Collaborative Professionalism

Chapter 7
Teacher Educators Using Cogenerative Dialogue to Reclaim Professionalism

Deborah Heck, Helen Grimmett and Linda-Dianne Willis

Abstract Teacher education is a space that is constantly in flux as it responds to the increasing requirements of governments to improve the quality of teachers and teaching in specific and measurable ways. The burden of this work falls to academic staff who then must balance their engagement with research, teaching and service within a higher education sector that has a different set of measures and requirements. Against this background, we (authors) have aimed to identify ways to work together to reclaim our professionalism as teacher educators. This chapter recounts one of our experiences as three teacher educators from different parts of Australia and our use of cogenerative dialogue (interactive social space for dialogic exchange) that included material objects to support our collaboration. Vygotsky's conception of individual cognition being connected to social interactions and speech provided a theoretical context for our explorations. Using metalogue as our methodological approach, we document how using material objects during cogenerative dialogue allowed us to reflexively consider possible ways to improve our practice of research and teaching. The implications of this self-study identify the importance of cogenerative dialogue to support teacher educators to reclaim their identity and academic agency as professionals in an era of measurement.

1 Introduction

There is increasing international emphasis on the quality of the teaching profession that has been articulated through government policies as a long list of compliance

D. Heck (✉)
University of the Sunshine Coast, Sippy Downs, QLD, Australia
e-mail: dheck@usc.edu.au

H. Grimmett
Monash University, Clayton, VIC, Australia
e-mail: helen.grimmett@monash.edu

L.-D. Willis
The University of Queensland, Brisbane, QLD, Australia
e-mail: l.willis@uq.edu.au

© Springer Nature Singapore Pte Ltd. 2019   137
A. Gutierrez et al. (eds.), *Professionalism and Teacher Education*,
https://doi.org/10.1007/978-981-13-7002-1_7

requirements for teacher educators. While Aubrey and Bell (2017) identify recognition of qualifications and a drive for professional status as positive outcomes of the policy agenda, there are also concerns about the implications for the profession. They note the significant gap between the compliance agenda of government and the democratic professionalism and personal philosophies of teacher educators that have often led to acts of resistance towards implementation. In response to the call to reclaim teacher educator professionalism by Heck and Ambrosetti (2018) and inspired by the work of Biesta (2015, 2017), we (authors) have endeavoured to identify ways to engage with our professionalism through research and practice. This chapter recounts our experience as three teacher educators from different parts of Australia and the way we dialogued cogeneratively to improve our practice of research and teaching in a bid to reclaim professionalism.

2   Literature Review

The move to accountability and measurement of performance has impacted on what it means to be a professional in the context of teacher education. Education philosophers such as Biesta (2015) challenge us to reflect on and balance the three purposes of education, namely qualifications, socialisation and subjectification, in our work. How this can be achieved in the context of government policy that has focussed on generating new processes and procedures that quantify and measure the quality of education is unclear. These new processes privilege what can often be measured, narrowing the focus to the qualifications purpose of education. In the context of teacher professionalism, Sachs (2016) suggests that the increasing emphasis on compliance and audit is indicative of a lack of trust in the profession. These same notions can be applied in the context of teacher education where increased energy expended on compliance leads to de-professionalisation. Evetts (2011) describes the shift towards standardisation and managerial responses as the emergence of organisational professionalism with an emphasis on market and organisational imperatives. Occupational professionalism is an alternative conception of professionalism, focussed on the way a profession identifies itself based on the collegiality of the group, trust and partnership with an emphasis on how the profession protects the interests of the public. In the context of education, alternative terms have been used, for example democratic professionalism rather than the current emphasis on managerial professionalism (Sachs, 2016). The challenge remains for teacher educators to navigate the terrain. While the theory may offer various names to professionalism, we also need to acknowledge the requirement to navigate the teacher education landscape and identify the possibilities for us to generate a hybrid *third space* for our professional work (Forgasz, Heck, Williams, Ambrosetti, & Willis, 2018). Generating a third space is important to afford us opportunities for the collaborative development of new possibilities that we cannot achieve in isolation.

Creating a third space will require us to develop a deeper understanding of the impact the compliance and measurement focus has on perceptions of professionalism more generally. Research emerging from the United States by Bair (2016) advocates that teacher educators and graduates have a restricted view of professionalism that contrasts with status professionalism in nursing and activist professionalism in social work. Hence, the need for work on teacher educator professionalism is substantiated as a gap in the research literature that requires further exploration. This gap requires further examination of the teacher educator professional identity that goes beyond accounts of teacher educators' experiences of meeting registration requirements (Boei et al., 2015) and moves towards the exploration of our roles as teacher educators engaged in meaningful self-study to reclaim our professionality (Jónsdóttir, Gísladóttir, & Guðjónsdóttir, 2015).

Understanding more about the role of academic agency in the context of our professionalism provides a further theoretical lens. Our work draws on the definition of human agency advanced by Emirbayer and Mische (1998):

> the temporally constructed engagement by actors of different structural environments—the temporal relational contexts of action—which, through the interplay of habit, imagination, and judgment, both reproduces and transforms those structures in interactive response to the problems posed by changing historical situations. (p. 970)

This definition provides a lens for exploring academic agency in terms of how our actions connect with the past, the future and the present. Emirbayer and Mische (1998) identify these three interrelated components of human agency as the iterational element, projective element and practical-evaluative element. Theories of practice (Ortner, 1984) explain the iterational element where our personal and professional histories impact our actions both as routines and conscious reflection on the past. Projective elements relate to creatively planning for future actions in both the short and longer term. The final element incorporates the practical-evaluative aspects of agency referring to present judgements and actions based on an evaluation of the range of alternatives in the context of past and future issues, challenges and opportunities. This ecological view of agency has been used to consider teacher agency regarding curriculum development in school contexts (Priestley, Biesta, & Robinson, 2013). These different notions of agency provide a theoretical frame to reflect on how we critically shape our engagement with the problem of reclaiming academic professionalism.

At the same time, we are interested in how working together on problems or issues can influence professionalism and agency. Hence, we also drew on the role of relational agency (Edwards, 2007, 2009) to support theorisation of our work. Relational agency emphasises collaboration. As teacher educators, we have worked together on a previous project that explored the challenges of professional experience partnerships in the context of teacher education (Willis, Grimmett, & Heck, 2018). As part of this project, we re-engaged with our work on developing and sustaining professional experience partnerships using cogenerative dialogue as an example of relational agency. We described our developing idea of cogenerative dialogue as "the interactive social spaces—actual and virtual—set up by participants to enable dialogical exchange" (Willis et al., 2018, p. 51). Our developing ideas about cogenerative dialogue acknowledge the use of the approach in both the context of research and practice within the field of teacher education (Elden & Levin, 1991; Roth & Tobin, 2004; Siry, 2011; Tobin, 2006). Building on the insights of the previous work, we then sought to explore additional ways to enable cogenerative dialogue as a possible third space with application to our practice both as teacher educators and as researchers of teaching.

An opportunity to explore alternative ways to engage in curriculum design in higher education emerged from participation in a conference workshop led by Habel (2017). He provided a workshop that introduced the use of LEGO® Serious Play® (LSP) for educational purposes and explored the underlying philosophy and practice of this now open source approach (LEGO Group, 2010). While initially used to inspire future generations of engineers (Grienitz, Schmidt, Kristiansen, & Schulte, 2013) and in business settings to develop the process of creating and solving problems (Hadida, 2013), there is a move towards use in higher education. In this context, it has been adapted for use in the context of student personal development (Anthoney, Stead, & Turney, 2017) and application in coursework where reflection on practice is required (Peabody & Noyes, 2017). We were keen to explore how we might draw on the playfulness of LSP as a way to create opportunities for creativity (Pirrie, 2017). In particular, we were keen to explore LSP as a tool for stimulating cogenerative dialogue for both ourselves and our preservice teachers.

3   Research Design and Theoretical Framework

Vygotsky's (1987) conception of individual cognition being connected to social interactions and speech provided a theoretical context of our explorations. Building on our previous work using cogenerative dialogue and metalogue (Heck, Willis, & Grimmett, 2017; Willis & Exley, 2016; Willis et al., 2018), the chapter recounts our self-study of exploring LSP as a tool for cogenerative dialogue on our journey to reclaim professionalism in teacher education by creating cogenerativity and exploring academic agency. We use the term, *cogenerativity*, to refer to an ongoing process that occurs when we enter into dialogic spaces with others in ways that continue and expand each other's knowledge and understanding in new, different and even unexpected ways (Willis, 2016). Willis (2016) wrote, for example, that: "As people talk, their ideas become enmeshed with others' so that their interactions and transactions may lead to changes in an individual's consciousness or perspective" (p. 127). Cogenerativity thus brings different participants together to enable new learnings and insights leading to more action possibilities than one person could likely achieve alone (Willis et al., 2018). We use the term, *metalogue*, to describe analytical conversations we have about the transcribed texts of our original cogenerative dialogues. Roth and Tobin (2004) identify both cogenerative dialogue and metalogue as appropriate ways to engage in practice and also undertake research reflexively. Our work is based on Bateson's (1972) approach to metalogue requiring conversation focussed on the exploration of a problematic subject, and in which the form of the conversation also reflects the subject of the conversation. The analytical conversations, sometimes conducted as additional conversations in real time and sometimes as exchanges of emails or working asynchronously on written texts, take these original dialogues to the theoretical level—dialoguing about our dialogues to produce theoretical understandings of our insights.

Using metalogue as our methodological approach, we recorded an initial conversation as we explored the use of LSP materials and methodology. During this exploration, we used cogenerative dialogue to support our practice, problematising the topic in the context of our work as initial teacher education academics. The problem posed was "What is metalogue?" We used LSP materials to individually construct a model in response to the question and then shared our models and reflected on the question posed. This conversation took place in person and was recorded and subsequently transcribed. Photographs and video of our explanations of our LSP models were also taken to support the rereading of the transcription. The transcribed text was then revisited and reshaped (through later Skype conversations about the transcript and while taking it in turns to prepare the manuscript of this chapter) to form the findings as well as the discussion (metalogue) which connects the findings to the literature on teacher educator agency, professionalism and cogenerative dialogue.

4 Findings and Discussion

This findings and discussion section demonstrates our cogenerative process and is presented in three sections. Each section presents an excerpt of our original conversation after exploring the LSP materials, followed by metalogue (Parts 1–3) which provides links to literature and theoretical insights identified during our later analytical discussions about the transcript. In the first section, we focus on the LSP process, share our individual photographs and explanations of our built models and provide an example of the ensuing conversation. The second section focuses on the role of metaphor and the limitations and opportunities that are inherent in the LSP materials. The final section focuses on the importance of making space for dialogue as part of our professional practice.

4.1 Creating Cogenerative Dialogue About Metalogue Using LSP

As part of our initial exploration, we followed the four essential steps of the LSP *Core Process* (Frick, Tardini, & Cantoni, 2013, p. 8):

Step 1: Posing the question—In this case, our question was, "What is metalogue?"—although it could just have easily been about anything. Questions we typically use with our preservice teachers are, "What is learning?" "What is good teaching?" et cetera.

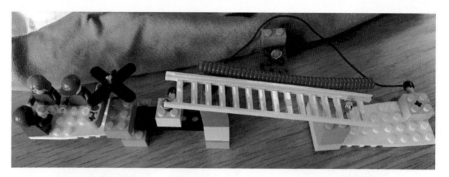

Fig. 1 Metalogue representation by Deb

Step 2: Construct—We each spent about 15 minutes simultaneously using the LSP materials to build our own individual construction representing the idea of metalogue. Although we worked alongside each other, we did not engage in discussion during this time.

Step 3: Sharing—We then took turns to talk about our own model, explaining the meaning and story behind our representation of metalogue.

Step 4: Reflection—Open discussion about each other's models and what they illuminated about the topic.

After these four steps, we broadened our discussion into a cogenerative dialogue about the process we had experienced and the possibilities this could hold for our own teaching with preservice teachers.

This core process forms the basis of the LSP methodology that was extensively field tested and researched from the mid-1990s until 2010 while the LSP materials and methodology were only available to be used by trained facilitators (Frick et al., 2013). LSP materials are now openly available for public purchase, and methodology documentation and manuals are available to download free of charge through a Creative Commons Licence (LEGO Group, 2010). The question posed and the process used to generate the LEGO models were articulated in the research design section. Hence we pick up the process here at Step 3—Taking turns to share recounts of our representations of metalogue.

The model created by Deb is represented in Fig. 1. Deb begins:

> I'll go first. Well, I suppose I tried to pull together the idea of a bit of, "How does metalogue work as a process?" So, I kind of saw myself at this end of the model being people gathering together, and I tried to make those people look all different. They could be all different walks of life, different kinds of people, but that then they actually have the opportunity to take this journey together. There will be gems along the way and the gems [pointing out the gold pieces] are actually in different locations. The gold represents knowledge or wisdom, but there are potentially different pathways that the group could take or that individuals might take along this journey of the metalogue, but that it all comes together at the end. So, some of these journeys are a bit more tenuous [pointing to the wire], and are a bit more problematic. Some of them are a challenge if you are a little bit claustrophobic [pointing to the tube]. Others of them are quite unstable but that everyone pulls together at the end and ends up in a location with a richer view, collecting the relevant gems along the way. You might not

Fig. 2   Metalogue representation by Helen

collect all of them, because no one might take that path, and that's actually okay. But that's the representation. The spinning wheel here is just that there are obstacles in the way that might impede your journey [Debbie spins the wheel and suddenly all the pieces collapse]. And these are all very tenuous. As you see, they fall apart at the blink of an eye!

Helen's model is represented in Fig. 2 and the conversation continues:

Okay. So, when I think of metalogue I think about it as layers. You do a first round of talking, so each person is bringing their little brick of input or information, and that's sort of that first layer of metalogue. And then from there you do a bit more input, and everyone's input is getting a little bit closer towards this one meaning that you're heading for. And another layer, and then you come to a shared product or something [pointing to the flag at the top of the structure] and you might think of that as, "Hooray, we've reached the pinnacle." The purpose of this thing [pointing to the pole and white brick that looks like a street lamp] is to shine new light on your experiences and your understandings. But actually, from here, although it's a pinnacle in a sense that you've created this metalogue, it's actually also then a springboard to new journeys, to new seas, new lands [pointing to the wires connecting outlying platform pieces]. There you go. But yeah, that layered thing was what I was thinking about.

Linda then explains the final model of metalogue Fig. 3.

Okay, I suppose I started with what we talked about yesterday as a thorny problem. So I put my thorny problem in the middle. <laughter> That's what that is down there [pointing to the plant-like shape at the base of the structure]. I also started with a platform, and I thought about the three of us, so I started with each of these big platforms to represent our body

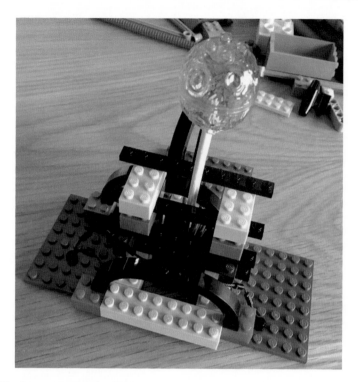

Fig. 3 Metalogue representation Linda

of work and where we each are, and then to try and show that somehow when we work together we step into this cogenerative space. These ones, the black ones [arch shaped piece, centre front], I used to show the idea of when we make connections; they're the bridges and represent the idea of the process being iterative. So, it's sort of backwards and forwards. This one [flexible connecting piece] is a little bit more contorted and, in some ways, the material suggested that process, because I couldn't get it to work anyway. But I thought the process sometimes loops back and goes forward, but all the while moves towards some greater understanding among those involved. And, I guess, these were the layers [pointing to the heights of the pieces], and these were the connections [horizontal black piece, top back] as bridges form between and across our work. And ultimately, this doesn't quite do what I wanted it to do, but I wanted it to represent, not so much an outcome, but a problem that was thorny and messy, to one that's become clearer and more compact, yet complex. Everything is still complex, but because of the process of metalogue, we have a greater understanding of the thorny problem.

Following the presentations of each of our representations of metalogue, a cogenerative dialogue naturally ensued among the group that represents the reflection stage in the LSP process:

Helen　[Speaking about Linda's creation] Yeah. But I think what's interesting is, because we've been cogeneratively thinking about this notion, it's not unusual therefore that the kinds of images that we have of what metalogue looks like have been more distilled into that space that you've got there in that model? Do you know what I mean? That we are going someplace and that's not unusual.

Linda   Yeah. No, I think we used similar but different metaphors to show that, didn't we? You [speaking to Deb] used the metaphor of a journey. I don't think you used that, Helen. Did you use "the journey"?

Helen   No. But mine is more coming up, whereas yours [speaking to Deb] is

Deb   Going someplace.

Linda   Yes. You [speaking to Helen] specifically used other metaphors. I was just trying to think what you used. But you used different ones. We both use layers.

Deb   And that's why mine has different heights.

Linda   Yes, the heights.

Deb   Like, it went up and down and around.

Linda   Yes. There was a sense of the process, trying to represent that in each of our models, and the sense of connected to something that's not connected to other things, but then all of these things coming together, and then also a point that we reached. There was an endpoint. There was a celebration, or there was insight, and, for me, there was still this complexity, but it was clearer, whatever the complexity was. <laughter>

Deb   You could actually see through it [referring to the transparent sphere shape at the top of Linda's structure]. <laughter>

Linda   Yes, true.

Helen   And that endpoints are only endpoints for a moment in time, but actually are springboards to further things.

Linda   That's right. So that's where I was going, that this was going to keep going.

Deb   That's where I kind of was wondering where, if we looked at putting them together, you could almost say, "Well, these are a series of different ways of representing metalogue using the materials," and we move from one to the next to the next, as a cycle. And that was what I couldn't represent in the way I did it. I felt like it would be nice to go around in a circle. And if I'd had more time I would have recreated it to try and show that.

Linda   The iterations

4.1.1 Metalogue Part 1: Creating Cogenerative Dialogue About Metalogue Using LSP

Our individual models and stories provided multiple perspectives of what metalogue is as both a process and a product and yet also highlighted shared understandings that were held by all of us. The LSP core process provided a structure that enabled all of our views to be expressed and shared on an equal footing. Rather than constraining and standardising our views, as the compliance measures that are imposed on our work as teacher educators so often do, this LSP structure flattened power hierarchies and opened up opportunities for going beyond preconceived ideas. Our conversation dipped back and forth between talking about our products (our models and our understandings) and our process of creating these. We felt a sense of agency, in that we were collectively creating our own meanings and understandings rather than having others' views imposed upon us.

This structure fits well with our pre-existing commitment to the value of cogenerative dialogue as a possible third space, but adds the new element of using materials to build physical models as *thinking tools*. This allows thinking to take place not just as a cognitive and verbal process, but also as a physical process of thinking with our hands, allowing manipulation of physical materials to construct understanding of our individual interior experience (Bürgi, Jacobs, & Roos, 2005). This is particularly useful when grappling with very abstract ideas and processes that are often difficult to explain verbally. The building process allowed our hands and materials to make "the invisible visible" (Hadida, 2013, p. 4), which then made verbalising the ideas easier.

4.2 The Role of Metaphor and Agency Emerge in the Limitations and Opportunities Inherent in the Materials

Our reflective conversation continued, providing further stimulus for thinking about how the materials facilitated creativity and provided a tool for cogenerative dialogue.

Helen Yeah. But it's true, the materials do dictate, to a certain extent. Like, I started doing one thing and couldn't make that work so I thought, "Oh, how do I do it with these materials?" And different materials start to suggest different things to you. You think, "Okay, I can go with that metaphor." I was trying to work out how to make something springing off and then I thought, "Yeah, I quite like these."

Linda Well, it's interesting, because I have one of those too [referring to the same piece as Helen], which I didn't talk about, but that's the tenuous connections where you can kind of see connection, but you're not quite sure.

Helen Yeah, and these can go in many different places and directions.

Linda Yeah. And this is nice because you've got that spiralling out as well. You've got that idea.

Helen I was surprised at the frustration of bits not going together in the way that you wanted them to go. But that actually is part of the process too. It represented metalogue as well, that it's unexpected or that you've got ideas about what you want something to be like.

Deb And it doesn't always work exactly the way you want.

Helen Yeah.

Deb And so therefore, what's my way around or how will I represent it?

Helen And sometimes, by what you can do with the materials, it presents new opportunities that you hadn't thought of before, which is exactly what happens. It's cogenerativity, in that the bringing together of the different ideas creates new possibilities that weren't in your individual head before. So, in a way, the materials are a new partner in that process that open up new spaces for thinking or doing or making.

Deb   And I think in terms of, not so much us, but in terms of working with preservice teachers around this kind of idea, is the fact that you actually have to make a product. It means that you've actually got something, a talking point, and it facilitates you to think, "Well, what do I think that looks like and what is something I can use to represent that?" Unlike when you ask preservice teachers to actually get together in a group and talk about something and by the time it gets around my idea is the same as everyone else's because they actually didn't think about it.

Helen   That's right.

Deb   And the busyness of your hands, I think. Even if you aren't really sure what you're doing to start with, I feel like you're collecting pieces, and I collected some pieces and started something and then went, "No, that's not what I want. I want this and I want that." But the actual ability to just do, rather than just sit and wonder was actually facilitated, "Well, why am I putting that like that? That connects like this and this is what I think."

Helen   Yep.

Linda   I think the level of concentration was very obvious, wasn't it?

Helen   Yeah.

Linda   I wondered whether down the track, if we were more familiar, we might say, "Hey, I'm collecting people. If you find any, give them to me." Like, I was collecting certain bits there, and we were all so quiet I didn't ask, but maybe in a group or if we did this more often I'd be saying, "Look, I'm collecting these long black bits," or something.

Helen   Yeah, like I had a sense that you had come to a finish and so you wouldn't mind helping me look for some links.

Deb   No. Yeah, exactly.

Helen   But also, the other thing was that at one stage I felt like I was finished. I nearly just stopped at my layers. But everyone else was still going so I thought, "Oh, okay. What else can I add?" and you probably did the same.

Deb   I did the same thing. I was going to put people and then I went, "I can't find some of those bits. I won't worry." Then there was more time and I went, "Well, now there's time, I will do that." So, I think if you're doing it with preservice teachers though we'd need to be pretty precise about the time to get it into our tutorial times. I think actually for us to then say, "Well, the similarities between what we did are amazing."

Linda   Well, that's interesting too. Getting back to the materials, two things, I wonder whether, when we're more familiar with what the materials can do, that allows us to make a model that better represents what we were trying to do, or our greater understanding of metalogue influences a change in what we use. And that would be interesting to sort of say, "If we come again, at some other point down the track, and re-represent metalogue, after we've had time to see what our preservice teachers do and more time for us to talk about it, what would we do differently? Would we choose things because we understand the materials better or would we have a different or better understanding of metalogue?

Deb   And that could be a good conversation to have at a later date.

Helen   But I think there is a thing about the time being a little bit longer than

Deb   Than is comfortable.

Helen   Yeah. Because it actually makes you think, "Oh, hang on." You sit with them for a second and think, "Okay, I think I'm done," and then realise, "I've got more time so I could just…"

Deb   And there's more pieces. I think that's also the thing, isn't it?

Helen   Yeah.

Deb   The amount of materials needs to be large.

Linda   Yes, for the choice.

Deb   So that there's choice, but there's also not competition.

Linda   Yeah, that's right. I think that was really important there was no competition about the pieces.

Helen   "I need that. I need that."

Linda   Yeah, not fighting over it. <laughter>

4.2.1   Metalogue Part 2: The Role of Metaphor and Agency Emerge in the Limitations and Opportunities Inherent in the Materials

In this part of our cogenerative dialogue, the role of metaphor emerged alongside a discussion about the limitations and opportunities of using the LSP materials. Metaphors permeate our language and culture and enable us to think more deeply about a topic or concept by drawing a comparison or analogy between things imaginary and/or concrete (Thomas & Beauchamp, 2011). In education, metaphors are deployed by teachers of every subject as powerful tools to enhance student conceptual learning. Metaphors used by teachers and preservice teachers, and in our case, teacher educators, can also provide a window into our beliefs, thoughts and actions. They can therefore support our practice in teaching and research by providing insight into our experiences and simultaneously contributing to the development and re-development of our individual and collective professional identity. When using LSP materials to represent metalogue, metaphors initially appeared to emerge in the context of the materials, specifically what the materials suggested they might *do*. That is, we each chose materials less for their colour and shape and more for their ability to "spring off," "connect," "go in different places and directions" and "spiral out." However, the materials we selected for construction were ones that aligned with our respective concept of metalogue. The words we used in conversation to describe what we did seemed to suggest our selection of materials focussed on the *processes* involved in metalogue and how the materials might best represent our understanding and experience of these. The metaphor of a journey was also evident. This featured beginning and end points as well as critical learnings (e.g. Deb's "gems") along the way. At the same time, we each used layers and/or height as metaphors to convey the challenges and complexities involved. Our models of metalogue thus represented processes and products simultaneously.

Seen through Emirbayer and Mische's (1998) three-pronged notion of agency, it would seem that our previous knowledge and experience of participating in cogenerative dialogue (iterational element) to produce metalogues (projective element) informed our decision making during the construction of our models (practical-evaluative element). Our use of relational agency as a further element became most visible when we engaged in cogenerative dialogue to talk together about our individual experiences of developing our models. During this dialogue, we showed how we supported each person's ideas by accepting what they said and responding in positive respectful ways. Turn taking and talk time were mostly equitably distributed among all three participants. Ideas were built upon and expanded in ways that built shared understandings. We thus intuitively used the experience of representing metalogue with materials as a way to illustrate cogenerativity in action (Willis, 2016; Willis et al., 2018). Our conversation also showed the potential for these representations to change and improve in relation to our changing knowledge of metalogue in future.

Emirbayer and Mische's (1998) notion of agency is also useful for thinking about our use of the materials themselves. We were familiar with metalogue but less so in using LSP materials. Although we discussed how the number and variety of pieces offered multiple different opportunities for our individual purposes and minimised competition between us, our dialogue showed that we were less secure in the knowledge of what different pieces could *do* (i.e. we lacked *technical* knowledge and skills to work with these materials). This was evident when we voiced our frustrations and unmet expectations about how pieces might fit together. In this way, our possible lack of previous knowledge and experience of manipulating LSP materials (iterational element) may have limited our possible representations of metalogue (projective element) and constrained decision making during model construction (practical-evaluative element). Nevertheless, we recognised that using hands-on materials may have increased our level of concentration and length of time on task during construction. Indeed, we discussed how more time not only seemed to increase familiarity and ease in using the materials, but also afforded more opportunities to be creative and open to new and different ideas than first thought. We later cogenerated about the possibilities of working in a group rather than individually and how this might further speed up the process of finding pieces and the processes of collaboration. Working individually initially thus constrained relational agency during construction but this was offset later during cogenerative dialogue by talking together about: the different experiences of playing with the materials; the variety of interpretations for the possible use of different pieces; and the limitations and opportunities for representing and cogenerative dialoguing about metalogue using the materials. As Helen noted above:

> It's cogenerativity in that the bringing together of the different ideas creates new possibilities that weren't in your individual head before. So, in a way, the materials are a new partner in that process that opens up new spaces for thinking or doing or making.

4.3   Creating Space for Dialogue

We continued our reflective conversation and explored the potential of LSP to create dialogue and connect with our sense of academic agency. We began with explorations of how LSP developed our own thinking about questions we posed as Step 1 of the process. Then, we explored connections and impacts on our past and future practice to explore our academic agency as teacher educators with both teaching and research responsibilities.

Helen   Using the materials does spark conversation.

Deb   It does.

Linda   But in different ways. A different kind of conversation than we'd be having. We'd be having much more of an academic conversation perhaps in that more abstract way, whereas I think this (LSP) anchors it a little bit more in the way we've represented metalogue and that gives us other language to talk about it.

Helen   And it's the starting point, isn't it, of the conversation?

Linda   Yeah.

Helen   Like, that's always the hardest thing. You go, "What do you say first?"

Deb   Yeah, and how do you get it going?

Helen   Everyone has something to say here.

Linda   I think if we think about an equitable conversation where people are able to have the same amount of time each and the same amount of input not just the same number of turns, but the length of turn-taking as well, which I think we're quite good at, quite naturally, because we're very respectful and we're also very respectful of this third space. And I think, Helen, coming back to that point of "everyone's had a turn" is equitable because, firstly, everyone's doing one and, also, it's yours. Everybody loves to talk about themselves, not in a selfish way or self-centred way, but because it's natural. It's just natural.

Helen   And even if they don't like it, it actually is a starting point. Your focus is on that [pointing to the model]. Your focus is not on looking at me.

Linda   That's right.

Helen   You're looking at that [model] as well.

Deb   It takes the pressure off.

Helen   That's right.

Deb   And what I thought was interesting as we progressed, is we built on the ideas of other people and so when you mentioned something about the model then, Linda, when you talked about your model you mentioned something about both models, and so we made the connections naturally through the conversation. It wasn't a tutorial activity that actually we had to say, "Do this, do this, and now bring the connections together." I think it will happen.

Linda   I tried not to, but I felt it was inevitable to mention all the models, but I think we could have discussed the connections even more so.

Deb   Yep, we could. And that's where I think the next stage is to say, "How do we bring these together? Can we bring them together in some way?"

Helen   I think it's actually important that everyone feels like, at first, they are just talking about their own, because otherwise they feel like they have to start bringing in everyone. So I think it's important, as a first stage.

Deb   Have bringing together and connecting as the next step. To actually have that conversation about, "What's the similarities? What's the differences?"

Helen   Yeah. And I think some of those do come up naturally in talking about your own anyway, but that then provides the springboard for the next conversation.

Deb   And I think that notion of the uniqueness about each one could link really nicely to that subjectification notion from Biesta (2015). "What's unique about them? What's similar, but what's unique?" So, the similarities are really in that socialisation of language and ideas. But the uniqueness could be a really interesting way of thinking about that.

Linda   So, my big challenge is to help our preservice teachers to recognise that teaching is not just about how to teach them to read. That there's a bigger purpose.

Deb   A bigger agenda.

Linda   And that they could make such an enormous difference to their communities, to the profession, if they weren't coming to it or exiting, possibly, from our programs thinking, "Okay, I've ticked all of those boxes. There's nothing more here." This kind of thing might actually enable those kinds of ways of bigger picture thinking about changing the world. I mean, we try and help them to think that's what you do with your students in your classrooms. We tell them that, "You can do anything," kind of attitude. But I think we should be helping our preservice teachers to see that's what they can do too.

Helen   And I think what this does is allows them to make a concrete object with materials to represent what they're thinking, and even if the complexity of what they've done doesn't even come to them until they speak about it and they maybe hear someone else say, "Oh, this means that," and they go, "Oh, okay. Well, why did I put that there? I can actually come up with a much more complicated description of what I've done." But if you'd actually sat there and asked them to explain, would a teacher, particularly a first year preservice teacher, be able to come up with that kind of language?

4.3.1 Metalogue Part 3: Creating Space for Dialogue

Our conversations and reflections on the use of LSP identified that a different kind of dialogue and discussion could be generated using this approach. LSP generated conversation that provided a third space for us to draw upon our past, imagine the future and evaluate these thoughts and ideas in the present moment through the construction of a model of our thinking about a problematic topic. The act of building and then explaining our model allowed us to connect our thinking with a representation that connected with each of us uniquely. Each model has its own story, and the process for sharing allowed each person to take centre stage to talk about their story and thinking. Within the third space that we created we had the opportunity to think about and consider the ways LSP might provide opportunities for us to work with preservice teachers in different ways to engage them beyond the narrow focus on ticking off the achievement of qualifications that is only one of the purposes of education (Biesta, 2015).

Our engagement with the LSP process identified that while we were able as professionals to draw together synergies between our emerging discussions, the process would require further scaffolding for preservice teachers. We identified the value of moving through the four steps in the LSP process and providing time for each person to speak. This process not only allowed for each person's model to be explored by the group but also facilitated cogenerativity. We reflected on Biesta's (2015) notion of subjectification and felt that the LSP process provided an opportunity for each person to talk about their own ideas highlighting their uniqueness. Although as teacher educators we were able to move between sharing and reflection, we identified the value when working with preservice teachers of keeping these aspects separate. We also identified that before moving on to the reflection stage where similarities and differences can be examined, we would need to redirect preservice teachers back to the initial question and provide them with a way to identify their uniqueness before moving on to more collective conversations.

We were drawn to the use of material objects for discussion as an extension of our own experiences of using cogenerative dialogue (Willis et al., 2018) and engagement with LSP (Habel, 2017) and the use of material objects in our own professional practice. We then connected these experiences with the current research on teacher talk that suggests regularly engaging students with classroom dialogue increases their participation and has a positive impact on student outcomes (Mercer & Dawes, 2014). We were drawn to the work of Alexander (2017) who challenges some of the dominant types of classroom talk that emphasise recitation. Our practice seeks to explore ways to move beyond question and answer that are limited to recall. We feel LSP offers the opportunity for the development of what Alexander defines as both discussion and dialogue. Discussion represents the opportunity to share ideas while dialogue moves towards the development of a common understanding. The four steps in the LSP process, in the context of cogenerative dialogue, offers opportunities for both of these kinds of teaching talk to take place in classrooms both at schools and in universities.

Our own academic agency became evident as we discussed how we could use LSP in our professional practice. We drew on our previous experiences with preservice teachers together with our understanding of theory and practice to signal the need for preservice teachers to consider their own understandings of what it means to be a teacher. Beauchamp and Thomas (2009) identified the need for initial teacher education programmes to begin the process of engaging with teacher identity. We see LSP in the context of cogenerative dialogue provides a mechanism for us as educators to engage in talk within the teacher education classroom that engages preservice teachers in a way that they can generate their story of teacher identity.

One of the challenges is the time required for these conversations in comparison with the recitation models of teacher talk that occur in many higher education classrooms.

5   Conclusion and Implications

The implications of this self-study identify the value and importance of cogenerative dialogue to support teacher educators to reclaim their identity as professionals in an era of measurement. The development of this work allowed us to create a third space for conversations about professionalism that connects with Evetts (2011) occupational professionalism and Sachs (2016) democratic professionalism rather than the managerial professionalism that is dominating teacher education. It allowed us to reflect on our own identity as teacher educators and consider the role of the past, the future and the present in the way academic agency connects with our practice. It also allowed us to use relational agency (Edwards, 2007, 2009) to build upon the expertise and ideas of each other, in effect creating new ideas and practices that were beyond our previous individual or shared practices. We identify implications here for our practice as teacher educators and the importance of relational agency as part of reclaiming our professionalism.

The LSP materials provided us with new ways to talk about topics we have problematised in our work and to reflect on our own academic agency. Similarly, the LSP processes offer opportunities for preservice teachers to begin the process of identifying their own developing story of becoming a teacher. The hands-on nature of using the LSP materials is engaging and provides a unique opportunity for all to participate in generating their story. A wide range of materials needs to be available to choose from during the creation process to ensure everyone has the opportunity to build their response. Time is an important factor in the individual building process and more time encourages more building. Lack of familiarity with the materials was a challenge; however, it was not insurmountable and often provided scope for improvisation. Using the LSP process in the context of a cogenerative dialogue approach throughout a program would provide some unique markers of preservice teachers' changing teacher identity.

This work demonstrates the value of LSP to provide additional resources and opportunities to structure cogenerative dialogue among teacher educators in ways that positively contribute to research practices and autoethnographic research. As evidenced by the metalogue in this chapter, this contribution identifies our academic agency with particular emphasis on the way the relational practices develop our work and thinking. We aim in our work to identify how we might continue to engage in authentic cogenerative ways to develop our research and teaching practice. It is this joint work that allows us to engage our academic agency in ways that meet the needs of academic managers in the current context of higher education practice.

In reclaiming our professionalism in the context of initial teacher education, our aim is to problematise aspects of work in relation to teacher education. We identify the importance of our own exploration of academic agency for connecting with the need for our preservice teachers to begin the work of exploring their teacher identity. Acknowledging to our preservice teachers that the work of academic agency and teacher identity development is never complete but an ongoing and continual process throughout our professional life is a challenging message. We feel that the use of material objects has deepened our engagement with cogenerative dialogue and allowed us to generate a rich metalogue. We also feel that it has helped us as teacher education researchers to develop our identity not just individually but also collectively. We have enhanced our understanding of these research practices and what we are able to achieve through them because of the way cogenerative dialogue together with metalogue enables deeper thinking and conversation and therefore learning and insights.

References

Alexander, R. J. (2017). *Towards dialogical teaching: Rethinking classroom talk* (Fifth ed.). Thirsk, UK: Dialogos.

Anthoney, J., Stead, R., & Turney, K. (2017). Making connections and building resilience: Developing workshops with undergraduates. *Knowledge Management & E-Learning, 9*(3), 404–418.

Aubrey, K., & Bell, L. (2017). Teacher education in further education 2000–2010: Subversion, avoidance and compliance. *Journal of Further and Higher Education, 41*(2), 99–111. https://doi.org/10.1080/0309877X.2015.1062846.

Bair, M. A. (2016). Professionalism: A comparative case study of teachers, nurses, and social workers. *Educational Studies, 42*(5), 450–464. https://doi.org/10.1080/03055698.2016.1219651.

Bateson, G. (1972). *Steps to an ecology of mind*. New York: Ballantine Books.

Beauchamp, C., & Thomas, L. (2009). Preparing prospective teachers for a context of change: Reconsidering the role of teacher education in the development of identity. *Cambridge Journal of Education, 39*(2), 175–189.

Biesta, G. (2015). What is education for? On good education, teacher judgement, and educational professionalism. *European Journal of Education, 50*(1), 75–87. https://doi.org/10.1111/ejed.12109.

Biesta, G. (2017). Education, measurement and the professions: Reclaiming a space for democratic professionality in education. *Educational Philosophy and Theory, 49*(4), 315–330. https://doi.org/10.1080/00131857.2015.1048665.

Boei, F., Dengerink, J., Geursen, J., Kools, Q., Koster, B., Lunenberg, M., et al. (2015). Supporting the professional development of teacher educators in a productive way. *Journal of Education for Teaching, 41*(4), 351–368. https://doi.org/10.1080/02607476.2015.1080403.

Bürgi, P. T., Jacobs, C. D., & Roos, J. (2005). From metaphor to practice: In the crafting of strategy. *Journal of Management Inquiry, 14*(1), 78–94.

Edwards, A. (2007). Relational agency in professional practice: A CHAT analysis. *Actio: An International Journal of Human Activity Theory, 1*, 1–17.

Edwards, A. (2009). Relational agency in collaborations for the well-being of children and young people. *Journal of Children's Services, 4*(1), 33–43. https://doi.org/10.1108/17466660200900004.

Elden, M., & Levin, M. (1991). Cogenerative learning: Bringing particiaption into action research. In W. F. Whyte (Ed.), *Participatory action research*. Thousand Oaks, California: Sage Publications. Retrieved from http://methods.sagepub.com/book/participatory-action-research, https://doi.org/10.4135/9781412985383.

Emirbayer, M., & Mische, A. (1998). What is agency? *American Journal of Sociology, 103*(4), 962–1023. https://doi.org/10.1086/231294.

Evetts, J. (2011). A new professionalism? *Challenges and opportunities. Current Sociology, 59*(4), 406–422. https://doi.org/10.1177/0011392111402585.

Forgasz, R., Heck, D., Williams, J., Ambrosetti, A., & Willis, L.-D. (2018). Theorising the third space of Professional Experience partnerships. In J. Kriewaldt, A. Ambrosetti, D. Rorrison, & R. Capeness (Eds.), *Educating future teachers: Innovative perspectives in professional experience* (pp. 33–47). Springer.

Frick, E., Tardini, S., & Cantoni, L. (2013). *White paper on LEGO® SERIOUS PLAY®: A state of the art of its applications in Europe.* Retrieved from https://www.researchgate.net/publication/262636559_White_Paper_on_LEGO_R_SERIOUS_PLAY_A_state_of_the_art_of_its_applications_in_Europe.

Grienitz, V., Schmidt, A.-M., Kristiansen, P., & Schulte, H. (2013). Vision statement development with LEGO® SERIOUS PLAY®. In *IIE Annual Conference. Proceedings*, 791–798.

Habel, C. (2017, 11–13 December). Envisioning the future of research-based curriculum design using Lego Serious Play. In *International Conference on Models of Engaged Learning and Teaching*. Retrieved from https://www.adelaide.edu.au/rsd/i-melt/papers/HabelIMELT2017paper.pdf.

Hadida, A. L. (2013). Let your hands do the thinking. *Strategic Direction, 29*(2), 3–5. https://doi.org/10.1108/02580541311297976.

Heck, D., & Ambrosetti, A. (2018). Reclaiming educator professionalism in and for uncertain times. In D. Heck & A. Ambrosetti (Eds.), *Teacher education in and for uncertain times* (pp. 1–13). Singapore: Springer.

Heck, D., Willis, L.-D., & Grimmett, H. (2017). *Using metalogue to develop an understanding of cogenerativity and school-university partnerships in initial teacher education.* Paper presented at the Australian Association for Research in Education Conference, Canberra. http://www.aareconference.com.au/wp-content/uploads/2013/11/AARE-2017-Conference-Program6.pdf.

Jónsdóttir, S. R., Gísladóttir, K. R., & Guðjónsdóttir, H. (2015). Using self-study to develop a third space for collaborative supervision of Master's projects in teacher education. *Studying Teacher Education, 11*(1), 32–48. https://doi.org/10.1080/17425964.2015.1013026.

LEGO Group. (2010). *Open-source: Introduction to LEGO® SERIOUS PLAY®.* Retrieved from http://seriousplaypro.com/docs/LSP_Open_Source_Brochure.pdf.

Mercer, N., & Dawes, L. (2014). The study of talk between teachers and students, from the 1970s until the 2010s. *Oxford Review of Education, 40*(4), 430–445. https://doi.org/10.1080/03054985.2014.934087.

Ortner, S. B. (1984). Theory in anthropology since the sixties. *Comparative Studies in Society and History, 26*(1), 126–166.

Peabody, M. A., & Noyes, S. (2017). Reflective boot camp: Adapting LEGO® SERIOUS PLAY® in higher education. *Reflective Practice, 18*(2), 232–243. https://doi.org/10.1080/14623943.2016.1268117.

Pirrie, A. (2017). The Lego story: Remolding education policy and practice. *Educational Review, 69*(3), 271–284. https://doi.org/10.1080/00131911.2016.1207614.

Priestley, M., Biesta, G., & Robinson, S. (2013). Teachers as agents of change: Teacher agency and emerging models of curriculum. *Reinventing the curriculum: New trends in curriculum policy and practice.* London: Bloomsbury.

Roth, W.-M., & Tobin, K. (2004). Coteaching: From praxis to theory. *Teachers and Teaching: Theory and Practice, 10*(2), 161–179. https://doi.org/10.1080/0954025032000188017.

Sachs, J. (2016). Teacher professionalism: Why are we still talking about it? *Teachers and Teaching, 22*(4), 413–425. https://doi.org/10.1080/13540602.2015.1082732.

Siry, C. A. (2011). Emphasizing collaborative practices in learning to teach: Coteaching and cogenerative dialogue in a field-based methods course. *Teaching Education, 22*(1), 91–101. https://doi.org/10.1080/10476210.2010.520699.

Thomas, L., & Beauchamp, C. (2011). Understanding new teachers' perspectives through metaphor. *Teaching and Teacher Education, 27*, 762–769. https://doi.org/10.1016/j.tate.2010.12.007.

Tobin, K. (2006). Learning to teach through coteaching and cogenerative dialogue. *Teaching Education, 17*(2), 133–142. https://doi.org/10.1080/10476210600680358.

Vygotsky, L. S. (1987). Thinking and speech (N. Minick, Trans.). In R. W. Rieber, & A. S. Carton (Eds.), *The collected works of L. S. Vygotsky: Vol. 1, Problems of general psychology* (pp. 39–285). New York: Plenum Press.

Willis, L.-D. (2016). Exploring cogenerativity for developing a coteaching community of practice in a parent-teacher engagement project. *International Journal of Educational Research, 80,* 124–133. https://doi.org/10.1016/j.ijer.2016.08.009.

Willis, L.-D., & Exley, B. (2016). Language variation and change in the Australian Curriculum English: Integrating sub-strands through a pedagogy of metalogue. *English in Australia, 51*(2), 74–85.

Willis, L.-D., Grimmett, H., & Heck, D. (2018). Exploring cogenerativity in initial teacher education school-university partnerships using the methodology of metalogue. In J. Kriewaldt, A. Ambrosetti, D. Rorrison, & R. Capeness (Eds.), *Educating future teachers: Innovative perspectives in professional experience* (pp. 49–69). Singapore: Springer Singapore.

Chapter 8
Teacher Emotional Rules

Jean Hopman

Abstract Who are teachers? What do teachers do and who, or what influences them? Equally important is, what do teachers feel and who, or what influences their feeling? Due to the tightly controlled nature of teachers' work, they are expected to follow practice blindly diminishing the emotional implications of the role. Acting, thinking and feeling are intimately enmeshed, and teachers navigate their work within a set of implied emotional rules that may be at odds with what a teacher may naturally feel. A collection of teacher emotional rules emerged from an action research project, which was also a narrative inquiry, researching teachers' emotional awareness and reflective practices. Six teachers from a Victorian Government secondary school came together over a year to share and inquire into their stories of teachers' day-to-day work. Each teacher's story featured a struggle that stems from the difficulty, yet the desire, to abide by institutionally derived emotional rules. Teachers live and work in tension and negotiating this tension is a struggle, but reflective practice, which is an essential aspect of teachers' self-understanding, can assist in uncovering the hidden emotional strain.

1 Introduction

> [Teaching] is a very personal profession I think (Blair).

Blair's opening statement suggests there is something more to teaching—something more than what is easily visible and something that is unique to each teacher. How do teachers understand their work and role? Who, or what compels them to do what they do? Equally important is, what do teachers feel and who, or what influences their feeling? Acting, thinking and feeling merge as teachers navigate their work within a set of implied emotional rules that may be at odds with what a teacher may naturally feel. The pull to feel or express emotion in a particular way is likely in tension with a teacher's impulses and provides a considerable struggle in teachers'

J. Hopman (✉)
Victoria University, Melbourne, VIC, Australia
e-mail: Jean.Hopman@vu.edu.au

© Springer Nature Singapore Pte Ltd. 2019
A. Gutierrez et al. (eds.), *Professionalism and Teacher Education*,
https://doi.org/10.1007/978-981-13-7002-1_8

work. This chapter is an exploration into such struggles and is a prompt for education professionals to consider the complex ways that teachers experience emotion in practice as well as a prompt for policymakers to consider the often unrecognised and unsupported aspects of teacher practice—emotional work. In Sect. 1 I turn to a range of authors—educational professionals, psychoanalysts, psychologists and sociologists—to frame "emotional work" in a contemporary context. Section 2 outlines the qualitative research project that led to the discovery of a specific set of implied emotional rules, which are listed in Sect. 3. The emotional rules stemmed from eight emotions that emerged as significant to teachers' work. The emotions and the implied rules are demonstrated through a specific teacher's story in Sect. 4. The story reveals the emotional implications of a teacher attempting to "control" a particular student's act of violence. Scrutinising the implied emotional rules within a teacher's story provides evidence that for teachers to attain self-understanding, reflective practice is required to uncover the hidden emotional strain.

2 The Teaching Profession

The exploration into teacher emotional rules stemmed from an action research project, which was also a narrative inquiry, researching how teachers' emotional awareness impacted on agency and whether the reflexivity required to enhance emotional consciousness could facilitate professional learning. Six teachers, Blair, Eden, Jesse, Kai, Marley and Taylor, from a Victorian Government secondary school and I, repeatedly came together over a year to share and inquire into our stories of teachers' day-to-day work. Blair's statement, as well as the following statements, were partial responses to a question I asked at our first meeting—"how would you describe your teaching practice?"

> Being in a classroom can sometimes feel like you are on a roller coaster depending on what's happening around you, but it's my job to make the classroom calm (Marley).
>
> I don't have a loud booming voice, and I don't punish a lot of students, but I am nurturing (Eden).
>
> Caring can be the best part of [teaching], but it can also be the worst (Kai).
>
> There are so many corners that you can cut, but it just wouldn't be me if I cut the corner (Jesse).
>
> I love seeing progress in the students. Getting good results (Taylor).

All the teachers described their work as "*hard*," that it had its "*ups and downs*," much like Marley's rollercoaster analogy, but that it also had its rewards such as the "*good results*" one might get from "*caring*." Keller, Frenzel, Goetz, Pekrun, and Hensley (2014) support that teaching is emotionally rewarding, but what are good results and who determines what these are? There is a set of norms and common knowledge drawn on to inform a teacher about how to "perform" (Edwards, 2017; Kelchtermans, 2009). Kemmis (2009) describes three incorporated elements of teacher practice: doing, saying and relating which are shaped by "practice architectures" (p. 466)—cultural-discursive, material-economic and social-political forces that inform practice. Where "doing" takes on a physical characteristic, the "saying" is the product of logical reasoning and "relating" has an ethical element related to engagement with others. Edwards-Groves, Brennan Kemmis, Hardy, and Ponte (2010) build on Kemmis's (2009) practice architectures by explaining that practice architectures are shaped by and in turn shape social interactions, suggesting that there are relational architectures infused in practice architectures. The relational and personal aspects of what teachers do are often eclipsed by the administrative and political aspects.

While there are a set of norms and common knowledge, a teacher's willingness to endeavour is still framed by personal biographies (Priestley, Edwards, Priestley, and Miller 2012). A sentiment that reiterates Blair's opening statement: *"[teaching] is a very personal profession I think."*

The teachers' statements imply certain expectations of their work. For example, Marley states, *"it's my job to make the classroom calm,"* Eden suggests that teachers might typically have *"loud booming voices"* and be punitive, and Taylor emphasises the importance of *"getting good results."* Winograd (2003) articulates similar expectations of teachers:

> [T]eachers are supposed to enjoy children, enjoy their work, maintain a patient and kind front, become angry with children infrequently and so on. These rules are not necessarily taught formally to teachers, but they are collaboratively constructed in the everyday work of teachers, students, principals, parents, and teacher educators. (p.1645)

Winograd (2003) uses the word "rule" to frame such expectations. Numerous researchers discuss the growing expectations of teachers to fit a mould (e.g. Biesta, Priestley, & Robinson, 2015; Burnard & White, 2008; Edwards, 2017; Groundwater-Smith, Mitchell, Mockler, Ponte, & Ronnerman, 2012; Hilferty, 2008; Johnson & Down, 2013; Priestley et al., 2012; Ryan & Bourke, 2013; White, 2010). The expectation that a teacher's "performance" will be measured against a preferred "script" of what to say and a long list of competency standards is very real but cannot replace teachers' "professional judgement or individual pedagogy," and ultimately reduces teachers' autonomy (White, 2010, p. 293). For instance, take Jesse's statement, *"There are so many corners that you can cut, but it just wouldn't be me if I cut the corner."* What if *"cut[ting] the corner"* was the expectation in a certain situation? Then, Jesse could no longer be *"me."* Edwards (2017) outlines that teacher agency, the potential for a teacher to take conscious action, is not an individual entity but a collective capacity that can thrive or dampen depending on how the demands of teaching are understood. Teacher agency is more than what a teacher "does," or how they "act," or how they "perform" but also depends on what is "expected" of them and how they are supported or limited by their professional relationships and environment. The expectations of teachers stretch far beyond the classroom walls and influence how a teacher perceives oneself and their work.

Teachers' work is framed by the inherent expectations affiliated with the dialectic of self and other. Winnicott (1965) explores the notion of a layered self in terms of a true self and false self. For Winnicott (1965), the true self is driven by instinct, and the false self is driven by the need to be accepted by others. The drive to be accepted by others is the catalyst for the false self to emerge and to keep certain aspects of oneself hidden. Whereas the true self is impulsive and expresses what is immediately desirable and comes naturally.

This "performance" of conformity includes how teachers might emote; for example, professional codes of ethics are often a disguised set of emotional rules as well as professional norms (Yin, Lee, Zhang, & Jin, 2013). Teachers are often expected to hide or fake their emotions (Hochschild, 2012; Stebbins, 2010; Taxer & Frenzel, 2015; Winograd, 2003). Emotion is an evolving dynamic merging how a person physically feels, a person's pre-dispositional way of expressing and appraising emotion, all within socially constructed emotional incidents (Fried, Mansfield, & Dobozy, 2015; Schutz, Aultman, & Williams-Johnson, 2009). In such circumstances, teachers may find themselves in a "struggle to reject normative discourses" and "find their own voice" (Zembylas, 2003, p. 229).

While a sense of endeavour is a rewarding aspect of teacher's work within that endeavour, there is a more complicated "struggle." The teachers prioritise the care, nurturing and love involved in their work—the emotionally rich aspects of their work—which in Kemmis' (2009) terms would be aspects of "relating" but the political and public expectations prioritise the "doings" because a teacher acting "professional" instils confidence in the performance (Groundwater-Smith et al., 2012; Kemmis, 2009).

The undercurrent in this struggle is that acting professional also means maintaining tight control of one's emotions; hence, teachers' work is in constant tension. So, how do teachers manage this tension and persist in the struggle? Teachers persist through emotional work, which is not a problem in itself—emotional work is a necessity of life—yet is not always well understood. This chapter does not propose a solution, but it does outline the mostly hidden or implied aspects of teachers' emotional work that can better prepare teachers' in their professional endeavours.

Hochschild (2012) has explored the notion of emotional rules and the "commercialisation of human feeling." She highlights that identifying wholeheartedly with one's work heightens the risk of burnout. For example, Shapiro (2010) described how "I began to sense that the longer I was a teacher, the less I might feel like a full human being. My professional identity was eclipsing my humanity" (p. 616). Teacher autonomy is reduced on every level, including an emotional level—the profession is being depersonalised. Furthermore, Hochschild (2012) outlines the potential harm of abiding by institutionally derived emotional rules that are not necessarily in alignment with personal emotional responses.

I am not suggesting that teachers should not have to feel certain things such as unpleasurable emotion. On the contrary, I suggest that all emotion is useful, and I avoid describing emotion as either positive or negative. For example, an expression of anger might typically be described as negative in a classroom but is not necessarily harmful and is more accurately described as unpleasurable. Anger may indeed be useful and impact positively in maintaining a power balance where the occasional expression of anger is an effective way to assert some control over a classroom that is increasingly getting out of hand (Keller, Frenzel, Goetz, Pekrun, & Hensley, 2014;

Winograd, 2003). Students may perceive emotional neutrality in such circumstances uncomfortably (Warner & Shields, 2009). While certain emotions are considered negative and harmful to the classroom environment, some emotions are considered "positive" and "useful" to the classroom environment. Teachers are expected to influence the emotional state of others by promoting enjoyment or enthusiasm or calming fear or anger while maintaining tight control on personal emotions based on professional norms (Hochschild, 2012; Winograd, 2003; Yin et al., 2013). Like Marley states, *"it's my job to make the classroom calm"* regardless of what one might be feeling.

Emotion is complex. What I mean by complex is that it has many facets that cannot be understood in complete isolation but do need to be understood individually in some way to make sense of the whole (Cochran-Smith, Ludlow, Grudnoff, & Aitken, 2014; Kincheloe, 2001). Emotion consists of a physical feeling, an appraisal of an emotional incident, and a display of emotion, which takes place within a collective context shaped by relational/practice architectures. What it means to be a teacher is shaped by these architectures, which are shaped by what teachers say, do and how they relate. Teachers' emotional work can only be understood, like teaching practice, by considering the individual within a collective, which is at the same time a collective of individuals.

There exist frameworks for emotional intelligence, emotional competence, emotional regulation, emotional labour and emotional resilience. For example, emotional regulation is a means to emotionally respond to something through a process of appraisal (Gross, 2013). So, emotion is felt, evaluated and then displayed through a process of emotion regulation. In some ways, each of these frameworks might weave in with a notion of teacher emotional rules, but what I want to emphasise is that while individuals experience emotion, it is also a collective experience through emotional rules, which are not determined by individuals. Kemmis (2009) states that "practice architectures are the densely interwoven patterns of saying, doing and relating that enable and constrain each new interaction" (p. 466). What I wish to add and demonstrate is that all teacher practice can be enabled or constrained by emotional rules because the emotional rules are part of the foundation to Edward-Groves, Brennan Kemmis, Hardy, and Ponte (2010) relational architectures.

Emotional rules divide into two categories; rules about what should be felt and rules about what should be displayed, and they are not necessarily the same for each emotional experience. I refer to "emotional rules" as an umbrella term for both display and feeling rules. The process of hiding and faking emotion is achieved through what Hochschild (2012) calls deep acting and surface acting. Deep acting enables a person to summon the expected emotion that is then felt and displayed; surface acting enables a person to either diminish felt emotions by hiding what is displayed or faking an emotion that is not naturally felt (Hochschild, 2012; Truta, 2014; Yin et al., 2013). Both deep acting and surface acting can be useful. For example, imagine a teacher about to take a class that has recently proven to be difficult; deep acting can provide the necessary happiness and enthusiasm to survive the class. Surface acting might be an act of kindness if, for instance, a teacher hides their laughter while watching a student attempting a task clumsily. Hagenauer & Volet (2014) assert that, depending on the social context, manipulating one's emotions is not necessarily harmful.

Though the manipulation of emotion is not necessarily unhealthy, the processes of hiding, faking and conjuring emotions to abide by institutional emotional rules renders a teacher somewhat blind to how they might be feeling. I will demonstrate such a process by sharing a specific story from the research later in this chapter. Hochschild's (2012) notion of hiding and faking emotions fits neatly with Winnicott's (1965) true and false self. We abide by emotional rules and employ faking, hiding and conjuring strategies to be accepted by others. These mechanisms can prove useful in personal circumstances but can be harmful if the person employing such ingrained mechanisms begins to feel like they are living a lie and detached from their reality—the false self begins to consume the whole self, which impacts on one's understanding of reality (Winnicott, 1965).

3   The Research Theoretical Underpinnings and Approach to Inquiry

I argue, like Fried, Mansfield, & Dobozy (2015), that emotion and thought are insep-arable; therefore, knowledge is laden with emotion. Kincheloe, McLaren, and Stein-berg (2011) suggest that knowledge is constructed in complex ways, and this was the theoretical framework of the research. Knowledge is complex, not just because of its inherent partnership with emotion, but because, like Edwards (2017) asserts, it is not always immediately apparent. To embrace theoretical complexity, where something is understood in reference to its parts, but those parts are only understood in reference to the whole, a theory of bricolage proves useful. Bricolage is a "critical, multi-perspectival, multi-theoretical and multi-methodological approach to inquiry" (Rogers, 2012, p. 1). Multiple perspectives from sociological, psychoanalytical and psychological theory were drawn on to pull together an understanding of teachers as thinking, acting and feeling individuals that are part of a teacher collective profiled by social, political and cultural aspects.

Multiple approaches to research design such as narrative inquiry and action research were also utilised. As the study set out to capture the experience of emo-tion within an emotional context, narrative inquiry was undertaken as it is a way of understanding experience (Clandinin, 2013). The methods, outlined in the follow-ing section, allowed the teachers and me to share our stories through individual and group interviews. Clandinin (2013) states that co-constructing knowledge entails co-composing narratives. Each story told includes multiple stories—a lived story, and its threads of the past, present and future, as well as a story told, heard and retold. All of these stories are slightly nuanced in a way that means that a story is dynamic. The other aim of the research was to determine a reflexive strategy that might facilitate professional learning collaboratively, so the teachers and I were actively seeking new understandings about ourselves and each other, which is why the project also necessitated a participatory action research approach. In participatory action research, multiple voices are considered in the evolving path that the project follows (Groundwater-Smith et al., 2012). The teachers and I were co-participants and co-researchers. It was due to the layered nature of the stories—my stories would inevitably weave in with the teachers' stories—that meant that I also had to be scrutinised through the research.

4 The Project

Blair, Eden, Jesse, Kai, Marley, Taylor and I came together to engage in the research project. This chapter includes gender-neutral pseudonyms and pronouns due to the small number of participants. The participants formed two groups consisting of two females and one male each. The teachers chose to participate in the research after attending an information seminar at their school and became known as participants of the research. The aim was to understand better how teachers' emotional consciousness impacted on agency and whether the reflexivity required to enhance emotional consciousness could facilitate professional learning.

Before three action research cycles commenced, each teacher participated in a background interview. Each cycle consisted of four phases, planning, acting, observing and reflecting (Kemmis & McTaggart, 1982; Groundwater-Smith et al., 2012). The aim of the first action research cycle (ARC1) was to gauge how emotionally conscious we were in a professional context and how reflection on emotion might best be facilitated on a one-to-one basis. In ARC1, I worked individually with the first three teachers who volunteered to participate in the project. We came together for an hour-long semi-structured conversation. In some ways, each session was like a mini action research cycle that we collectively engaged in, though the action and observation took place concurrently in the sessions. Specific interview questions were not applied, but the teachers were asked to share a critical incident, which was not critical in that it required "critique," but it was significant and somehow felt important to the teacher. Teachers were advised that the critical incidents should not be thought of as simply "difficult" incidents. The incidents could be anything that struck the teacher as important. For example, "*I thought it was important for me to correct the uniform because that was my job as a teacher*" (Marley) or "*I did a really awesome thing today*" (Kai).

The second action research cycle (ARC2) had the same three teachers and I come together in a small group. For ARC2, our semi-structured conversations gained more structure as we had developed a draft of a reflexive process to illuminate the conflictual and hidden aspects of our work, which became known to us as a Collaborative Inquiry Process (CIP). In ARC2, I facilitated the CIP process.

The third action research cycle (ARC3) saw two CIP groups running concurrently. By ARC3, the CIP process was further fine-tuned. Details of the CIP will not be explained in this chapter other than to outline that there were four stages:

(1) a teacher shared a story; (2) the group identified strengths in the story; (3) we each shared a similar story; (4) we inquired into our collective similar—but not the same—experience. The first group comprised of the same three teachers and me, but the difference was that I did not act as the facilitator. The teacher participants took turns to facilitate. The second CIP group comprised of three new teacher volunteers to trial the CIP process. ARC2 was about determining if the CIP was generally useful and whether the CIP could be managed and sustained by the participating school.

Thirty-three hours of conversation was recorded and transcribed in a combination of one-to-one interviews and group semi-structured conversations. The CIP was a process that challenged each of us—it forced us to confront our underlying emotion critically through a type of inquiry that Kelchtermans (2009) calls "discomforting dialogues." Care was required to create a safe enough space to share what was troubling while protecting the teacher participants. The project gained ethics approval by Victoria University and the Department of Education and Training.

5   The Emotions and the Rules

Through narrative inquiry and thematic analysis into the emotions discussed, explicitly and implicitly, eight notable emotions were identified in the teachers' work: defeat, contentment, frustration, worry, anger, sadness, happiness and love. This list of emotions is in order of how many times they were referenced. Though I have named these emotions, which runs the risk of reducing the complexity of emotion, they are not isolated entities. For example, a feeling of shame depends on the intensity and constellation of emotions that feed into it such as fear, anger and sadness (Turner, 2009). As the intensity or constellation of emotion might shift, the initial shame could shift into feelings of guilt or alienation. The usefulness of naming emotion is not to define it in general terms but to be able to talk about it because what feels like anger to one person might feel like frustration to another. People experience specific emotions uniquely, and each experience will be nuanced depending on the context of the experience.

Fifty-one emotions were discussed throughout the CIP sessions and interviews. I analysed the transcripts through NVivo software (QSR, 2015) and considered emotion holistically. I did not seek out specific emotions—the eight notable emotions emerged through the teachers' stories. When analysing the transcripts, I looked for emotional experiences. For example:

> [the student's poem] was really poignant and sweet and I read it and [I] burst into tears on the spot, well you know, you hide it but that was the impulse (Blair).

In such experiences, the emotion is often implied, for instance, the word "*sweet*" implies delight and perhaps affection, while "*poignant*" implies sadness as does "*bursting into tears.*" A fragment of conversation such as this was categorised in multiple ways. Emotion was sometimes discussed explicitly and sometimes implied, which was the discovery that led to understanding the existence of teacher emotional rules.

Some emotions are only subtly different, and if the words were interchanged, the meaning of the surrounding sentence would not necessarily change. Emotions were deemed similar on this basis, and the 51 emotions became 33. For instance, *"overwhelmed," "challenged," "overworked," "difficult," "fight"* and *"hard"* were used to describe a similar feeling, so these categories became one called "defeat" (for a complete list see Hopman, 2017). The eight notable emotions were differentiated from the complete list of 33 because those eight emotions were present in over half of all of the sessions. I carefully deliberated over the word choices, and "defeat" may seem a strange word to attribute to an emotion. Darwin (cited in Brenner, 1974, p. 542) describes having no hope of relief as "despair"; Turner (2009) relates "shame" to the vulnerability of a struggle. Defeat captured the feeling of a struggle on a continuum, although despair and shame were likely clustered in the feeling of defeat. Defeat was referenced 302 times throughout the sessions, the highest out of the eight notable emotions, and ranged from a feeling of threatening defeat but the struggle on the cusp of being overcome; or, a feeling of holding ground; or, a feeling of losing the struggle; or, the struggle as lost—defeating to defeated. For example:

> I'm having more work time than everything else… I usually have to work in the holidays as well… But I've done a little bit more this year, and I think it was too much… I totally overworked myself, and I was totally run down… I've got to try and cut down, but I don't know how (Marley).

"Overworked", "too much", "run down" signals that Marley is feeling at the defeated end of the continuum, but that another struggle and maybe hope for the future exist, because Marley will still *"try and cut down"*.

Pleasurable emotions featured throughout the sessions as well. The teachers discussed a general feeling of satisfaction and pleasure which I named "contentment." Contentment was referenced 122 times throughout the sessions and what was discovered is that pleasure and unpleasure often co-exist. Defeat was expressed in all 33 sessions, and contentment was expressed in 29 of the 33. For instance, the following quote discusses *"good"* or *"great relationships"* and *"pride,"* signalling a feeling of contentment.

> I've got really good relationships with some of the boys … who can be pretty rough … I take a bit of pride knowing that it took a lot of work, but Ive established these great relationships (Jesse).

On the other hand, a threat of defeat still lingers because building relationships with *"pretty rough"* students takes *"a lot of work."* This co-existence of pleasure and unpleasure reiterates Kai and Marley's respective statements from the beginning of this chapter: *"Caring can be the best part of [teaching], but it can also be the worst"* and *"being in a classroom can sometimes feel like you are on a roller coaster."* It is also evident in Blair's quote where the student's poem was *"poignant and sweet."* Challenge is helpful to drive one forward but teachers being asked to remove the "personal" element of the profession by following tight emotional rules makes the role impossible.

Interestingly this work of exploring specific emotions led to an important discovery about emotional limits and catalysts of emotion. In the background and debrief interviews, teachers were prompted to discuss emotional experiences in their practice. In the CIP sessions, teachers were prompted to discuss experiences first, and the emotion was explored later in the session. There was a discrepancy between how teachers reported on their emotional experiences when prompted, compared to the emotional experiences naturally recounted. Each emotional experience was categorised into either a teacher–student interaction or a teacher–teacher interaction. When prompted to discuss emotional experiences in their teaching practice the teachers reported that teacher–student relationships were the catalyst for their emotional experiences, aside from love. Attributing emotion to teacher–student relationships rather than teacher–teacher relationships is not surprising given that Shapiro (2010) noticed teacher conversation was often restricted to "two main topics—student misbehavior [sic] and reality television" (p. 616). The emotional experiences discussed in the CIP sessions told a different story—often teacher–teacher relationships were the catalyst for the many emotions discussed.

There was also some discrepancy in what emotions could be discussed in which context. For example, some emotions were more easily examined in the one-to-one session compared to the group sessions. Sadness, for instance, was discussed overwhelmingly relating to student relationships and was comfortably discussed with teacher peers, whereas discussion of anger was mostly restricted to the one-to-one sessions suggesting that anger is not readily talked about and expressed among teacher colleagues. This restriction aligns with Winograd's (2003) statement where teachers ought to "become angry with children infrequently" (p. 1645); however, according to this analysis teachers ought to "become angry" infrequently if at all.

Teachers hide their emotions. It is a predicament explicitly detailed in Blair's quote: "*[I] burst into tears on the spot, well you know, you hide it but that was the impulse.*" Another interesting discovery was how the teachers were inhibited to discuss love in relation to people. Considering that overall, the catalyst for emotional experiences was either teacher–student or teacher–teacher relationships, love was mostly discussed in reference to non-human objects. This resistance to acknowledge love was surprising because relationships entail a level of attachment, and love is the result of an attachment (Bowlby, 2012; Winnicott, 1969). Like the other emotions, such as fear or anger, love varies in intensity and is often clustered with sadness, such as Blair's quote. I am not suggesting that everyone in a school feels intense love for each other but that it is human nature to form some level of attachment with other humans. The expressions of love mostly took the following form:

I'd sort of fallen in love with this place (Jesse).

I do love teaching the kids … (Marley).

I love the day when I've got [subject] (Kai).

Teachers could express love for the school, love for the act of teaching and love for their discipline areas but not for people. Stebbins (2010) believes that educational institutions promote non-attachment, diminishing the loving feelings because love is regarded as an obstacle to learning. Instead, teachers are compelled to remain emotionally "safe but shallow" (Shapiro, 2010, p. 616). It was through the exploration outlined above that the following list of teacher emotional rules surfaced.

1. Frustration, worry, sadness and anger are evoked by student interactions;
2. Teachers should not feel or display fear;
3. Teachers should not display anger;
4. Teachers should not display sadness to students;
5. Contentment is evoked by the act of teaching, students and other teachers;
6. Happiness is evoked by the act of teaching and students;
7. Love is evoked by the act of teaching;
8. Teachers should not feel or display love for their students or other teachers; and
9. Defeat is inherent in teaching but must not be shown.

The rules show that some emotions are suitable to feel but not display, other emotions are not proper to feel or display. Some emotions are appropriate in relation to students, or teachers, or the act of teaching, or a combination of the three. These rules are not the end of the exploration. Analysing emotion in such a way highlighted the hidden emotions but gaining an understanding of how emotions are faked required a more in-depth look, mainly, since teachers employ deep acting strategies to conjure up certain emotions. For example, defeat, while the most prominently expressed emotion was the least explicitly discussed and permeated every other emotion. Either a threat of defeat or defeat was felt in every experience shared, yet was not readily talked about. Since defeat should not be shown, could it be possible that contentment is conjured? If this is the case, how would we ever know, if in such circumstances teachers are hiding the feeling of defeat from themselves? So, the significance of any of the emotions discussed may have been emphasised by faking processes, as Hollway and Jefferson (1997) suggest, and are not necessarily the teachers' intrinsic impulses.

I do not think there is anything unusual in finding that a feeling of defeat is prominent in teachers' work, particularly because defeat, or the threat of it, is the feeling associated with a struggle. Teaching is a struggle because a struggle is inherent in life, as is unpleasure. No human can be immune from unpleasure as it serves a purpose (Adler & McAdams, 2007). The aim is to strike a balance between pleasure and unpleasure; for example, Ramvi (2010) asserts: "[t]he challenge faced by every human being is to integrate love and hate" (p. 339). In every story, there was a line drawn somewhere and the teachers struggled to maintain the balance. On one side of the line, the teachers overcame the struggle, in which case the teacher may have felt contentment or happiness, depending on how agentic they perceived oneself to be. But on the other side, it was lost. Worry was evoked as to whether or not the line was going to be crossed or maintained. The struggle itself, especially if it was being lost, spurred frustration, anger and sadness. These experiences were usually part of a larger struggle, and the teachers jumped the line backwards and forwards continuously.

The difficulty for teachers is not that therein lies a struggle but that the teachers are constrained to feel and display their emotions in particular ways, rendering some emotion unavailable. To say that a person has control over their emotions is far too strong and to have such institutional emotional rules demanding such control is like a demand for perfection. The aim for a balance between pleasure and unpleasure and the acknowledgement of vulnerability is far more sustainable than a target for perfection, which is likely to lead to exhaustion and exaggerated imperfection (Shapiro, 2010). While the balance may tip from time to time, teachers might better understand the balance and how to maintain it through emotional consciousness, since thought and emotion are entwined, and emotion is often a more viable excavation point (Pitt & Brushwood Rose, 2007).

6   The Rules in Action

I shall turn to a teacher's story which highlights the teacher emotional rules in action. The expectation to keep the classroom calm is real, as underlined in Marley's opening statement: *"it's my job to make the classroom calm."* Teachers are compelled to respond to the expectation. Difficulty in meeting such an expectation is voiced in Eden's story:

> So, [Berna, a student,] came into my class and she was pretty annoyed. ... it's really hard to control her behaviour as well. She was mouthing off back and forth to [another student, [Dell], and it was getting threatening—really hostile. She did exit herself but when she throws a threat in the class, it seems like there's this energy bouncing back and forth, and they are so mad at each other that they're blinded with a white light in their face. They can't even tell that there's a teacher there, so I feel like I have no presence and I feel like the only way to get presence would be to be the loudest, like the dog with the loudest bark or something. I don't want to go that way because if I calmly got her to go away and get back on track—it feels like it was the only thing that I could think to do other than yelling and screaming and getting really out of hand. So, I don't know. ... she just did all this swearing and yelling and walked out, relatively calmly, the normal way that she does, because she can be really aggressive, and she'll hit something or someone. ... That also makes me freeze up and makes me—fight or flight—and I freeze! Because I don't know what to do about it (Eden).

The aim is to have a calm classroom, even while it is very hard *"to control [Berna's] behaviour."* The struggle in this story is trying to control everyone's emotional state and is attributed a feeling of defeat. Eden froze and implied that control was lost. Fortunately, Berna exited the room of her own volition. While such violence is not a typical occurrence in a classroom, it does happen, and teachers are expected to manage it by meeting the expectations within limitations. The expectation is to keep the classroom calm by *"calmly"* getting Berna *"back on track"* while allaying the other student's fears in the face of such a *"threat."* Eden states, *"I don't know"* demonstrating worry over whether Eden handled the situation appropriately. Eden's story is like a question—did I do the right thing? But consider the options; (1) keep Berna in the class and perhaps *"be the loudest"* to take *"control,"* which is necessary to reduce the *"threat"*; or (2) let Berna exit the classroom—and go where and do what? I am not suggesting that Eden acted inappropriately or "lost" in any way. What I am saying is that the feeling of defeat stemmed from the perceived loss. A sense of defeat is present in the story though it is implied rather than explicitly stated because, as Rule 9 suggests, defeat is inherent in teaching but must not be shown. As a group, we explored the scenario and shared similar experiences. Taylor shared a similar experience where two students started to fight in class and Taylor stepped between the two students to diffuse the situation. It was a different response to Eden, but Taylor was still left asking oneself a similar question: "*should [I] have been more proactive to reduce the risk of conflict?*" It is this experience of being caught between expectations and limitations that is the catalyst for conflictual emotions and spurs on deep acting as a response.

There were emotional rules at play in this story, for instance, Rule 2—teachers should not feel or display fear—and Rule 3—teachers should not display anger. The aim to keep the classroom calm meant that anger should not be visible. Eden indicated that they felt compelled to yell—"the only way to get presence would be to be the loudest"—but could not do so. Fear is present in Eden's story though it was minimised and described more like worry, which was minimised further still. Eden states, "*it was getting threatening—really hostile.*" Eden was asked to expand on what was meant by "*fight or flight*":

> I never want to admit it—to the students, but I think it's not so much a fear. I'm not worried about her hitting me or anything. She could if she wanted to, I wouldn't do anything back, but I think that it's more fear about—it's way beyond my control (Eden).

"Fight or flight" is a fear response but it is as though Eden is conjuring contentment and resigning himself to the fact that Berna "*could [hit me] if she wanted to.*" Taylor minimised the fear in their experience too so that even though Taylor's body was on the line as a student was "*getting quite aggressive toward [them], and [they were] sort of back-pedalling,*" Taylor described themself as feeling "*a little bit threatened.*" The act of back-pedalling or freezing is like a controlled flinch—the fear is implied. But the fear has to be hidden from students and oneself, as Eden states, "*I never want to admit it,*" where "*it*" refers to the feeling of fear. Taylor concurs: "*you don't want students to ever think that you're scared*" so courage has to be conjured instead.

Another implied emotional rule is Rule 8—teachers should not feel or display love for their students or other teachers. Eden states "*I'm not worried about [Berna] hitting me*" suggesting a level of trust and also later in the conversation explains that they are "*fairly proud of [Berna] for [exiting the classroom herself].*" To be proud of someone suggests that the teacher–student relationship affords pleasure or satisfaction and it is because of these feelings that Eden toils hard to "*work out what to do for [Berna].*" There is a demonstration of care, affection and attachment that is a form of love, which is an oversight in the stories.

Rule 4—teachers should not display sadness to students—is also an undercurrent of these stories. Blair's earlier statement "*[I] burst into tears on the spot, well you know, you hide it but that was the impulse*" already suggests its existence. In Eden's story, sadness was less obvious but was present and is tied up with the loving feelings Eden has for Berna. Eden wanted to protect Berna and wanted to think the best of her, so, on the one hand, Eden felt proud of her for exiting, but disappointed in the repercussions of her actions. For example:

> It makes me sad that [people] think that [bad behaviour] is all that she's boiled down to, just one or two mistakes that she's made in her life (Eden).

This statement does acknowledge the sadness Eden feels but not explicitly about Eden's relationship with Berna, it is more about Berna's relationships with others. Also, the rule suggests that sadness cannot be displayed to students, and because the teachers are expected to "*keep calm*" sadness and then disappointment must be kept at bay. A teacher outlining their disappointment in such a predicament might make way for sadness to emerge. Sadness and tears must be kept from classrooms.

7   Conclusion

> I failed at this, I did something and it was wrong (Kai).

All of the shared teacher stories contained a similar thread of sense of "failure." Not that the teachers actually did do anything "wrong"—something they were able to realise after inquiry into the emotional tension underlying each story. Even the story Kai shared where they "*did a really awesome thing today,*" contained an element of failure. The story featured an interaction Kai had with a student that led to a moment where, with some cajoling, the student expressed a talent. Kai was concerned that they had exposed the student in a way the student might not have wished to be exposed and had overstepped a mark. Kai's loving feelings had led to a sense that an emotional boundary was crossed. Similar to Eden's story, love for students should not be felt or displayed, so being compelled to act out of love is going to feel like a failure. A feeling of defeat is inherent in teaching because a teacher cannot physically, mentally and emotionally control every aspect of their practice, yet they are expected to follow a script, and if they deviate from that script, they are perceived as "wrong."

Perhaps it seems harsh to think of these experiences as failures, but it does not change the reality that these rules in some shape or form exist and if overstepped the "feeling" of failure or imperfection will ensue. While these stories transpired in a specific school, with particular teachers in a moment in time, there is evidence that teachers are bound by emotional rules—even if not the distinct rules outlined in this chapter. Recognising the "failures" was the difference between them remaining "failures" or becoming learning experiences through reflexive practice. A threat to a person's sense of self—that the false self was unable to keep the true self at bay—is discomforting and the natural urge might be to turn away from it. But as Shapiro (2010) states, to turn away would require a denial of humanity because vulnerability and imperfection is a condition of living.

Emotion is like a sixth sense. The word "feel" is used like a sense of touch. For example, Kai stated, "*I felt battered*" after an emotionally taxing experience. Thought and physical sensation are mediated by emotion (Schutz, Aultman, & Williams-Johnson, 2009). Teachers are either enabled or constrained by practice/relational architectures, which are permeated by teacher emotional rules. They can only sense their way forward by being alert to emotion, and teachers being alert to emotion counter to the expectations in practice. What became apparent is that teachers are conflicted between what is expected of them and what they desire to be, do or feel. Teaching is like performing, and the teachers aimed to act, think and feel in line with the emotional rules; however, the process of hiding and faking emotion renders some emotion hidden as well as the related thoughts, even from oneself. To increase teacher agency' teachers should be encouraged to reflect on and inquire into, who am I, what do I do and how do I feel?

References

Adler, J., & McAdams, D. P. (2007). Telling stories about therapy: Ego development, wellbeing and the therapeutic relationship. In R. Josselson, A. Lieblich, & D. P. McAdams (Eds.), *The meaning of others: Narrative studies of relationships* (pp. 213–236). Washington, DC: American Psychological Association.

Biesta, G., Priestley, M., & Robinson, S. (2015). The role of beliefs in teacher agency. *Teachers and Teaching: Theory and Practice, 21*(6), 624–640. https://doi.org/10.1080/13540602.2015.1044325.

Bowlby, J. (2012). *A secure base*. Hoboken, NJ: Routledge.

Brenner, C. (1974). On the nature and development of affects: A unified theory. *The Psychoanalytic Quarterly, 43*(4), 532–556.

Burnard, P., & White, J. (2008). Creativity and performativity: Counterpoints in British and Australian education. *British Educational Research Journal, 34*(5), 667–682. https://doi.org/10.1080/01411920802224238.

Clandinin, J. (2013). *Engaging in narrative inquiry*. United States of America: Left Coast Press Inc.

Cochran-Smith, M., Ell, F., Ludlow, L., Grudnoff, L., & Aitken, G. (2014). The challenge and promise of complexity theory for teacher education research. *Teachers College Record, 116*(5), 1–38.

Edwards, A. (2017). The dialectic of person and practice: How cultural-historical accounts of agency can inform teacher education. In J. Clandinin & J. Husu (Eds.), *The Sage handbook of research on teacher education*. Thousand Oaks, CA: Sage Publications.

Edwards-Groves, C., Brennan Kemmis, R., Hardy, I., & Ponte, P. (2010). Relational architectures: recovering solidarity and agency as living practices in education. *Pedagogy, Culture & Society, 18*(1), 43–54. https://doi.org/10.1080/14681360903556814.

Fried, L., Mansfield, C., & Dobozy, E. (2015). Teacher emotion research: Introducing a conceptual model to guide future research. *Issues in Educational Research, 25*(4), 415–441.

Gross, J. J. (2013). *Handbook of emotion regulation* (2nd ed.). New York: Guilford Publications.

Groundwater-Smith, S., Mitchell, J., Mockler, N., Ponte, P., & Ronnerman, K. (2012). *Facilitating practitioner research. Developing transformational partnerships*. Hoboken, NJ: Taylor and Francis.

Hagenauer, G., & Volet, S. (2014). "I don't hide my feelings, even though I try to": Insight into teacher educator emotion display. *Australian Educational Researcher, 41*(3), 261–281. https://doi.org/10.1007/s13384-013-0129-5.

Hilferty, F. (2008). Theorising teacher professionalism as an enacted discourse of power. *British Journal of Sociology of Education, 29*(2), 161–173. https://doi.org/10.1080/01425690701837521.

Hochschild, A. R. (2012). *The managed heart: Commercialization of human feeling.* Berkeley, CA: University of California Press.

Hollway, W., & Jefferson, T. (1997). Eliciting narrative through the in-depth interview. *Qualitative Inquiry., 3*(1), 53–70.

Hopman, J. (2017). *Emotional work: Applying reflexivity in teacher practice.* (Doctoral dissertation, Victoria University, Melbourne, Australia). Retrieved from http://vuir.vu.edu.au/34909/.

Johnson, B. & Down, B. (2013). Critically re-conceptualising early career teacher resilience. *Discourse: Studies in the Cultural Politics of Education, 34*(5), 703–15. https://doi.org/10.1080/01596306.2013.728365.

Kelchtermans, G. (2009). Who I am in how I teach is the message: Self-understanding, vulnerability and reflection. *Teachers and Teaching, 15*(2), 257–272. https://doi.org/10.1080/13540600902875332.

Keller, M., Frenzel, A., Goetz, T., Pekrun, R., & Hensley, L. (2014). Exploring teacher emotions: A literature review and an experience sampling study. In P. Richardson, S. A. Karabenick, & H. M. G. Watt (Eds.), *Teacher motivation: Theory and practice* (pp. 69–82). New York: Routledge.

Kemmis, S. (2009). Action research as a practice-changing practice. *Educational Action Research, 17*(3), 463–474.

Kemmis, S., & McTaggart, R. (1982). *The action research planner.* Waurn Ponds, VIC: Deakin University.

Kincheloe, J. L. (2001). Describing the bricolage: Conceptualizing a new rigor in qualitative research. *Qualitative Inquiry, 7*(6), 679–692. https://doi.org/10.1177/107780040100700601.

Kincheloe, J. L., McLaren, P., & Steinberg, S. R. (2011). Critical pedagogy and qualitative research. In N. K. Denzin & Y. S. Lincoln (Eds.), *Handbook of qualitative research* (pp. 163–73) (4th ed.), USA: Sage Publications.

Pitt, A. J., & Brushwood Rose, C. B. (2007). The significance of emotions in teaching and learning: On making emotional significance. *International Journal of Leadership in Education, 10*(4), 327–337. https://doi.org/10.1080/13603120701373656.

Priestley, M., Edwards, R., Priestley, A., & Miller, K. (2012). Teacher agency in curriculum making: Agents of change and spaces for manoeuvre. *Curriculum Inquiry, 42*(2), 191–214. https://doi.org/10.1111/j.1467-873X.2012.00588.x.

QSR (2015). *NVivo (Version 10.2.2) [computer software].* QSR International Pty Ltd.

Ramvi, E. (2010). Out of control: A teacher"s account. *Psychoanalysis, Culture & Society, 15*(4), 328–345. https://doi.org/10.1057/pcs.2009.7.

Rogers, M. (2012). Contextualizing theories and practices of bricolage research. *Qualitative Report, 17*(48), 1–17.

Ryan, M. & Bourke, T. (2013). The teacher as reflexive professional: Making visible the excluded discourse in teacher standards. *Discourse: Studies in the Cultural Politics of Education, 34*(3), 411–423. https://doi.org/10.1080/01596306.2012.717193.

Schutz, P. A., Aultman, L. P., & Williams-Johnson, M. R. (2009). Educational psychology perspectives on teachers" Emotions. In P. A. Schutz & M. Zembylas (Eds.), *Advances in teacher emotion research: The impact on teachers" lives* (pp. 537–587). New York: Springer.

Shapiro, S. (2010). Revisiting the teachers" lounge: Reflections on emotional experience and teacher identity. *Teaching and Teacher Education, 26,* 616–621. https://doi.org/10.1016/j.tate.2009.09.009.

Stebbins, A. (2010). Freud, Lacan and erotic desire in education. *Atlantis: Critical Studies in Gender, Culture & Social Justice, 34*(2), 159–167.

Taxer, J. L., & Frenzel, A. C. (2015). Facets of teachers" emotional lives: A quantitative investigation of teachers" genuine, faked, and hidden emotions. *Teaching and Teacher Education, 49,* 78–88. https://doi.org/10.1016/j.tate.2015.03.003.

Truta, C. (2014). Emotional labor and motivation in teachers. *Procedia—Social and Behavioral Sciences, 127,* 791–795. https://doi.org/10.1016/j.sbspro.2014.03.356.

Turner, J. H. (2009). The sociology of emotions: Basic theoretical arguments. *Emotion Review, 1*(4), 340–354. https://doi.org/10.1177/1754073909338305.

Warner, L. R., & Shields, S. A. (2009). Judgements of others" emotional appropriateness are multidimensional. *Cognition and Emotion, 23*(5), 876–888. https://doi.org/10.1080/02699930802212365.

White, J. (2010). Speaking "over" performativity. *Journal of Educational Administration and History, 42*(3), 275–294. https://doi.org/10.1080/00220620.2010.492960.

Winnicott, D. (1965). *The maturational processes and the facilitating environment: Studies in the theory of emotional development.* London: The Hogarth Press.

Winnicott, D. (1969). The use of an object. *International Journal of Psychoanalysis, 50,* 711–716.

Winograd, K. (2003). The functions of teacher emotions: The good, the bad, and the ugly. *Teachers College Record, 105*(9), 1641–1673.

Yin, H., Lee, J. C. K., Zhang, Z., & Jin, Y. (2013). Exploring the relationship among teachers" emotional intelligence, emotional labor strategies and teaching satisfaction. *Teaching and Teacher Education, 35*(1), 137–145. https://doi.org/10.1016/j.tate.2013.06.006.

Zembylas, M. (2003). Emotions and teacher identity: A poststructural perspective. *Teachers and Teaching: Theory and Practice, 9*(3), 213–238. https://doi.org/10.1080/13540600309378.

Dr. Jean Hopman currently works in Initial Teacher Education at Victoria University and researches teacher emotional work, which was the topic of her doctorate. She is invested in exploring the, often hidden, underlying layers of a teacher's role in support of their work. Prior she completed a Bachelor of Primary and Secondary Education and a Graduate Diploma in Child Psychotherapy Studies. She has taught and counselled in diverse educational settings, including government schools, private schools, international schools, alternative education settings and universities since 2000.

Chapter 9
Teacher-Targeted Bullying and Harassment in Australian Schools: A Challenge to Teacher Professionalism

Rochelle Fogelgarn, Edgar Burns and Paulina Billett

Abstract In this chapter, we consider how teacher professionalism is challenged by teacher-targeted bullying and harassment (TTBH) in Australian schools. Informed by findings from our exploratory mixed method study of TTBH in Australia, the incidence of student bullying towards teachers suggests that conventional views of professionalism need rethinking. International research reveals that TTBH occurs irrespective of an individual's innate gifts, talents, experience, commitment or traits. TTBH has been attributed to a range of factors external to personal professional expertise and its incidence undermines or compromises the sustained practice of victimised teachers. Yet, in our neoliberal climate of governmentality, where performativity pressures inhibit disclosure of struggle, TTBH has been *invisibilised*. In a culture dominated by managerialism, standards and compliance, the right of teachers to a safe workplace needs urgent redress. Until government policy explicitly addresses the provenance and extent of this issue, teacher vulnerability to student and parent-enacted TTBH threatens teacher well-being.

1 Introduction

People enter teaching for a variety of reasons, including a desire to make a social contribution; a belief that education has an intrinsic value and an interest in working with young people (König & Rothland, 2012). The traditional narrative of the teaching profession assumes that students will appreciate teacher knowledge and pedagogical expertise and consequently be receptive and cooperative (Tirri & Puolimatka, 2000). Notwithstanding teachers' noble motivations, teaching is becoming increasingly complex and challenging due to changing societal norms, values, expectations

R. Fogelgarn (✉) · E. Burns · P. Billett
La Trobe University, Melbourne, VIC, Australia
e-mail: r.fogelgarn@latrobe.edu.au

E. Burns
e-mail: e.burns@latrobe.edu.au

P. Billett
e-mail: p.billett@latrobe.edu.au

© Springer Nature Singapore Pte Ltd. 2019
A. Gutierrez et al. (eds.), *Professionalism and Teacher Education*,
https://doi.org/10.1007/978-981-13-7002-1_9

and conditions (Gu & Day, 2013). Frustration borne of the difficulty inherent in trying to effectively direct a diverse and complex learning environment, can impact negatively on teachers' energy, well-being and professional practice (Bowles & Arnup, 2016). Moreover, stressed teachers are vulnerable to the anti-social behaviour engendered by frustrated students making the "game of school" challenging for both parties (Fried, 2005). In certain circumstances, teacher-targeted anti-social student behaviour may be perceived by teachers as bullying and harassment. Indeed, teacher victimisation by students and parents is rapidly becoming a universal twenty-first century threat to teacher well-being (Espelage et al., 2013).

In addressing the increasing vulnerability of teachers, this chapter shifts the focus away from framing teachers within either traditional or neoliberal views of professionalism. The intention here is to move away from blaming or ignoring teachers, or the mostly covert view that some teachers need to face up to reality or toughen up and leave the profession. We wish to pose a question: Why can't we say that teachers feel bullied and harassed by students? In this chapter, we consider teacher professionalism and how it is challenged by the presence of teacher-targeted bullying and harassment (TTBH) in Australian schools. TTBH is defined in our study as

> a communication process that involves a real or perceived power imbalance where a teacher is subjected, by one or more students or their parents, to interaction that he or she perceives as insulting, upsetting or intimidating (Kauppi & Pörhölä, 2012) which may be verbal, nonverbal or physical in nature; a single or recurring instance; and of short or long duration'.

TTBH occurs internationally (Espelage et al., 2013), notwithstanding an individual's innate gifts, talents, experience, commitment or expertise (Chen & Astor, 2008; Vaaland & Roland, 2013). TTBH is attributable to a range of factors external to personal professional excellence that undermine or compromise the contribution of individual teachers by structuring the teaching context in ways that are inimical to good teaching for students, teachers and the betterment of society.

2 Teacher Professionalism

There are many ways of construing teacher professionalism and its benefits and liabilities (Demirkasımoğlu, 2010). Recent scholarship documents the increasing complexities of teaching in contemporary, neoliberal contexts (Hult & Edström, 2016; Mockler, 2012; Whitty, 2006). Sachs (2016) contends that "teacher professionalism is shaped by the external environment and that, during periods of increased accountability and regulation, different discourses of professionalism will circulate and gain legitimacy and impact on how professionalism is conceived and enacted" (p. 414). Sociologists, psychologists and education scholars continue to theorise professions and professionalism (Burns, 2007; Dent, Bourgeault, Denis, & Kuhlmann, 2016; Hilferty, 2008; Liljegren & Saks, 2016; Swann, McIntyre, Pell, Hargreaves, & Cunningham, 2010). Professions universally offer a model of professionalism based on some combination of normativity and knowledge—that is, professional goodness (altruism, service and benefit to the community) and expertise (skill, content, solutions). Decades of neoliberal emphasis on the necessary practical functions of teaching and classrooms fail to recognise that this vision of teacher performance can only ever be half the story. This is because theoretically speaking, it is an internalist account of teacher practice—from within the person. The reality of teaching is significantly governed by other factors than those internal to the teacher.

Teacher professionalism thus functions between:

- internal drivers of the teacher's own actions and the contextual drivers of student behaviour;
- processes and external demands and expectations; and
- the values that drive and sustain excellent teachers and their professional work.

In the neoliberal culture of performativity (Ball, 2016), fundamental shapers of performance and specialised professional knowledge and experience for teachers sit within the structures of school; school communities including students' families; the diverse environments of classrooms; and the policy settings of state and national guidelines and governing bodies (Bronfenbrenner, 1979). School teaching is no longer negotiated primarily in a closed classroom between a teacher and their class of students. Connell (2009) has observed that 'the divisiveness of the neoliberal agenda for education is clear, and many experienced educators are deeply unhappy with it…[but] in the complex task of defining educational futures, an important focus is to develop a better conception of "good teachers"' (p. 221). "Good teachers" effectively organise and manage the learning environment so that student engagement is optimised (Muijs et al., 2014). It has become evident, however, that committed, organised, professional teachers may yet be unwitting victims of students who are determined to undermine, compromise, threaten or even destroy their teachers' professional influence (Chen & Astor, 2008; Vaaland & Roland, 2013). Contemporary neoliberal emphasis on school governance defaults to micro-management, targets, audit procedures and performance metrics. The stress of compliance disempowers many teachers from implementing creative and innovative practices which demand more time but would likely improve engagement and minimise TTBH (Espelage et al., 2013). The destructive power of the neoliberal perspective is that it renders these effects not only on the educational sector but on other sectors of contemporary society as well (Mockler, 2012).

Sociology of education scholarship has considered the role that individual attributes and expertise; professional context and practice; and character and personal values play in accomplishing professionalism. We suggest that these views of professionalism are limited and limiting for integrating thinking about the challenge teacher-targeted bullying and harassment presents to conventional notions of teacher professionalism. In this chapter, we identify three main ways that prevailing models of teacher professionalism, particularly those set by accreditation bodies, may impede understanding regarding the reasons teachers are subjected to TTBH. Further, such inadequate theorisation also hinders the capacity to resist, confront and overcome bullying and harassment which targets teachers. Each of the three following views is a necessary component of excellent teaching. However, if any one of the three is treated as the primary lens through which teachers view themselves or their work, the limiting nature of this focus may change an asset into a liability. We posit that what was previously held to be a protective, professional competence, may become a disability that harms or hinders the bullied teacher from overcoming the corrosive effects of TTBH.

2.1 Individual Traits

This view of teacher professionalism refers to the set of professional attributes which constitute the classic individualistic professional identity. These traits include pedagogical expertise, commitment, integrity, motivation and teamwork (Hattie, 2008). Teachers may possess desirable student-oriented traits; however, neoliberalism views accountability to systemic targets as the primary trait of professionalism (Bricheno & Thornton, 2016; Connell, 2013; Fournier, 1999). This concern with professionalism as compliance has been widely debated (Connell, 2009). Education scholars including Goodson and Hargreaves (1996) and Ball (2004, 2017) emphasise the impacts of neoliberal shifts and post-modern dimensions on contemporary teaching. Ball excoriates top-down management by a culture of targets, budgets and highly quantified, but misleading, outcomes. The hollowing out of content and human values in the focus on money and efficiency creates what Ball calls "depthlessness". Teachers blame neoliberal accountability measures such as standardised testing for consequent narrowing of curriculum, restriction in the range of skills and competencies learnt by students and constriction of pedagogical approaches (Polesel, Rice, & Dulfer, 2014). Thus, individual traits may not be sufficient protection in a system which has teacher performance determined primarily by the standardised test results of their pupils (Connell, 2013).

2.2 Classroom Practice

This second view represents professionalism as primarily being about the professional skills needed for effective classroom practice (Muijs et al., 2014). The field of classroom management appropriately takes the microcosm of the day-to-day interaction between teachers and students as its primary focus for effective teaching and learning (Allen, 2010; Ross, Romer, & Horner, 2012). The contextual relational elements of teaching are often invisible; hence, the mistake of ignoring their influence in conventional thinking about teacher professionalism is not immediately obvious (Roffey, 2012). Efficacy in classroom management is often rated as low by new teachers (Allen, 2010). Difficult behaviours challenge the best of teachers but whilst veteran practitioners may perceive potentially problematic issues and make timely and effective responses in appropriate ways, early career teachers may expend inordinate energy endeavouring to maintain a conducive learning environment (Buchanan et al., 2013). The complexities of managing diverse learning needs and behaviours may cause some teachers to give up and leave the profession before reaching a sustainable level of professional expertise (Vaaland & Roland, 2013). Being repeatedly publicly harassed or belittled by students can corrode self-efficacy and perceptions of professional competence (Espelage et al., 2013). Thus, the extent to which individual traits and motivation to be an excellent teacher can inure teachers from attack is limited in the dynamic context of classroom practice.

2.3 Human Values

This view refers to professionalism in the tradition of the heroic professional whose humanity, integrity and willingness to go the extra mile epitomise this kind of professionalism—it's not about money, power or prestige. Wholeheartedness, goodness, caring and altruism are attributes valued in more holistic views of pedagogical service (Nias, 1996; Noddings, 2012; Palmer, 2007). Film and television images of actors Robin Williams in *Dead Poets' Society*, Edward Olmos in *Stand and Deliver* and Hilary Swank in *Freedom Writers* illustrate this idealised model of passionate, empathic teaching. Motivational as these portrayals may be, they depict only a fraction of the reality of the complexities of everyday professional teaching (Allen, 2010). Without disputing the energising effects of such stories, if relied upon as the essence of teacher professionalism, this idealised view's limitations do not provide resilience or inoculation against bullying and harassment by students and parents. At the very least, preservice teachers need to deeply appreciate that teaching involves complex understandings of pedagogy, learning, behaviour management, the impact of external influences and a very intentional approach towards effective classroom practice (Loewenberg Ball & Forzani, 2009).

2.4 Teacher Professionalism and Vulnerability

The obvious desirability of teachers being responsible for meeting and maintaining high standards of professional conduct (VIT, 2018) is a positive aspect of the drive to increase teacher professionalism. However, the emphasis on professional standards and performativity has left many teachers feeling uncertain of their professional identity and the extent to which professional standards regulate practice and curtail creative pedagogical thinking (Connell, 2013). A symbiotic relationship between professional and personal identity is part of a holistic view of teacher professionalism (Day and Gu, 2007; Day, Sammons, Stobart, Kington, & Gu, 2007). Without a holistic framing of teacher professionalism, our point in the present discussion is that teachers' professional ability to recognise and effectively respond to the onset of bullying and harassment is disarmed.

Treating teacher professionalism as being primarily defined by the person who is *doing* the teaching is a truncated view of professionalism and the experience of teachers. Individual traits and specialised training alone do not inure teachers to the risks inherent in trying to address the breadth of student diversity in an educational climate which privileges inclusion. Secondly, viewing teacher professionalism as confined to the pedagogical work teachers do in their classrooms—or equivalent learning environments—ignores the impact of what can be termed the occupational hazards of teaching in a complex and often volatile human context. As Benefield (2004, p. 22) observes, school teaching is "clearly a particularly hazardous" profession. Thirdly, an altruistic view of teacher professionalism principally focussed on the primacy of human values may not accord sufficient agency to teachers to protect themselves from the vicissitudes of teaching in a complex, contemporary context.

Focussing predominantly on any one of these views about the teaching professional and what a teacher *should* do, means that teachers are not conceptually prepared for the adverse and negative aspects of teaching, including TTBH (Woudstra, van Rensburg, Visser, & Jordaan, 2018). These untoward effects do not necessarily reflect a lack of teacher training or teacher professionalism. Nor are they indicative of a lack of good values or personal commitment by teachers. Instead, these impacts of TTBH derive from the various contextual elements which are almost inevitably beyond the individual teacher's personal control. The lack of language to name this phenomenon makes coping with it more difficult for victimised teachers. Moreover, the non-existence in theoretical terms of TTBH in Australian schools challenges the adequacy of contemporary views of teacher professionalism. A dissonance between contemporary reality and an idealised narrative of teaching somehow allows TTBH to occur without systemic recognition or sanction.

The three views of teacher professionalism described above each have a dark side in which professionalism entraps rather than liberates educators. First, the classic model of professionalism that references practitioner autonomy and a series of traits, such as expertise, knowledge and commitment, is not realistic in any profession, let alone teaching (Day, Sammons, Stobart, Kington, & Gu, 2007). This view fails to take into account the professional context which involves elements beyond the teacher's control. Second, viewing teacher professionalism as primarily focussed on professional practice similarly fails to recognise the affective dimension of teaching and the personal needs of the practitioner and how these may collide with the personal needs of students. This view valorises the investment made in acquiring the specialised knowledge and training required to teach effectively when many graduate teachers actually feel inadequately prepared to protect themselves against the often harsh reality of the job (Bowles & Arnup, 2016). Third, the idealisation of teachers as good, noble and caring humans who model prosocial values and behaviours (Noddings, 2015; Palmer, 2017) can indeed be seen as necessary and desirable for good education. However, even with a requisite skill set for teaching practice, and an appropriately managed context (which is often problematic), this attenuated version of professionalism still leaves the teacher vulnerable to abuse in the workplace.

2.5　*TTBH Challenges Conventional Notions of Teacher Professionalism*

Our research into TTBH calls into question a variety of conventional views of teacher professionalism. Differing conceptions of professional identity orient teachers in different ways. These ideas may have been developed before becoming a professional teacher. Preservice teachers may have imbibed perceptions of teaching from family members or from lecturers or mentors during preservice training. Attitudes may be derived from media representations or come from general cultural knowledge or from previous contact with teachers and earlier schooling experience. Thus, both formal and informal acquisition of what it means to be a professional teacher intersects with professional learning and expectations. Evolving understandings of teacher professionalism may be due to a process of osmosis and may be deeply held by the preservice teacher (Brownlee, Boulton-Lewis, & Purdie, 2000). Importantly, traditional conceptions of the teacher–student dynamic, which typically portrays the teacher as the authority holding the power, may not prepare teachers for the reality of being a victim of student-enacted aggression or violence.

For many teachers, it is not until they experience TTBH in the workplace that they find that this encounter directly challenges the adequacy of their professional self-identity. Being challenged by TTBH reveals the disconnect between teachers' implicit conceptualisation of being a professional and what is needed to enable and support robust and competent professional practice. TTBH may thus disconcertingly undermine the model of professionalism preservice teachers may have been taught. We acknowledge that as TTBH takes many forms, deriving from different sources, this makes it hard to convey to preservice teachers the likelihood that at some stage in their career, circumstances will likely conspire to disrupt their professional work. It is important for novice teachers to recognise that self-efficacy, teacher identity and expectations of teacher professionalism may be difficult to disentangle when confronted with TTBH. Our data demonstrate that student or parent-enacted bullying and harassment undermines any simple framework of efficacious (Greenberg & Krusché, 2006), harmonious (Rothstein-Fisch & Trumbull, 2008) and positive teacher identity (Day et al., 2007) and learned views of teacher professionalism.

3　The Phenomenon of Teacher-Targeted Bullying and Harassment (TTBH)

In the neoliberal Australian education environment (Murphy, 2015), well-meaning, macro-scale recommendations about improving student achievement abound. Measures including innovative online assessment programs, increasing professional autonomy and the creation of a new national education research and evidence institute have been proposed (Gonski, 2018). Even fully implemented, these and the other recommendations would likely have little practical purchase in overcoming the problematic aspects presented by teaching tomorrow's techno-savvy, variably engaged, increasingly diverse, student cohort. Gonski 2.0 (2018, p. 58) affirmed that "for teachers to fulfil their role as expert educators, schools need to be seen as professional learning organisations". By any calculation of the cost in the personal lives of teachers on the one hand, and to the teaching profession and education sector on the other, TTBH creates a multiplier effect such that bullying and harassment have consequences and further effects and costs over long periods of time.

Within this context, TTBH by students in Australia remains largely invisible in the academic arena in part because notions of professionalism are focussed on individual teacher attributes. Indeed, the negative elements noted above are mostly seen in terms of the individual teacher and not as a function of the classroom, the school, mediatised popular culture and government education policies. Additionally, people have trouble believing teachers are bullied or harassed by students and parents (Riley, Duncan, & Edwards, 2011; Woudstra, van Rensburg, Visser, & Jordaan, 2018). The reality is that students can, and do, subvert the power balance in both primary and secondary school learning environments (Garrett, 2014). Teachers are generally perceived as occupying a position of power (Vaaland, 2017), which may obscure the incidence of teacher-targeted bullying in both physical and virtual settings. Aside from a sprinkling of brave websites, little is said about the dark and difficult topic of TTBH (See for example theteachersareblowingtheirwhistles.com). Within discussions of teacher well-being (McCallum & Price, 2016), intermittent allusions to some of the less positive aspects of teaching are made but do not meaningfully presage the possibility of intentional victimisation by students or their parents.

The dominant traditional pedagogical narrative celebrates the school and its classrooms as the locus wherein the incontestable right of students to a safe learning environment is enabled. The emergence of teacher well-being research points to a parallel narrative; that teachers also have the right to a safe school and classroom working environment. Being harassed or bullied by students or parents is inconsistent with this professional right. A literature search conducted as part of our exploratory study reveals that whilst Australian researchers have not explicitly interrogated the incidence of TTBH by students or parents, numerous international researchers have produced disturbing evidence of this phenomenon which leaves many teachers feeling physically or emotionally unsafe in their workplace (Byers, 2012; Chen & Astor, 2008; Kauppi & Pörhölä, 2012; Kõiv, 2015; Kyriacou & Zuin, 2016; Moon & McCluskey, 2016).

The international literature identifies significant numbers of teachers who are vulnerable to frequent episodes of bullying and harassment from students or parents with many feeling compromised in reporting such incidents since their professional capacity may be questioned. Thus, at least two inhibiting factors inherent in TTBH challenge an individual teacher's sense of professionalism. Victimised teachers suffer a double dose of helplessness: feeling attacked whilst being unable to escape the situation and feeling powerless due to a perceived risk to their reputation in reporting the incident. A further concern is the possibility that for some victims of TTBH, the stream of sometimes minor, yet repetitive, expressions of disrespect, micro-aggression, ridicule or indolence, renders school an unsafe work environment. It is these ambiguous and ill-defined tensions that teachers face that James et al. (2008, p. 168) refer to in saying that:

> it is difficult for anyone to admit they are being bullied and for teachers it is particularly difficult as they are alone in the classroom and are expected to deal with it. Admitting experience of being bullied to a colleague or manager could be seen as failure. Teachers are often expected to deal with difficult classes with little training. Bullying is difficult for an individual to deal with on their own so why are teachers expected to deal with it alone?

Studies investigating the nature and prevalence of teacher-targeted bullying and harassment by students have been conducted in many countries with similar patterns and results emerging despite varied cultural contexts. In his pioneering study twenty years ago, Terry (1998) decided to test the hypothesis that "pupils may bully their teacher" (p. 256). His study of one hundred and one school teachers yielded evidence that students may "achieve considerable power over their teachers under certain circumstances" and furthermore, that "when such power imbalances occur, and are abused, then bullying may be predicted with some degree of certainty" (p. 266). Terry calls this phenomenon *bully-abuse by pupils.*

Terry (1998) defined bullying in his study as what

> occurs in situations where the victim cannot easily escape. It occurs when an uneven balance of power is exploited and abused by an individual or individuals who in that particular circumstance have the advantage. Bullying is characterised by persistent, repetitive acts of physical or psychological aggression (p. 261).

In response to being asked if teachers had experienced being bully abused by pupils at least once in the preceding school term, 56.4% answered affirmatively, whilst 35.6% said sometimes (p. 263).

Many international studies since that time have found TTBH by students to be a real and detrimental issue to teacher well-being (Garrett, 2014). In an American study, Dinkes, Cataldi, Kena, and Baum (2006), found that approximately 7% of teachers reported being threatened with injury and 4% were physically assaulted by students during the previous year. Another study in Luxembourg found that teachers had been subjected to rude or disrespectful behaviour with nearly 25% reporting being victims of strong verbal attacks; 19.4% reporting perceived defamation and 7.0% sexual harassment (Steffgen & Ewen, 2007, p. 86).

Hoel and Cooper (2000) found that teachers are among the most likely profession to experience bullying and abusive behaviour. Benefield's New Zealand study (2004) found that a third of teachers experience minor bullying on a weekly basis and 85% reported less frequent, but more significant forms of teacher-targeted bullying. Benefield noted that "teachers work in a complex work environment where the possibility of encountering aggression is arguably far greater than that encountered by most other employees" (p. 22).

Studies exploring the nature and prevalence of TTBH by students have been undertaken in many countries with their findings showing similar patterns and results. A sampling of international research includes studies conducted in Turkey (Özkiliç,

2012); Taiwan (Chen & Astor, 2008); South Africa (de Wet, 2012), the UK (Terry, 1998); Luxembourg (Steffgen & Ewen, 2007); Korea (Moon & McCluskey, 2016), New Zealand (Byers, 2012); (Benefield, 2004); Finland (Kauppi & Pörhölä, 2012) and Ireland (James et al., 2008). This literature demonstrates the cross-cultural incidence of TTBH and the deleterious effects it has on teacher well-being and related student outcomes. Teachers who perceive they have been victims of TTBH report decreased professional performance; lower efficacy in the classroom; depleted emotional and/or physical well-being; negatively impacted student outcomes and feelings of having been unprepared to effectively manage student violence (Espelage et al., 2013).

4   Our Exploratory Study

Our exploratory, mixed method study into TTBH was conducted with the support of the Association of Heads of Independent Schools of Australia and the AEU Victorian branch. We aimed to gather empirical data relating to the experiences of Australian teachers who had been victims of TTBH by either students or parents during the twelve-month period preceding the survey (mid-2017 to mid-2018). The survey was live for a one-month period during May–June 2018 and returned both quantitative and qualitative data. Qualitative information for this study was coded and analysed using Nvivo statistical software. Anonymous quantitative data were analysed using SPSS. Three research questions guided the survey design:

- Is there evidence of teachers experiencing student and parent-enacted bullying and harassment in Australian schools?
- What type of bullying and harassment are teachers experiencing in their day-to-day classroom interactions? and
- What effects, if any, does teacher-targeted bullying and harassment have on teachers' sense of self-efficacy and well-being?

4.1   Recruitment

Around 9000 teachers were approached through a month-long social media campaign which included an invitation to participate in an online survey circulated Australia wide (see Appendix for full survey). The survey was open to all teachers between the ages of 21–70 currently registered to teach in Australia or who had held registration within the last two years. The online campaign targeted individuals who identified in their online profiles as teaching professionals. The list of key identifying words included: primary, secondary, Principal, Assistant Principal, teacher. Identified individuals were invited to participate by clicking on the dedicated website link to take the survey. Teachers from Victoria were also able to indicate willingness to take part in an additional 1-hour online interview to further explore their experiences and perceptions of TTBH in more depth. University ethics approval was sought and obtained for both the online survey and interview components of the project.

4.2   Participants

Five hundred and sixty individuals participated in the survey. About 51.6% of respondents were from the secondary sector, 40% from the primary sector and 7.7% worked across both primary and secondary sectors. About 82.3% of respondents identified as teachers, 11.6% as head teachers, 3% as deputy principals and 3.1% as principals. The most common age bracket was 36–40 years of age. About 53.9% of participants had been registered teachers for ten years or longer; 46.2% had been registered for four years or less; only 2.1% had been registered for less than one year.

Our respondents identified predominantly as female (85.9%) with only 14.1% identifying as male. Female teachers were relatively evenly distributed across primary (42.3%) and secondary (48.6%) levels. Male respondents predominantly worked at secondary level (65%), with only 28% teaching in primary classes. These findings align with current gender distributions found more generally in Australian schools (see McKenzie et al., 2014). In terms of geographic location, respondents hailed from each Australian state and territory: Victoria 26.8%; Queensland 26.8%; New South Wales 16.6%; South Australia 7.6%; Western Australia 3.3%; ACT 1.1%; Tasmania 1.1% with 10.7% of participating teachers working in multi-states or territories (including the Northern Territory).

4.3   Incidence of TTBH

The survey recorded the incidence of bullying and harassment by students and parents over a 12-month period. Respondents were asked if they had experienced TTBH during: the last fortnight, the past month, two to five months, six to eight months and nine to 12 months prior to the survey. Participants were asked if the behaviour was a one-off incident or had been perpetrated by a repeat offender during each time period. This chapter reports survey data recorded for the nine to twelve-month period preceding survey completion. During this time period, 80% of respondents recorded having experienced some form of student or parent-enacted TTBH.

Eighty-five-point two per cent of participants believe that TTBH by students and parents is a problem in Australian schools. A further 13.0% felt that TTBH may be a problem. Fewer than 2% of participants believe that student and parental TTBH may not be a problem for teachers in Australian schools. In the preceding 9-12 months, 55.6% of teachers reported experiencing TTBH from both students and parents; 13.4% had experienced student-enacted TTBH and 12.4% reported experiencing parent-enacted TTBH. Parent/guardian-enacted TTBH was more common for teachers working in the primary sector, with 62.9% of primary school teachers having experienced bullying or harassment from a parent or carer in the 9-12 month period preceding the survey. Secondary teachers suffered more student-enacted bullying and harassment with 77.6% of respondents reporting having been bullied or harassed by a student in the past nine to 12 months.

4.4   Types of TTBH Experienced by Survey Participants

The survey recorded evidence of twelve different forms of TTBH, including yelling, swearing, hitting or punching, damaging personal property, disparaging remarks (verbal), disparaging remarks (social media), standing over/invading personal space, organising others against a teacher, lying to get a teacher into trouble, harassing phone calls or text messages, discriminatory behaviour and students engaging parents to argue on their behalf.

Verbal aggression was the most commonly reported form of student-enacted TTBH. About 28.6% of respondents recorded being sworn at by a student in the past nine to 12 months; 28% reported being the target of yelling and 25.5% endured disparaging verbal comments. Whilst reports of physical aggression were lower than for other types of behaviour, 10% of teachers had been hit or punched by a student in the last year, 12.5% had a student damage their personal property and 16.6% had a student stand over them or invade their personal space. First year teachers seemed to experience the lowest levels of TTBH by students of any cohort with mid-career teachers reporting the most abuse. Verbal abuse in the form of yelling, swearing and disparaging remarks was the most often recorded experience of student enacted TTBH for all career stages excepting teachers who had been teaching for 15–19 years. Early career teachers (registered for 4 years or less) recorded the lowest levels of a student engaging a parent to argue on their behalf. Hitting or punching was recorded most often by mid-career teachers (5–14 years registration). Late career teachers (15–20 +) reported the highest incidence of students engaging parents to argue on their behalf, using standing over tactics or invading personal space.

4.5   Impact of TTBH on Participants

For the participating teachers in this study, TTBH was experienced as a one-off or a series of disrespectful or insensitive events, which wear teachers down and erode teaching self-confidence, professional efficacy and fulfilment in the workplace. Many teachers lamented having lost their enthusiasm to teach due to ongoing TTBH issues and several found they were unable to re-motivate themselves. About 83.1% of teachers reported considering a different career path due to the perceived prevalence of teacher-targeted bullying and harassment by students and parents.

TTBH enacted by parents was regarded as an unwarranted challenge to a teacher's abilities and professionalism. Several teachers suggested that the ongoing, and at times relentless, advocacy performed by parents compromised a teacher's ability to manage poor student behaviour. This was experienced as humiliating and disempowering. Student-enacted TTBH is reportedly often attributed to poor classroom management; shifting blame from students to vulnerable, compromised and often victimised teachers. However, student-enacted TTBH was experienced by a large proportion of respondents from both primary and secondary sectors, across all genders, all age groups and extent of teaching experience. This would suggest that the issues being faced by teachers in the classroom are beyond any individual teacher's professional ability and are part of a much larger and complex set of societal issues.

Victimised teachers reported suffering symptoms of anxiety, depression, PTSD, panic attacks, uncontrollable shaking and nausea. Many had taken stress and sick leave (one or more days), unpaid or holiday leave to avoid experiencing ongoing bullying and harassment. TTBH was reported to affect all aspects of a teacher's life, including being fearful for their safety within school grounds, with some respondents also suggesting feeling unsafe in their local areas. Individuals who had taught in rural and regional schools also suggested that the visibility of individuals in close-knit communities was a factor in the distress caused by TTBH.

4.6 Teachers' Perceptions of Support

Participants reported a perceived lack of support from management and leadership as being a major hurdle to resolving instances of TTBH. Most teachers believed that interventions to end TTBH were only sometimes (56%) or almost never (31.8%) effective, with only a minimal percentage believing that action taken was successful (2.9%). The feeling that interventions were only partly effective was shared among respondents teaching at primary level (46.6%), secondary level (47.5%) and those teaching across both levels (50%). Participants also felt that a policy framework to protect teachers is currently non-existent, and there is an urgent need for policy change to overcome the adverse impacts of TTBH on the teaching workforce. The experience of unwarranted student-enacted TTBH was reported by survey participants as a very different experience when senior leadership had time and energy to intervene or actively support the victimised teacher. At the same time, senior teachers and principals may be stretched by similar dynamics themselves, often being called into situations that involve demanding or intransigent stakeholders (Riley, 2014). It is acknowledged that these human stressors combine with budgetary and management demands.

5   Implications for Policy and Further Research

Despite the research reported from a range of countries, until now, TTBH in Australian school has essentially been *invisibilised*. Our survey data indicate that the incidence, nature and impact of the TTBH phenomenon align with international research findings. Clearly, TTBH is an issue which from a social justice perspective can no longer be ignored. Every teacher deserves to be able to teach to their best of their ability in a conducive, professional environment (Gonski, 2018). With 80% of respondents reporting having experienced some form of student or parent-enacted TTBH in the recent past, more needs to be done to protect and support teachers in their workplace.

We note four elements of our study which justify larger-scale examination. First, the predominant majority of respondents are still teaching. The voices of teachers who have given up, changed jobs, retired or left the profession are not being heard in this survey. Many of those who have left teaching may have experienced the tougher end of TTBH. Second, we are not hearing the voices of teachers still in the profession who may feel too bruised or too at-risk to respond to such a research instrument. Third, teachers we have already interviewed, at all levels from junior to senior positions, have said they have colleagues who would participate in studies of TTBH but who simply do not have the time or energy to engage. Fourth, this exploratory study was intentionally available for a relatively short period of time, limiting opportunity for response. Even given the obvious limitations inherent in a preliminary project, the vividness of the portrayal of the TTBH phenomenon in this study of 560 teachers is striking.

On the strength of the evidence from our pilot study, teacher-targeted bullying challenges conventional models of teacher professionalism. Given the incidence of TTBH both locally and internationally, policy and governmental thinking must shift if we are to create a sustainable education workforce. It is not a matter of ramping up "more professionalism", whether in the classic sense of good and expert, or in the more neoliberal sense of control and accountability (Fournier, 1999). Policies relating to professional teachers must recognise the necessity of creating respectful and professional teaching environments. Until that is achieved, an unfair and insufficient teacher preparation and support model will persist. Given the key role teachers play in enabling relational well-being in classrooms, negative impacts on teacher well-being need to be reduced or eliminated.

Many factors have been suggested attempting to explain teacher employment churn. Empirical evidence from our mixed method, online survey of 560 teachers suggests continual bullying and harassment may play a role in teachers' decisions to leave the profession. Many teachers who initially entered teaching feeling passionate about making a difference to learners' lives are demoralised by the increasing incidence of bullying and harassment, exacerbated by a perceived lack of leadership support (de Wet, 2012; Garrett, 2014). Future Australian studies of TTBH are needed to better understand what motivates students and parents to bully and harass teachers and what the education sector can do to stem this wave of aggressive, intimidating anti-social conduct.

TTBH challenges current models of teacher professionalism. As traditional notions of authority and professional respect are eroded by social media and the prevalence of digital devices, boundaries are rapidly being blurred between informal and formal conduct, discourse and attitude (Kyriacou & Zuin, 2016). On entering the school context, many teachers report that the challenges they face are overwhelming (Buchanan et al., 2013). Teachers must often teach a disparate array of students, some with pronounced special needs and some who come to school without their basic human needs being met. Constant, low level disruptive behaviour saps teachers' vitality and time available in class for engaged teaching and learning. When teachers feel bullied or harassed by disengaged or discouraged students, any perceived lack of leadership support further tarnishes the vision of empowering learners which led them to invest four or more years into earning professional registration. The absence of policy addressing the scourge of TTBH is stark. Broad policy documents and platforms, such as Gonski (2011, 2018), that do not explicitly address the provenance and extent of this issue, are thereby limited in their capacity to improve teachers' individual working lives and the viability of teaching as a profession. Teacher vulnerability to student-related occupational hazard is a reality which requires urgent policy redress.

The often-hazardous nature of being a teacher has not gained appropriate acknowledgement or consideration within education or public discourse. We advocate change to the theoretical and policy framing of teacher professionalism because facilitating optimal learning opportunity for all in the classroom is significantly undermined when teachers are the targets of TTBH. Thinking through the issues of TTBH must go beyond unjust, individual blaming of teachers who are attacked, undermined, vilified or confronted by students or parents. Cost, efficiency and social justice perspectives regarding teachers having safe work environments justify further research. We thus see value in extending our exploratory study to better understand the impact of TTBH on Australian education.

This study was undertaken in 2018 with funding from the DVC(R) Research Engagement Income Growth Fund and HuSS IRGS Supplementary Support Fund.

Appendix—TTBH Survey Questions 2018

Investigation into Teachers' Experiences of Bullying and Harassment in Australian Schools

Q2 What is your gender?

Male
Female
Other

Q3 What is your age bracket?

21–30
31–35
36–40
41–50
51–60
60–70
70+

Q4 How long have you held registration as a teacher?

Less than 1 year
1–4 years
5–9 years
10–14 years
15–19 years
25+ years

Q5 Which educational level are you employed in? Tick all that apply

Primary school
Secondary School

Q6 which area do you teach into? Tick all applicable

Technology
Sport and Health
Humanities/Social Sciences
Math
English
Science
Art
Languages
Information Technology
Generalist
Specialist
Other

Q7 In what role are you currently employed

Teacher
Head Teacher
Deputy Principal
Principal

Q9 In which state/territory(s) have you taught? Please select more than one if applicable

Queensland
New South Wales
Australian Capital Territory
Victoria
South Australia
Western Australia
Norther Territory
Tasmania

Q10 Over the last twelve months, have you experienced bullying or harassing behaviour(s) from a student?

Yes
No

	In the last fortnight		In the last month		In the previous 2 to 5 months		In the previous 6 to 8 months		In the previous 9 to 12 months	
Yelling	Repeat aggressor	Once off instance	Repeat aggressor	Once off instance	Repeat aggressor	Once off instance	Repeat aggressor	Once off instance	Repeat aggressor	Once off instance
Swearing										
Hitting or punching										
Damaging personal property										
Disparaging remarks (verbal)										
Disparaging remarks (social media)										
Standing over/invading personal space										
Organising others against a teacher/principal										
Lying about a teacher/principal to get them into trouble (9)										
Harassing through phone calls or text messages										
Discriminatory behaviour										
Student engaging a parent to argue on their behalf										

Q14 Did you receive support from any of the following sources? (Tick all relevant)

Department of education or other governing institution
Teachers Union
Head teacher
Other staff members
Parents
Partner or family
Other (please specify)

Q15 Over the last twelve months, have you experienced bullying or harassing behaviour(s) from a parent/guardian(s)?

Yes
No

Q16 Which of the following behaviour(s) from a parent/guardian(s) have you experienced and in what frequency? (Tick all relevant)

	In the last fortnight		In the last month		In the previous 2 to 5 months		In the previous 6 to 8 months		In the previous 9 to 12 months	
Yelling	Repeat aggressor	Once off instance	Repeat aggressor	Once off instance	Repeat aggressor	Once off instance	Repeat aggressor	Once off instance	Repeat aggressor	Once off instance
Swearing										
Hitting or punching										
Damaging personal property										
Disparaging remarks (verbal)										
Disparaging remarks (social media)										
Standing over/invading personal space										
Organising others against a teacher/principal										
Lying about a teacher/principal to get them into trouble (9)										
Harassing through phone calls or text messages										
Discriminatory behaviour										
Student engaging a parent to argue on their behalf										

Q17 Have your own experiences of bullying and harassment by parents/guardians ever made you want to leave the teaching profession?

Yes
At times
No

Q18 Please tell us a little about the impact your own experiences of bullying and harassment by parents/guardians has had on you and your desire to teach

Q19 Did you receive support from any of the following sources?

Department of education or other governing institution
Teachers Union
Head teacher
Other staff members
Parents
Partner or family
Other (please specify)

Q22 Do you feel that bullying and harassment of teachers by students and their parents is an issue for schools in Australia?

Definitely yes
Probably yes
Unsure
Probably not
Definitely not

Q23 When a teacher, feels bullied or harassed at your school, is any action generally taken?

Always
Sometimes
Almost Never
Never

Q24 In what way is action taken and by whom?

Q25 Do you feel when action is taken, that the response is effective?

Always
Sometimes
Almost never
Never

Q26 What type of action do you feel your school could take to more effectively address bullying and harassing behaviour from students and/or their parent/guardians towards teachers?

Q27 What is the Index of Community Socio-Educational Advantage (ICSEA) score for your school? This will not in any way identify you or your school.

To view your school's scores click here (a new window will appear) and enter your school's details and press view profile. Your school's ICSEA value will be displayed on the centre of the page next to "School ICSEA value" (If your school value is not available please add NA)

Q28 Would you like to participate in a one-hour interview to discuss teachers' experiences of bullying and harassment in Australian school with one of our researchers?

Yes
No

Q32 Are you currently teaching in a state, independent or Catholic school in Victoria?

Yes
No

Q33 Please add your first name, email and best contact day/time in the box below.

References

Allen, K. P. (2010). Classroom management, bullying, and teacher practices. *The Professional Educator, 34*(1), 1.

Ball, S. (2004). Education for sale! The commodification of everything? *King's Annual Education Lecture* (pp. 1–29). London: University of London.

Ball, S. (2016). Neoliberal education? Confronting the slouching beast. *Policy Futures in Education, 14*(8), 1046–1059.

Ball, S. (2017). *The education debate* (3rd ed.) Bristol, UK: Policy Press.

Benefield, J. (2004). Teachers–the new targets of schoolyard bullies? Paper to New Zealand Association for Research in Education Conference, 24–26 November, National Conference, Westpac Stadium. Wellington, New Zealand.

Bowles, T., & Arnup, J. (2016). Should I stay or should I go? Resilience as a protective factor for teachers' intention to leave the teaching profession. *Australian Journal of Education, 0004944116667620.*

Bricheno, P., & Thornton, M. (2016). *Crying in cupboards: What happens when teachers are bullied?*. Kibworth-Beauchamp, England: Troubador Publishing Ltd.

Bronfenbrenner, U. (1979). *The ecology of human development*. Cambridge, MA: Harvard University Press.

Brownlee, J., Boulton-Lewis, G., & Purdie, N. (2000). Core beliefs about knowing and peripheral beliefs about learning: Developing an holistic conceptualization of epistemological beliefs. *Australian Journal of Educational and Developmental Psychology* (2), 1–16.

Buchanan, J., Prescott, A., Schuck, S., Aubusson, P., Burke, P., & Louviere, J. (2013). Teacher retention and attrition: Views of early career teachers. *Australian Journal of Teacher Education, 38*(3), n3.

Burns, E. (2007). Positioning a post-professional approach to studying professions. *New Zealand Sociology, 22*(1), 69–98.

Byers, E. (2012). *Evaluation of the impact that teacher targeted bullying has on individual safety perceptions and stress*. M.Sc. Thesis. University of Canterbury, Christchurch, New Zealand.

Chen, J.-K., & Astor, R. A. (2008). Students' reports of violence against teachers in Taiwanese schools. *Journal of School Violence, 8*(1), 2–17.

Connell, R. (2009). Good teachers on dangerous ground: Towards a new view of teacher quality and professionalism. *Critical Studies in Education, 50*(3), 213–229.

Connell, R. (2013). The neoliberal cascade and education: An essay on the market agenda and its consequences. *Critical studies in education, 54*(2), 99–112.

Day, C., Sammons, P., Stobart, G., Kington, A., & Gu, Q. (2007). *Teachers matter: Connecting lives, work and effectiveness*. Berkshire, England: McGraw-Hill.

Day, C., & Gu, Q. (2007). Variations in the conditions for teachers' professional learning and development: sustaining commitment and effectiveness over a career. *Oxford Review of Education, 33*(4), 423–443.

Demirkasımoğlu, N. (2010). Defining "Teacher Professionalism" from different perspectives. *Procedia-Social and Behavioral Sciences, 9, 2047–2051.*

Dent, M., Bourgeault, I. L., Denis, J.-L., & Kuhlmann, E. (2016). *The Routledge companion to the professions and professionalism*. Routledge.

de Wet, C. (2012). Risk factors for educator-targeted bullying: A social-ecological perspective. *Journal of Psychology in Africa, 22*(2), 239–243.

Dinkes, R., Cataldi, E. F., Kena, G., & Baum, K. (2006). *Indicators of school crime and safety: 2006. NCES 2007-003*. National Center for Education Statistics.

Espelage, D., Anderman, E. M., Brown, V. E., Jones, A., Lane, K. L., McMahon, S. D., et al. (2013). Understanding and preventing violence directed against teachers: Recommendations for a national research, practice, and policy agenda. *American Psychologist, 68*(2), 75–87. https://doi.org/10.1037/a0031307.

Fournier, V. (1999). The appeal to 'professionalism' as a disciplinary mechanism. *The Sociological Review, 47*(2), 280–307.

Fried, R. (2005). The game of school: *Why we all play it, how it hurts kids, and what it will take to change it.* San Francisco: Jossey-Bass Inc Pub.

Garrett, L. (2014). The student bullying of teachers: An exploration of the nature of the phenomenon and the ways in which it is experienced by teachers. *Aigne, 5,* 19–40.

Gonski Report. (2011, December). *Review of funding for schooling.* Department of Education, Employment and Workplace Relations, Canberra, ACT, Australia. Review Panel Chair: D. Gonski. https://docs.education.gov.au/system/files/doc/other/review-of-funding-for-schooling-final-report-dec-2011.pdf.

Gonski 2.0 Report. (2018, March). *Through growth to achievement: report of the review to achieve educational excellence in Australian schools.* Australian Government Department of Education and Training, Canberra, ACT, Australia. Review Panel Chair: D. Gonski. https://www.appa.asn.au/wp-content/uploads/2018/04/20180430-Through-Growth-to-Achievement_Text.pdf.

Goodson, I., & Hargreaves, A. (Eds.). (1996). *Teachers' professional lives.* London: Falmer.

Greenberg, M., & Krusché, C. (2006). Building social and emotional competence. In S. Jimerson & M. Furlong (Eds.), *Handbook of school violence and school safety* (pp. 395–412). Mahwah, NJ: Erlbaum.

Gu, Q., & Day, C. (2013). Challenges to teacher resilience: Conditions count. *British Educational Research Journal, 39*(1), 22–44. https://doi.org/10.1080/01411926.2011.623152.

Hattie, J. (2008). *Visible learning: A synthesis of over 800 meta-analyses relating to achievement.* London: Routledge.

Hilferty, F. (2008). Theorising teacher professionalism as an enacted discourse of power. *British Journal of Sociology of Education, 29*(2), 161–173.

Hoel, H., & Cooper, C. L. (2000). Destructive conflict and bullying at work: Manchester School of Management, UMIST Manchester.

Hult, A., & Edström, C. (2016). Teacher ambivalence towards school evaluation: promoting and ruining teacher professionalism. *Education Inquiry, 7*(3), 30200.

James, D., Lawlor, M., Courtney, P., Flynn, A., Henry, B., & Murphy, N. (2008). Bullying behaviour in secondary schools: What roles do teachers play? *Child Abuse Review: Journal of the British Association for the Study and Prevention of Child Abuse and Neglect, 17*(3), 160–173.

Kauppi, T., & Pörhölä, M. (2012). School teachers bullied by their students: Teachers' attributions and how they share their experiences. *Teaching and Teacher Education, 28*(7), 1059–1068.

Kõiv, K. (2015). Changes over a ten-year interval in the prevalence of teacher targeted bullying. *Procedia-Social and Behavioral Sciences, 171,* 126–133.

König, J., & Rothland, M. (2012). Motivations for choosing teaching as a career: Effects on general pedagogical knowledge during initial teacher education. *Asia-Pacific Journal of Teacher Education, 40*(3), 289–315. https://doi.org/10.1080/1359866X.2012.700045.

Kyriacou, C., & Zuin, A. (2016). Cyberbullying of teachers by students on YouTube: Challenging the image of teacher authority in the digital age. *Research Papers in Education, 31*(3), 255–273.

Liljegren, A., & Saks, M. (2016). *Professions and metaphors: Understanding professions in society.* London: Routledge.

Loewenberg Ball, D., & Forzani, F. M. (2009). The work of teaching and the challenge for teacher education. *Journal of Teacher Education, 60*(5), 497–511.

McCallum, F., & Price, D. (Eds.). (2016). *Nurturing wellbeing development in education.* London: Routledge.

McKenzie, P., Weldon, P. R., Rowley, G., Murphy, M., & McMillan, J. (2014). Staff in Australia's schools 2013: Main report on the survey.

Mockler, N. (2012). Teacher professional learning in a neoliberal age: Audit, professionalism and identity. *Australian Journal of Teacher Education, 38*(10), 35–47.

Moon, B., & McCluskey, J. (2016). School-based victimization of teachers in Korea: Focusing on individual and school characteristics. *Journal of Interpersonal Violence, 31*(7), 1340–1361.

Murphy, P. (2015). *Universities and innovation economies: The creative wasteland of post-industrial society.* Farnham, UK: Ashgate.

Muijs, D., Kyriakides, L., van der Werf, G., Creemers, B., Timperley, H., & Earl, L. (2014). State of the art–teacher effectiveness and professional learning. *School effectiveness and school improvement, 25*(2), 231–256.

Nias, J. (1996). Thinking about feeling: The emotions in teaching. *Cambridge Journal of Education, 26*(3), 293–306.

Noddings, N. (2012). The caring relation in teaching. *Oxford Review of Education, 38*(6), 771–781.

Noddings, N. (2015). *The challenge to care in schools* (2nd ed.). New York: Teachers College Press.

Özkiliç, R. (2012). Bullying toward Teachers: An example from Turkey. *Eurasian Journal of Educational Research, 47,* 95–112.

Palmer, P. J. (2007). *The Courage to Teach.* San Francisco, CA: Jossey-Bass.

Palmer, P. J. (2017). *The courage to teach guide for reflection and renewal.* New York: Wiley.

Polesel, J., Rice, S., & Dulfer, N. (2014). The impact of high-stakes testing on curriculum and pedagogy: A teacher perspective from Australia. *Journal of Education Policy, 29*(5), 640–657.

Riley, P. (2014). *Australian principal occupational health, safety and wellbeing survey: 2011–2014 data.* Melbourne: ACU.

Riley, D., Duncan, D. J., & Edwards, J. (2011). Staff bullying in Australian schools. *Journal of Educational Administration, 49*(1), 7–30.

Roffey, S. (2012). Pupil wellbeing—Teacher wellbeing: Two sides of the same coin? *Educational and Child Psychology, 29*(4), 8.

Ross, S. W., Romer, N., & Horner, R. H. (2012). Teacher Well-Being and the Implementation of School-Wide Positive Behavior Interventions and Supports. *Journal of Positive Behavior Interventions, 14*(2), 118–128. https://doi.org/10.1177/1098300711413820.

Rothstein-Fisch, C., & Trumbull, E. (2008). *Managing diverse classrooms: How to build on students' cultural strengths.* Alexandria, VA: ASCD.

Sachs, J. (2016). Teacher professionalism: Why are we still talking about it? *Teachers and Teaching, 22*(4), 413–425.

Steffgen, G., & Ewen, N. (2007). Teachers as victims of school violence—The influence of strain and school culture. *International Journal on Violence and Schools, 3*(1), 81–93.

Swann, M., McIntyre, D., Pell, T., Hargreaves, L., & Cunningham, M. (2010). Teachers' conceptions of teacher professionalism in England in 2003 and 2006. *British Educational Research Journal, 36*(4), 549–571.

Terry, A. (1998). Teachers as targets of bullying by their pupils: a study to investigate incidence. *British Journal of Educational Psychology, 68*(2), 255–268.

Tirri, K., & Puolimatka, T. (2000). Teacher authority in schools: A case study from Finland. *Journal of Education for Teaching: International research and pedagogy, 26*(2), 157–165.

Vaaland, G. S. (2017). Back on track: Approaches to managing highly disruptive school classes. *Cogent Education, 4*(1), 1–21.

Vaaland, G. S., & Roland, E. (2013). Pupil aggressiveness and perceptual orientation towards weakness in a teacher who is new to the class. *Teaching and Teacher Education, 29,* 177–187.

VIT. (2018). Maintaining professional practice. *Victorian Institute of Teaching,* Melbourne, Vic. https://www.vit.vic.edu.au/.

Whitty, G. (2006). *Teacher professionalism in a new era.* First General Teaching Council for Northern Ireland Annual Lecture, Belfast, Ireland.

Woudstra, M., van Rensburg, E., Visser, M., & Jordaan, J. (2018). Learner-to-teacher bullying as a potential factor influencing teachers' mental health. *South African Journal of Education, 38*(1).

Web Pages

Theteachersareblowingtheirwhistles. Retrieved from https://www.theteachersareblowingtheirwhistles. com/.

Dr. Rochelle Fogelgarn is a lecturer in teacher education La Trobe University, Bundoora, Australia. After more than twenty years of teaching and school leadership, Rochelle moved into teacher education, specialising in classroom management, creating and supporting safe, inclusive and engaging classrooms, developing teacher readiness and reflexive professional practice. Her doctoral research investigated what sustains expert teachers' practice in an increasingly challenging workplace.

Dr. Edgar Burns Edgar is a senior lecturer in sociology at La Trobe University, located in Bendigo, Australia, who has researched professions over many years. He is currently finalising a sole-authored book provisionally titled "Theorising professions". He is also working on a project examining Ph.D. publications by Australian sociology students 2013–8. Edgar has substantial experience in the development of data collection tools, academic writing and conference presentations.

Dr. Paulina Billett is a lecturer in Sociology in the Department of Social Inquiry at La Trobe University, Victoria. Her research centers on women's lives and their lived experiences. Her research interest include violence against women, issues of identity formation, and the meaning of womanhood in the 21st century.

Chapter 10
Using the Student Engagement and Teacher Reflection App (SETRA) as a Teacher Professional Learning Tool: A Pilot Study

Jeanne Allen, Glenda McGregor and Donna Pendergast

Abstract This chapter reports on a pilot study conducted into the potential effectiveness of an application (app), titled the Student Engagement and Teacher Reflection App (SETRA), which is being developed as a professional learning tool to assist teachers to cater for the diversity of students in contemporary schools through engaging all young adolescents in learning. Drawing from the evidence-based Young Adolescent Engagement in Learning (YAEL) Model, the app serves to support teachers' growth in professional learning, which is an important characteristic of teaching and teacher professionalism. The YAEL Model, developed in 2016 by members of the research team, provides a professional learning approach for secondary school teachers to engage all students in their learning, including those at risk of disengagement. In order to facilitate teachers' access to, and implementation of the many dimensions and characteristics of the Model, SETRA has since been developed as a tool to provide teachers with real time, "anywhere, any place" professional learning. A pilot study subsequently determined proof of concept of the baseline version of the app, as well as its potential effectiveness as a teacher professional learning tool. In this chapter, the YAEL model is first overviewed and then the findings from the SETRA pilot are discussed.

1 Introduction

Teacher professionalism has been conceptualised and defined in different ways since teacher education came under the auspices of universities in the 1960s, at which time teachers were elevated to professional status and teacher preparation began to acquire

J. Allen (✉) · G. McGregor · D. Pendergast
Griffith University, Brisbane, QLD, Australia
e-mail: jeanne.allen@griffith.edu.au

G. McGregor
e-mail: g.mcgregor@griffith.edu.au

D. Pendergast
e-mail: d.pendergast@griffith.edu.au

© Springer Nature Singapore Pte Ltd. 2019
A. Gutierrez et al. (eds.), *Professionalism and Teacher Education*,
https://doi.org/10.1007/978-981-13-7002-1_10

academic legitimacy. Among the developments to emerge this century has been an increased and increasing emphasis on ongoing professional learning as a key feature of teachers' work. Requirements for teachers to participate in and provide evidence of performance in professional learning initiatives and activities have become mandated in many countries, including in Australia where the Australian Professional Standards for Teachers (Australian Institute for Teaching and School Leadership [AITSL], 2011) encompass engagement in professional learning as one of seven standards stipulating what teachers should know and be able to do before qualifying as teachers and advancing though the career stages. Similar professional learning requirements exist under teacher standards in New Zealand (New Zealand Education Council, 2017), the United Kingdom (United Kingdom Department of Education, 2011) and the United States (National Board for Professional Teaching Standards, 2018).

This continuing shift in what it means to be a teacher inevitably impacts on the types of professional learning initiatives deemed worthy of implementation and uptake in schools and other educational contexts. As with many other features of schooling, evidence of impact has become a focus. In addition to having a clear purpose and being able to engage teachers in meaningful ways, professional learning must also be designed to positively impact their practice and enhance their capacity to effect optimal student engagement and achievement. Schools in Australia and internationally have introduced teacher research, often centring on action research methodologies, as a standard criterion of teachers' work. This and other types of targeted professional learning innovation can address the needs of teachers, both as individuals and as a school collective, and may serve to "challenge existing beliefs, attitudes and understandings, and … result in changed professional practice for the benefit of students" (Timperley, 2011a, p. 4).

In this chapter, we step into this space by reporting on a pilot study conducted into the potential effectiveness of an application (app), titled the Student Engagement and Teacher Reflection App (SETRA), which is being developed as a professional learning tool to assist teachers to cater for the diversity of students in contemporary schools through engaging all young adolescents in learning. Drawing from the evidence-based Young Adolescent Engagement in Learning (YAEL) Model, which has been developed and implemented during the past three years, SETRA is a professional learning tool that teachers can access in real time, anywhere and at any place. As discussed in this chapter, it has the potential to make a significant contribution to assisting teachers in engaging and working with students in the endeavour of learning and teaching.

2   Teacher Professionalism

Discourses around teacher professionalism are contested, with many differing voices and viewpoints entering the debate about how it can and should be conceptualised and characterised, now and into the future. British sociologist Julia Evetts (2008, p. 20) identifies three broad interpretations that have developed over time: "professionalism as an occupational value; professionalism as an ideology; and professionalism as a discourse of occupational change and managerial control." Australian researcher Judyth Sachs (2016) agrees that a top-down approach to teacher professionalism has come to characterise the work of teachers during the past decade, arguing that teacher standards have failed, and will likely continue to fail, to act as a "catalyst for authentic professional learning." According to Sachs (2016), this type of managerial approach neglects the need for teachers to develop the kinds of attitudes and sense of commitment that might enable them to act as self-regulated, responsive and confident professionals.

The Organisation for Economic Co-operation and Development (OECD) (2016) claims that, while standardisation and externally imposed accountability measures impacted heavily on the profession in the twentieth century, the twenty-first century has seen a renewed and intensified emphasis on teacher professionalism as a leading feature of educational reform. This movement, generated in large part by the perceived need to raise teacher quality as the key to improving student outcomes, represents a fundamental change to how teachers' work is conceived and carried out. As early as the 1990s, evidence began to emerge that educational reforms, which were no longer stopping "at the classroom door" (Ashenden, 1994, p. 13), were leading to a significant reconceptualisation of what schools should be and what teachers should do (see, e.g. Hinton, 1997; Seddon, 1999; Seddon & Brown, 1997). Cranston (2000) noted that the changes taking place represented "alterations at the very 'heart' of schools in the learning-teaching enterprise, generating major challenges to the work and professionalism of teachers" (p. 123). These claims by commentators at the turn of the century have proven prescient, with teacher professional learning emerging as one of the principal factors in current-day conceptions of teacher professionalism.

3   Teacher Professional Learning

Teacher professional learning is also conceived in many different ways, according to context and time period, as well as educational, social and political trends. New Zealander Helen Timperley (2011b) suggests that, in current times, it commonly encompasses "both formal and informal opportunities for teachers and leaders to deepen professional knowledge and refine professional skills as described in the relevant Standards" (p. 4). This approach is evident in Australia where AITSL, in the *Australian Charter for the Professional Development of Teachers and School Leaders*, describes effective professional learning in the following way:

> Professional learning is the formal or informal learning experiences undertaken by teachers and school leaders that improve their individual professional practice, and a school's collective effectiveness, as measured by improved student learning, engagement with learning and wellbeing. At its most effective, professional learning develops individual and collective capacity across the teaching profession to address current and future challenges. (AITSL, 2012, p. 2)

Equipped with insights of this type, we are in a position to develop professional learning resources and tools that best respond to the needs of teachers, in and beyond the present time. Past responses have taught us important lessons, of which we highlight two in particular. First, the intensification of work in recent decades has led to a time "squeeze" for teachers, such that they often feel unable to fit professional learning into their schedules, regardless of the value they place on it. In 2014, an OECD report (OECD, 2014) listed conflicts with work schedules as one of the most commonly cited reasons why teachers across a broad range of countries and economies fail to participate in professional learning activities. Secondly, one-off professional development activities, which have been commonly used as an approach to teacher learning, have come under heavy criticism. The evidence shows that they often fail to result in a positive impact on teaching and learning outcomes (King, 2016; Lovett & Cameron, 2011; Yuen, 2012), with teachers reporting them as being isolated, disconnected and often irrelevant to the work they do in schools (Allen, McGregor, Pendergast, & Ronksley-Pavia, in press; Avalos, 2011; Korthagen, 2017). Possibly of greatest concern are the research findings that demonstrate these professional development activities have limited impact on practice and, therefore, student outcomes (Timperley, 2011c).

The study on which we report in this chapter seeks to respond to these types of issues and, additionally, aligns with thinking of the current digital age around changing the modalities in which teachers learn and work.

4 Background

The SETRA app serves as a teacher professional learning tool that draws from the YAEL Model. Developed by members of our research team in 2016, the YAEL Model provides a holistic approach to the provision of support for young adolescent learners, based on the understanding that all students should be supported to learn, flourish and develop the requisite skills and attitudes to lead fulfilling, productive and responsible lives. The Model was developed from an extensive review of the international student engagement evidence base, as well as findings from a large research study conducted in an Australian educational jurisdiction, also in 2016. All government high schools across the jurisdiction were included in the study, with the sample comprising 107 teachers, students, school leaders, parents/carers, education departmental staff and consulting professionals. Data collection focused on gathering the views of a range of stakeholders about engaging young adolescents in their learning, including those at risk of disengaging from schooling. Focus groups, individual face-to-face and telephone interviews and school site visits were conducted. The empirical study generated significant findings about a wide range of issues associated with young adolescent engagement and achievement in schools (see Allen et al., in press).

Conceived as a layered ecosystem of over-arching dimensions, sub-dimensions and components of provision of educational support, the Model is intended for whole-school, cluster or system adoption and implementation. Figure 1 provides a graphic representation of the Model, which is further delineated below.

Layer 1 represents the foundation and starting point of the Model, namely a school culture that seeks to provide requisite levels of support to *all* young adolescents in secondary school, and to ensure the best possible provision of learning support to all students, through attending to the core characteristics of *school structure and school community, student well-being* and *teaching, teachers and leaders*. Within each of these three over-arching dimensions, situated at Layer 2, are a number of sub-dimensions: whole-school reform; practical and network supports; visionary school leadership with the education department/system; family and community involvement; meaningful curriculum for young adolescent learners; appropriate pedagogies for young adolescent learners; teaching structures and professional learning; inclusive school culture; positive relational climate; and social, emotional, psychological and health support. The three components of educational provision are situated at Layer 3 and are conceptualised along a continuum of intensifying levels of student support: *five core elements for young adolescent engagement, flexible learning provision support* and *alternative provision*, with provision for students to transition in both directions, particularly from the first to the second component, according to individual need throughout adolescence. Table 1 outlines the purpose and intent of the components.

Since the start of 2018, the Model has been progressively implemented across the 26 high schools in the jurisdiction for which it was initially developed. A preliminary external evaluation of the Model as a means of lifting student engagement across the behavioural, emotional and cognitive dimensions is planned for mid to late 2019 and findings will be reported in due course.

5   SETRA

Having developed the YAEL Model as a means to promote and sustain students' engagement in school and development as learners, the research team acknowledged the need to ensure that the Model became readily accessible to teachers. Although designed for a range of individuals and groups holding a stake in the engagement of young adolescent learners, the Model is deemed particularly valuable for teachers seeking to engage students in ways that are highly effective and evidence based. Therefore, in 2017, members of the research team, in conjunction with university-based app designers, designed and developed the baseline SETRA app, aimed at enabling teachers to draw on the YAEL Model to enhance their skills in engaging and retaining students in learning. SETRA facilitates teacher professional learning through connecting teachers' classroom observations with frameworks of best practice support for the three main dimensions of student engagement: behavioural, emotional and cognitive (Gibbs & Poskitt, 2010). The key strengths of the app are that it: is evidence based and data driven; provides personalised just-in-time professional learning for teachers; is accessible anywhere and anytime; and promotes

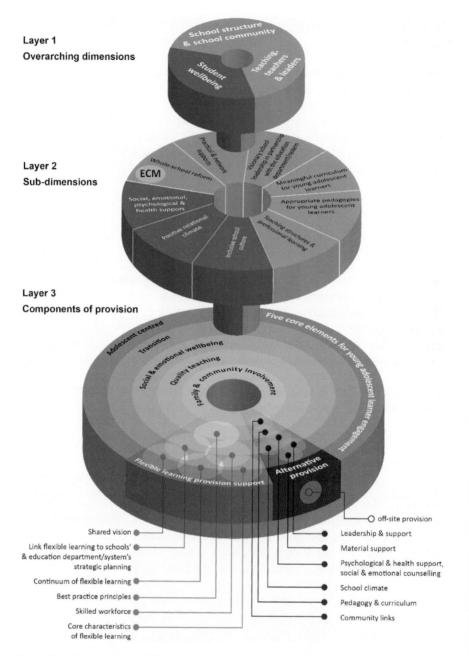

Fig. 1 The Young Adolescent Engagement in Learning Model (Allen et al., in press)

Table 1 Components of provision of the YAEL Model

Component of provision	Purpose & intent
1. Five core elements for young adolescent engagement	Intended as the mainstream approach for all secondary school students
	Acknowledges that all young adolescents are at risk of disengagement or underachievement
	An over-arching approach to enable a learning ecosystem intentionally designed to be responsive and appropriate to the full range of needs, interests and achievements of young adolescent students
	When elements of Component 1 are in place, there is less likelihood that students will need additional and/or alternative learning provision
2. Flexible learning provision support	Serves as early intervention measures and intended to address the needs of those students deemed to be at risk of disengaging from education, but not to the point of requiring alternative provision
	Strategies are most effective when professional learning communities are created in which classroom teacher/s and support staff work with students to address low-level, but persistent misbehaviour and off-task behaviours
	Provided within the context of early interventions through: • tailored pedagogies • targeted programs
	Structured so that students who are not at risk may choose flexible learning support as electives or extension activities
3. Alternative provision	Intended for students whose needs are best met outside of the general classroom environment within fit-for-purpose contexts → represents a corrective approach to learning disengagement
	The Model defines the parameters of two suggested types of alternative educational provision: on-site and off-site
	Provides a holistic model of support for all students but with increasing levels of assistance and alternative educational pathways for students with increasing behavioural, emotional, psychological and educational needs
	Emphasises the need to work collaboratively with community agencies, families, parents/carers and students within fit-for-purpose contexts

Adapted from Allen et al. (in press)

teacher reflection across the dimensions of student engagement. It is anticipated that
teachers will use the app following a class or sequence of teaching, in a similar
way to how they might consult a textbook or other source of professional support.
In its baseline form, the SETRA app prompts teachers to reflect on their teaching
through asking them to consider responses to a range of questions focusing on the
behavioural, emotional and cognitive dimensions of student engagement. Teachers
are able to record and review their reflections made after each lesson or sequence
of lessons. For example, having taught a class, teachers are asked to provide brief
textual responses to questions such as the following:

- How did the lesson go?
- Were the students on task?
- Were they behaviourally engaged?
- Were they emotionally engaged?
- Were they cognitively engaged?
- How do I know?

A series of clicking screens also enables teachers to reflect on specific areas
of student engagement across the dimensions, in response to the question "Which
of the following behavioural/emotional/cognitive components could be observed?"
The components include, for example in the behavioural dimension, "participation"
and "on task"; in the emotional dimension, "reactions to teachers" and "reactions
to classmates"; and, in the cognitive dimension, "volition" and "investment and
willingness to exert effort."

Drawing from the YAEL Model, the baseline app then provides tiered sequences
of proactive and supportive support strategies for teachers to consider, based on their
reflections, such as:

- Your students could be responding in this way because …
- You can potentially enhance their engagement by … or …
- If the strategies you use are not altogether effective, you could …
- If required, you might refer your students to …

It is important to note that the baseline app was developed at low cost and for proof
of concept only. It represents the first "pilot" version of a first-of-its-kind, innovative
and sophisticated app, to be fully developed and tested in partnership with teachers
and other school staff to serve the professional learning needs of teachers in our
contemporary schools.

6 Theoretical Framework

This chapter draws from the work of classical sociologists such as George Herbert
Mead (1934) and Herbert Blumer (1969) to provide insight into the function of
teacher education. As in previous work (see, e.g. Allen, 2009), we derived the theoretical orientation of this study from the interpretive school of thought of symbolic

interactionism, which enabled us to focus on the professional learning of teachers as they described their experiences in using the SETRA app to reflect on, and develop knowledge and skills in engaging young adolescents in learning. Symbolic interactionism was appropriate for this particular study because it provides a means of elucidating how individuals give contexts and situations meaning through their interactions with others (Blumer, 1969). It aims to reveal the subjective meaning of human behaviour and underlines the role that language and thought play in individuals' interactions in social contexts.

Mead's (1934) concept of role taking was also used in framing this study, based on the understanding that reflective learning is part of the professional role that teachers adopt. Described as one of the "specifically social expressions of intelligence" that shape the interpersonal nature of people's work (Mead, 1934, p. 141), role taking involves an individual engaging in a self-reflective dialogue in order to act in a specified role. The reflective thinking undertaken in professional learning shapes the actions of the individual teacher by enabling them to develop and sustain a role through structuring and reacting to their own experiences (O'Connor, 2008).

7   Research Aims and Methods

In order to determine proof of concept, the SETRA baseline app was trialled late in 2017 via a pilot study. Researchers were granted ethical clearances from the university and educational jurisdiction before undertaking the study. All reported data have been anonymised to ensure non-identification of the school and participants.

The aims of the pilot were to trial the baseline model of the SETRA app and to evaluate its potential effectiveness as a teacher professional learning tool to engage students in learning. The research questions were as follows:

1. In the views of participants, how effective is the SETRA app as a professional learning tool to facilitate student engagement and prevent student disengagement?
2. In what ways does the SETRA app enable teachers to identify, and reflect upon effective student learning engagement strategies?

The study comprised a sample of six secondary school teachers in one urban government school in south-east Queensland. Participants, who were nominated by the school principal, used the dual-platform app across two weeks as a professional learning tool to engage students in one selected class from Years 7 to 9, in subject areas including Humanities, English, and Health and Physical Education (HPE). Details are provided in Table 2.

A briefing meeting was held before the start of the trial in order to demonstrate the app, describe the study and fulfil ethical requirements, for example, gaining informed consent. Participants were asked to engage with the app before and after four lessons with a designated class. This involved making brief written reflections about student engagement and responding to questions about students' cognitive, emotional and

Table 2 Participant details

Participant	Gender	Subject	Year level
1	Male	Humanities	8
2	Female	English	7
3	Female	HPE	9
4	Female	Humanities	8
5	Female	English	8
6	Male	HPE	9

behavioural engagement via dropdown boxes. They were also asked to make field notes, to be included in the data analysis.

Individual semi-structured interviews were held with the participants at the end of the pilot study. The interview schedule can be found at Appendix 1. With participant permission, all interviews were digitally recorded, and the recordings were subsequently transcribed. Using a member checking approach (Cohen, Manion, & Morrison, 2018), participants were offered a copy of the relevant transcript and given the opportunity to amend it. Three participants also provided field notes, which were included in the data set. The data were analysed using a thematic approach (Patton 2015), which involved two members of the research team each separately reading the interview transcripts to identify and record patterns that responded in some way to the research questions. Subsequently, the two sets of recorded patterns were compared and contrasted, with inconsistencies resolved through further interrogation of the data, both by the two researchers and an additional member of the research team. This iterative process resulted in the generation of a number of themes, providing insight into the effectiveness of the SETRA app, both in terms of its functionality and its benefits as a teacher professional learning tool to engage young adolescent learners in schooling.

8   Findings

Data analysis resulted in four key findings: SETRA serves to promote teacher reflection and provides powerful student engagement strategies; an app such as SETRA is an effective, timely and innovative teacher professional learning tool to engage students in learning; SETRA would be enhanced through the development of an associated website; and SETRA needs further development in terms of functionality. Findings are summarised in Table 3.

Table 3 Key findings from the SETRA pilot study

Finding	Overview
SETRA serves to promote teacher reflection and provides powerful student engagement strategies	• The capacity of the app to promote teacher reflection emerged as one of its most positive features • Participants commented that the app prompted them to reflect on how *they* were engaging students, rather than merely focusing on how well the students were engaged
An app such as SETRA is an effective, timely and innovative teacher professional learning tool to engage students in learning	• Five of six participants commented on the potential effectiveness of the SETRA app as a professional learning tool to assist them in engaging students in their learning • One participant engaged minimally in the study, stating that she did not use apps and other forms of mobile technology in her work
SETRA would be enhanced through the development of an associated website	• One of the goals of the full project is to incorporate a website that enables the generation of communities of practice and serves as a repository of resources • This was not mentioned to participants, yet four raised the prospect
SETRA needs further development in terms of functionality	• The SETRA app developed for the pilot study was of necessity cost-effective (low cost) and was intended to constitute a baseline version of the future "high tech," fully developed app • The latter will be developed commercially and will be budgeted at a funding increase of approximately 1400%

9 Discussion

In our YAEL empirical study (Allen, McGregor, Pendergast, & Ronksley-Pavia, 2016), it became clear that although teachers generally believe they are good at identifying at-risk and disengaged students, they often feel overwhelmed in finding an appropriate response to support these students' needs. Findings and evidence from this 2016 study and more broadly show that a strong, integrated, coherent and coordinated approach to student engagement is required (e.g. Allen, McGregor, Pendergast, & Ronksley-Pavia, 2016; Allen et al., in press), and that teachers can be assisted in raising levels of student engagement through targeted professional learning. This can be understood from a theoretical stance in that individuals experience reality through their definitions of it and "act towards things on the basis of the meanings that the things have for them" (Blumer, 1969, p. 2). That is, how individuals (teachers in this instance) define or give meaning to the things they encounter will shape their actions towards them. In other words, they do not respond directly to things but through the use of symbols, including language, attach meaning to things and then act on the basis of that meaning (Benzies & Allen, 2001). For the purposes of the current discussion, this points to the need for teachers to engage in purposeful reflection in order to make meaning of what is occurring in their classrooms, and then, where necessary, establish ways in which they might negotiate change.

According to pilot participants, the SETRA app was particularly effective in motivating them to engage in reflection of this kind, as exemplified in these comments:

> The best element that I got out of it was … with the stopping and the reflecting. It's been a very, very chaotic term in terms of really lifting the rigour of the student work. So it's been a really good opportunity to force me to stop and reflect. I think I really appreciated that because at times things get too busy or you're, oh, I've got to do this and I've got to do that, and you don't actually stop and go, was this good for my students? Did I get the most out of the lesson? What can I do better next time? (Participant [P] 2)

> … some of the [SETRA] strategies really made me think about how I was engaging the students, rather than how the students were engaging with the class. So what could I do to change? … It really made me reflect on how I was engaging the students, rather than just seeing their response was more like looking back at me as a teacher, which I guess is what this app is about. (P1)

Given that the app is informed by evidence-based approaches to student engagement incorporated in the YAEL Model, it would seem to have the potential to provide teachers with fit-for-purpose and actionable methods and strategies to enhance their teaching of particular classes in the short to medium term and to raise their levels of professional knowledge and skills from the present into the future.

Further, across the participant group, most teachers (5 of 6) deemed that the fully developed app would be an effective, timely and innovative teacher professional learning tool. One participant said it was much more effective than "just using Google or something like that" and that its main benefit for her would be that:

> … it tracks the progress of how you're dealing with these behaviours or engagement of students. I like that. It really makes you think about it in those different stages and what could you do next lesson, giving you those strategies to go with next lesson. Or how could you better engage your students that way. (P3)

Another commented that it would provide new ways of approaching her work with students, especially when other avenues had been exhausted:

> Particularly when you get to a point where sometimes people feel like, even as a group, we've tried everything, what's next? That *what's next* question would be definitely where it would be useful. (P4)

Looking forward, several noted how valuable an app such as SETRA would be for future generations of teachers, for example:

> It would be fantastic because apps are just - that's the way to go educationally. Kids are on their phones 24/7. So are we. Yeah, just finding a better use for it. Educationally, it would be great for teachers, especially beginning teachers. (P5)

While much more research is needed, we suggest that the app, when fully developed and functional, might well serve to overcome several well-identified shortcomings of traditional, one-off professional learning endeavours (e.g. workshops and seminars), such as being isolated and disconnected to teachers' everyday work (Avalos, 2011; Watson & Michael, 2016) and having limited impact on their practice (Timperley, 2011c).

It could also serve as a key enabling tool in the development of intra- and inter-school professional communities of learners, which have been shown to be effective in driving change in practice (Aylsworth, 2012). Several participants saw practical value in being able to use the app in collaboration with others to share and compare engagement strategies and their effectiveness with individual students and cognate/age groups. Prior to the pilot study, it had already been determined that the elaborated SETRA app would include links to purpose-built websites to address this professional need.

Tailored websites would provide additional benefits to teachers, including the facility to upload, store and share student engagement resources, links to other online materials and sites, and, most importantly, discussion boards and other asynchronous (and possibly synchronous) forms of collaboration. Participants alluded to these types of advantages, with one teacher noting how discussions and online video clips further enrich the learning she engaged in via SETRA:

> I think maybe talking through some of the elements, maybe giving examples of what that might look like in a classroom. ... Maybe if it, later on, it expanded [to include] a website, maybe the videos would come in really helpful with that element as well because I know that I particularly - I learn best when I'm hearing things and watching things visually as well ... If there was an option for some sort of local tutorial, talk-throughs or videos, that would take it to the next level. (P2)

As intended, participants used the app before and after (not during) lessons. Building an associated SETRA website would enable them to access a range of mobile technologies during these times:

> We've got our laptops with us. If you could access it and then [the app] could be connected, that would be even better. (P6)

Including collaborative measures as a way to enhance teachers' professional learning has been well demonstrated in practice and research (e.g. Kelly, 2006; Korthagen, 2017), and can also be understood theoretically through Meadian principles of emergence. The fundamental understanding involved in Mead's (1934) theory is that when an individual or living form of some kind interacts with its environment in a particular way, some new object or situation is likely to emerge. Different factors impact in different ways (along a positive-negative spectrum) on the individual, the environment, the nature of the interaction and, thus, on the new object or situation that emerges. In relation to the current discussion, the interaction of the individual (the teacher) with their (school) environment is likely to be *positively* impacted by the involvement of supportive colleagues and peers in giving rise to gains in professional learning (the newly emergent object/situation).

The final key finding in the pilot study was that the SETRA app needs further development in terms of functionality. This was not unexpected, given that the app had been developed as a baseline version and was of necessity cost-effective (low cost). The following comments point to the types of issues encountered by participants:

> But when I went in the first session, something happened and my phone glitched out and I had to get [back] into the program. I found that when I went back a couple of days later, my session one that I'd done wasn't there so I had to redo it. (P2)

> When I used it the first time I noticed when I was typing in the first bit I had a spelling mistake, and I couldn't tap just on the spelling mistake. You had to delete the whole lot, and I couldn't copy and paste, which was really irritating. That, to me, was like oh, my god, seriously! (P5)

This type of constructive feedback that we received is proving very useful in the development of a much more sophisticated version of the SETRA app with enhanced communication and search functionality, which is in process.

10   The Way Forward

Student engagement has been identified as one of the most reliable predictors of academic achievement and yet approximately 40% of Australian school students are deemed to be disengaged from education, increasing their vulnerability to unemployment and civic and social dislocation (Australian Productivity Commission, 2017). Teacher effectiveness in mitigating against student disengagement is crucial and developing teacher efficacy through targeted professional learning is therefore essential.

The research team, in partnership with interested schools, is currently finalising an application for an Australian Research Council Linkage grant to further develop the SETRA app and associated mobile technologies as professional development tools to assist teachers to engage students in their learning. Our proposed research builds on the YAEL evidence-based Model of best practice for adolescent student engagement, in order to develop personalised learning tools for teachers. The effectiveness of interactive technologies for teacher professional learning is of growing academic interest, yet remains seriously under-researched.

Immediate benefits of the research will include personalised professional learning; targeted strategies for student engagement; and conversion of best practice to common practice in schools. Long term, this project will address persistent community concerns about student achievement, made explicit most recently in the 2017 Australian Productivity Commission Report (Australian Productivity Commission, 2017).

11   Conclusion

The YAEL Model is the first-of-its-kind in that it has been developed from an evidence-based theorisation of teaching and learning that can inform the professional learning of teachers. Specifically, the Model can serve to establish and foster best practice in teachers in engaging students in learning through meeting the behavioural, emotional and cognitive needs of young adolescent learners. As such, in this chapter we contend that it offers potential for real innovation in the way teachers structure learning for young adolescents. The associated SETRA app has the potential to provide teachers with real-time access to supportive and reactive measures to address the particular learning needs of individual or groups of students, thus serving as a conduit between theory and practice.

The ongoing research study reported on in this chapter has the potential to make a significant contribution to the teacher education field in several ways. First, the research is contextualised in contemporary learning environments, with the YAEL Model having been developed for twenty-first century teachers and learners whose needs incorporate a range of skills vital to living, learning and working in a complex and technologically rich world. Via the SETRA app, it enables ready access to a continuum of pedagogical, curricular and social support measures for young adolescents. Second, the ongoing research has the potential to provide insight into teachers' digital competence and the integration of technology in teacher education and teaching practices, which are areas of increasing research focus internationally (e.g. Ferrari, 2012; Spiteri & Rundgren, 2017). Using mobile technologies such as the SETRA app and associated websites enables teachers to address their professional learning needs anywhere and at any time, regardless of their location and competing work demands.

Acknowledgements We acknowledge the valuable work undertaken by Dr. Michelle Ronksley-Pavia as a research assistant during this project.

Appendix 1: Pilot Study Interview Schedule

Thank you for participating in this interview. The interview should take about one hour.

There are two sets of questions. First, we would like to hear your views about the learning experiences you had in using the app, and then, secondly, we would like to hear about your experiences in using the app itself. Your answers will help us to modify and improve the app and its functionality.

A. The first four questions relate to your professional learning through the use of the app.

    1. To begin with, could you please explain your approach to using the app? In other words, what method did you find suited you best in accessing the app for your professional learning needs?

    2. Could you please describe some of the positive professional learning experiences you had in using the app?

    3. In what ways, if any, did you find that the app didn't meet your professional learning needs?

    4. How do you think we could improve the type of learning provided through the app in order to better meet your needs?

B. The following questions relate to the app itself.

    1. How easy, or otherwise, did you find it to use the app?

    2. Could you please describe some of the most positive features of the app?

    3. What were some of the challenges you encountered?

    4. Taking a 'blue sky' approach, how do you think we should re-design the app to provide maximum benefit?

This the end of the questions. Do you have any other points or questions you would like to raise?

Thank you for participating in this interview.

References

Allen, J. M. (2009). Valuing practice over theory: How beginning teachers re-orient their practice in the transition from the university to the workplace. *Teaching and Teacher Education, 25*(5), 647–654.

Allen, J. M., McGregor, G., Pendergast, D., & Ronksley-Pavia, M. (in press). Young adolescent engagement in learning: Supporting students through structure and community. London, UK: Palgrave-Macmillan.

Allen, J. M., McGregor, G., Pendergast, D., & Ronksley-Pavia, M. (2016). Student Engagement Continuum: Engaging high school students (Year 7–10). Commissioned by the ACT Government Education Directorate. Brisbane, QLD: Griffith University.

Ashenden, D. (1994, 19 October). Better schools begin with better classroom reform. *The Australian*, 13.

Australian Institute for Teaching and School Leadership (AITSL). (2011). *Australian Professional Standards for Teachers*. Carlton Sth, VIC: Ministerial Council for Education, Early Childhood Development and Youth Affairs (MCEETYA).

Australian Institute for Teaching and School Leadership (AITSL). (2012). *Australian charter for the professional development of teachers and school leaders: A shared responsibility and commitment*. Canberra, ACT: Author.

Australian Productivity Commission. (2017). *Shifting the dial: 5 year productivity review*. Canberra, ACT: Author.

Avalos, B. (2011). Teacher professional development in teaching and teacher education over ten years. *Teaching and Teacher Education, 27,* 10–20.

Aylsworth, A. J. (2012). Professional learning communities: An analysis of teacher participation in a PLC and the relationship with student academic achievement. (Graduate Theses and Dissertations. 12264), Iowa State University, Ames, IA.

Benzies, K. M., & Allen, M. N. (2001). Symbolic interactionism as a theoretical perspective for multiple research. *Journal of Advanced Nursing, 33,* 541–547.

Blumer, H. (1969). *Symbolic interactionism: Perspective and method*. Englewood Cliffs, NJ: Prentice-Hall.

Cohen, L., Manion, L., & Morrison, K. (2018). *Research methods in education* (8th ed.). London, UK: Routledge.

Cranston, N. C. (2000). Teachers as leaders: A critical agenda for the new millennium. *Asia-Pacific Journal of Teacher Education, 28*(2), 123–131.

Evetts, J. (2008). The management of professionalism. In S. Gewirtz, P. Mahony, I. Hextall, & A. Cribb (Eds.), *Changing teacher professionalism: International trends, challenges and ways forward* (pp. 19–30). Hoboken, NJ: Routledge.

Ferrari, A. (2012). *Digital Competence in Practice: An Analysis of Frameworks*. Seville, Spain: Joint Research Centre.

Gibbs, R., & Poskitt, J. (2010). *Student engagement in the middle years of schooling (Years 7–10): A literature review*. Report to the Ministry of Education. Ministry of Education: New Zealand.

Hinton, F. (1997). Winds of change: Teachers in the year 2007. *Unicorn, 23*(2), 18–24.

Kelly, P. (2006). What is teacher learning? A socio-cultural perspective. *Oxford Review of Education, 32*(4), 505–519.

King, F. (2016). Teacher professional development to support teacher professional learning: Systemic factors from Irish case studies. *Teacher Development, 20*(4), 574–594.

Korthagen, F. (2017). Inconvenient truths about teacher learning: Towards professional development 3.0. *Teachers and Teaching, Theory and Practice, 23*(4), 387–405.

Lovett, S., & Cameron, M. (2011). Schools as professional learning communities for early career teachers: How do early career teachers rate them? *Teacher Development, 15*(1), 87–104.

Mead, G. H. (1934). *Mind, self, and society*. Chicago, IL: University of Chicago Press.

National Board for Professional Teaching Standards. (2018). *National Board Standards*. Washington, DC: Author.

Council, New Zealand Education. (2017). *Our code, our standards: Code of professional responsibility and standards for the teaching profession*. Wellington, New Zealand: Author.

O'Connor, K. (2008). "You choose to care": Teachers, emotions and professional identity. *Teaching and Teacher Education, 24*(1), 117–126.

Organisation for Economic Co-operation and Development (OECD). (2014). *Talis 2013 results: An international perspective on teaching and learning*. Paris, France: Author.

Organisation for Economic Co-operation and Development (OECD). (2016). *Supporting teacher professionalism: Insights from TALIS 2013*. Paris, France: Author.

Patton, M. Q. (2015). *Qualitative research and evaluation methods* (4th ed.). Thousand Oaks, CA: Sage.

Sachs, J. (2016). Teacher professionalism: Why are we still talking about it? *Teachers and Teaching: Theory and Practice, 22*(4), 413–425.

Seddon, T. (1999). A self-managing teaching profession for the learning society. *Unicorn, 25*(1), 15–29.

Seddon, T., & Brown, L. (1997). Teachers' work: Towards the year 2007. *Unicorn, 23*(2), 25–38.

Spiteri, M., & Rundgren, C. S.-N. (2017). Maltese primary teachers' digital competence: Implications for continuing professional development. *European Journal of Teacher Education, 40*(4), 521–534.

Timperley, H. (2011a). *Realizing the power of professional learning.* Berkshire, UK: Oxford University Press.

Timperley, H. (2011b). *A background paper to inform the development of a national professional development framework for teachers and school leaders.* Melbourne, VIC: Australian Institute for Teaching and School Leadership.

Timperley, H. (2011c). *Using student assessment for professional learning: Focusing on student outcomes to identify teacher needs.* East Melbourne, VIC: State of Victoria (Department of Education and Early Childhood Development).

United Kingdom Department of Education. (2011). *Teachers' standards: Guidance for school leaders, school staff and governing bodies.* London, UK: Author.

Yuen, L. H. (2012). The impact of continuing professional development on a novice teacher. *Teacher Development, 16*(3), 387–398.

Jeanne Allen is an Associate Professor of Teacher Education at Griffith University. Her research expertise is in teacher education, standardised educational contexts, teacher identity, and student engagement and retention. She was an invited contributor to the prestigious *Sage Handbook of Research on Teacher Education* in 2017 and her co-edited book, *Learning to Teach in a New Era* (Cambridge), was highly commended in the 2018 Educational Publishing Awards. In 2018, she was named national leading researcher in the field of Teaching and Teacher Education by Australia's League of Scholars. She is currently the Co-Editor of the *Asia-Pacific Journal of Teacher Education*.

Dr. Glenda McGregor is a Senior Lecturer and Deputy Head (Academic) of the School of Education and Professional Studies, Griffith University. Her research interests include sociology of youth, school reform, curriculum and social justice and education. Her most recent book (co-authored) is *Re-imagining Schooling for Education: Socially Just Alternatives*, published in 2017 by Palgrave Macmillan. Alongside colleagues, Glenda has worked on two Australian Research Council projects investigating alternative and democratic schooling and has been a team member on Queensland Government projects and, most recently, one completed on behalf of the ACT Education Directorate.

Professor Donna Pendergast is Dean of the School of Education and Professional Studies at Griffith University. Her research expertise is educational transformation and efficacy with a focus on: middle years education and student engagement; initial and professional teacher education; and school reform. In 2015, she received the Vice Chancellor's Research Supervision Excellence Award; in 2017, a National Commendation from the Australian Council of Graduate Research for Excellence in Graduate Research Supervision and in 2018 the Australian Council for Educational Leadership Miller-Grassie Award for Outstanding Leadership in Education.

Chapter 11
What Does It Mean to Be an English-as-an-Additional-Language Teacher? Preservice and in-Service Teachers' Perceptions

Minh Hue Nguyen

Abstract This qualitative study explores the ways in which the work of English-as-an-additional-language (EAL) teachers is understood by preservice teachers (PSTs) and in-service teachers (ISTs) of EAL. The PSTs were completing a Master of Teaching programme at a large university in Australia, which would qualify them to work as EAL teachers. They were asked to reflect on the role of the EAL teacher before and after a three-week practicum. The ISTs, who are EAL practitioners in secondary schools in the state of Victoria, were each asked in an interview to reflect on their role as an EAL teacher. Results indicate that the PSTs demonstrated some level of understanding of the complexities of teaching EAL based on their theoretical knowledge and limited exposure to EAL in context. The ISTs' reflection was based more specifically on their contextualised teaching experiences. The chapter discusses implications for EAL teacher education in terms of supporting growth in professional understandings and teacher identity.

1 Introduction

Like other English-speaking countries, Australia has large immigrant inflows (Phillips & Simon-Davies, n.d.), and 21% of Australians speak languages other than English at home in 2016 (Australian Bureau of Statistics, 2017). Therefore, there has been a strong need for English language instruction in Australia (Oliver, Rochecouste, & Nguyen, 2017). In the state of Victoria, approximately 13% of students in government schools are part of an English-as-an-Additional-Language (EAL) programme taught by a specialist EAL teacher (Department of Education and Training, 2018). These students have highly diverse linguistic, cultural and educational backgrounds, which impact on how teachers identify and perform their role (Johnson, 2009). From a socio-cultural perspective on second language teacher education, what the teachers

M. H. Nguyen (✉)
Faculty of Education, Monash University, Clayton, VIC, Australia
e-mail: minh.hue.nguyen@monash.edu

© Springer Nature Singapore Pte Ltd. 2019
A. Gutierrez et al. (eds.), *Professionalism and Teacher Education*,
https://doi.org/10.1007/978-981-13-7002-1_11

bring to their job, such as teacher education experience, professionalism and amount of teaching experience, also plays an influential role in shaping their identity and practice (Johnson, 2009).

National data suggest a number of areas that Australian teacher education institutions need to address in their efforts to prepare classroom ready teachers (TEMAG, 2014). One of the important steps towards classroom readiness is developing a good understanding of the future professional role. This has been considered an essential dimension of teacher identity (Anspal, Eisenschmidt, & Löfström, 2012; Lasky, 2005). There is a growing body of research on second language teacher identity, with participants including both preservice teachers (PSTs) and in-service teachers (ISTs) (Barkhuizen, 2017). However, there have only been periodic studies on language teachers' role identification (Gross, Fitts, Goodson-Espy, & Clark, 2010; Linville, 2016). Gross et al. (2010) used a qualitative survey to examine how teacher candidates identified, defined and constructed their roles at different times while completing their degrees. The study found that the participants' perceptions of their role as a teacher became more elaborated and specific over time, and multiple practicum experiences in different settings contributed significantly to the development of their contextual understandings. Also surveying PSTs of English language, Linville (2016) examined specifically how the participants conceptualised their roles as advocates for English language learners in different contexts. Linville found that the PSTs rated their role as advocates in the classroom and school as more important than in the community. Both studies offer valuable insights into PSTs' understanding of their future role as English language teachers. However, more research of this type is needed to enrich the field's database. In addition, there is a dearth of research on how experienced English language teachers conceptualise their role and how that compares with PSTs' role conceptualisation.

As the author of this chapter, I have been teaching an EAL method unit as part of an EAL teacher education course at a Melbourne-based university. This Master of Teaching programme prepares EAL teachers for secondary teaching in Australia. After several weeks of coursework, each PST completes a three-week practicum in a secondary school in Victoria. The PSTs then return to university to continue with the EAL method unit for the remaining weeks of the semester. During the practicum, I also visit a number of schools where I interact with experienced EAL teachers. My observations of the PSTs during my university teaching and my interactions with experienced EAL teachers during my school visits have prompted me to think about the varying conceptualisations of role among the PSTs and ISTs. I have wondered what similarities and gaps exist in their understandings of the role and how, as teacher educators, we could develop programs to support PSTs' professional understandings and identity development. "How can we narrow the gaps in professionalism so that PSTs are well prepared when they enter the profession?" is the question that has driven my research and practice. As a result, I conducted a research study to investigate the following questions:

1. How do preservice EAL teachers understand the role of an EAL teacher at different stages of teacher education?

2. How do in-service EAL teachers understand their professional role?
3. What similarities and gaps are identified in the role understandings of the participants at different stages of teacher education and career?

2   Theoretical Framework

To investigate the questions listed above, the research draws on positioning theory (Davies & Harré, 1990) and the notion of self (Anspal et al., 2012; Kelchtermans, 1993; Lasky, 2005) as an underpinning theoretical framework. Positioning theory (Davies & Harré, 1990) offers elements that can support the analysis of teachers' understanding of their professional role in the current study. According to Davies and Harré (1990), there can be reflexive positioning and interactive positioning in conversations. Reflexive positioning occurs when a person positions himself/herself, while in interactive positioning one positions another. The current study draws on the principles of reflexive positioning to uncover the participants' positioning of self, which offers insights into their understanding of EAL teacher work. To this end, the notion of self can complement the idea of reflexive positioning by Davies and Harré (1990) in the analysis of teachers' understanding of their work. The notion of self involves (1) how teachers define themselves to themselves and (2) how teachers define themselves in relationships with others (Lasky, 2005, p. 901). The first aspect (i.e., how teachers define themselves to themselves) is useful for analysing teachers' self-image and self-esteem (Kelchtermans, 1993). The second aspect (i.e., how teachers define themselves in relationships with others) can be used to analyse how teachers define their role in relation to students, colleagues and the classroom contexts (Kelchtermans, 1993).

3   Research Methods

3.1   Participants and Settings

Two unrelated groups of participants took part in this qualitative study. The first group includes 28 PSTs attending an EAL method unit and a practicum unit as part of their Master of Teaching programme at a Melbourne-based university. The PSTs had been admitted into the Master of Teaching based on their first degree in an area related to one of their two teaching methods, one of which is EAL. Some of the PSTs had experience doing private tutoring to EAL students, but none had engaged in formal teaching of EAL. In the teacher education programme, they were completing general education units, two EAL method units, two second method units and four rounds of practicum. The data for this chapter were collected from PSTs through two reflective writing pieces during the first EAL method unit and an associated three-week practicum.

The second group includes three ISTs (referred to in this chapter as Mrs Clarks, Mr. Thomas and Mrs. Williams using pseudonyms), with at least ten years of experience in teaching EAL. At the time of data collection, the EAL practitioners were working in three different government secondary schools in Victoria, Australia after spending a number of years teaching English language to different learner groups in different overseas contexts. Mrs. Clarks had taught English language for over ten years, including in Turkey, England and Japan, before she moved to Victoria, Australia to work as an EAL teacher in a secondary school. Mr. Thomas had a degree in Teaching English to Speakers of Other Languages (TESOL) and 17 years of extensive EAL teaching experience in schools both in Hong Kong and Australia. Mrs. Williams had a double-major qualification in teaching EAL and mainstream English. She had 15 years of experience in teaching EAL to secondary students and adults in Italy and then secondary students in Victoria, Australia.

3.2   Data Collection and Analysis

Before and after the practicum, the PSTs completed two pieces of reflective writing on the EAL teacher role by responding to guiding questions as part of their class activities in the EAL method unit. The reflective writing was collected and formed a basis for other class activities within the unit. For the purpose of this research, as the lecturer I had obtained ethics approval for using these reflective entries as data. Integrity and justice were the key principles of ethical research conduct in this study. After explaining the research, I distributed a consent form to each of the class members. They completed the consent form and returned it to a professional staff member who assisted with the consent process. He then put all signed consent forms into an envelope, sealed and kept it until the final results of the unit had been released. At this point, the professional staff member returned the sealed envelope to me. The consent forms show that all the 28 PSTs had given consent for their reflections to be used as data, and at that point, data analysis commenced. Each of the ISTs, with ethics approval and informed, written consent, participated in a 30-min individual interview at their school during my school visit. The interviews were transcribed, and then, data from both sources were analysed using content analysis to determine themes corresponding to the research questions. The analysis drew on the theoretical framework, which comprises of the concept of reflexive positioning (Davies & Harré, 1990) and how teachers define themselves to themselves and in relationships with others (Kelchtermans, 1993; Lasky, 2005). The key themes include PSTs' understanding of role before and after the practicum, ISTs' understanding of role, understanding of role at different stages of teacher education and understanding of role at different career stages.

4 Findings and Discussion

4.1 EAL PSTs' Role Identification Before the Practicum

Before the practicum, the PSTs responded to the question "What is the role of the EAL teacher?" Analysis of the data reveals four roles which were identified by the PSTs, including teaching the language and facilitating English language learning, developing cultural understanding, facilitating transition into the new society, and being understanding and supportive. These identified roles show the PSTs' positioning of self in relationships with EAL students (Anspal et al., 2012; Davies & Harré, 1990; Kelchtermans, 1993; Lasky, 2005). The reflections show that, according to the PSTs these are inter-related roles of an EAL teacher. However, for the purpose of analysis, these roles are presented separately in this section.

4.1.1 Teaching the Language

Teaching the English language was consistently identified, from the PSTs reflections, as the primary role of an EAL teacher. Typically, PST12 writes, "*firstly, and most obviously, to teach the English language!.*" More specifically, another participant comments on their role in teaching the four macro language skills,[1] which ultimately aims to develop the students' higher English proficiency:

> The students are taught how to complete English written tasks, reading comprehension, listening and oral tasks as a benchmark to lift up their competence in English. (PST21)

It is interesting to note that for the majority of the PSTs, teaching the language does not only involve the act of imparting knowledge but also requires the teacher to assume a facilitator role. The PSTs used a number of verbs, such as *facilitate*, *help* and *assist*, to refer to this role. For example:

> This [The role of the EAL teacher] could include helping students with their English literacy, such as reading, writing, speaking, comprehension, communication, and other ways of forming and responding to language. (PST2)

> The role of the EAL teacher could be to assist a non-native learner or student to develop the theoretical, practical and analytic skills required in order to communicate in an oral, verbal or written manner. (PST9)

The extracts above show the PSTs' understanding that EAL students come from non-English-speaking backgrounds, and they need to develop English language skills to function effectively in the Australian society and schooling. The data also show their understanding of the learners as active participants in the learning process and not as empty vessels to be filled with knowledge.

---

[1]The four macro language skills refer to listening, speaking, reading, and writing.

4.1.2 Developing Cultural Understanding

Many PSTs identify that developing cultural understanding is an important part of EAL teaching. This is succinctly captured in the following extract:

> The EAL teacher provides understanding of the English language and Australian culture because language and culture are strongly correlated. The way Australians speak English is different from the way the British and American speak which is influenced by their respective culture. (PST1)

This comment is further reinforced by some other PSTs who recognise that, *"introducing local culture and helping to familiarise the way of living in the new environment"* (PST7) and *"introducing the students to the life and culture of Australia"* (PST21) are among important responsibilities of an EAL teacher. Another PST has a more pedagogical approach to the task of developing cultural understanding when identifying the need for the EAL teacher to provide materials and knowledge that are suitable for developing both the language and culture and that are based on the learners' goals and needs:

> The EAL teacher should provide the cultural language materials and insights into "English" language and culture – depending on the English goals and needs of the learner. (PST4)

For another PST, EAL teaching goes beyond developing cultural understanding. It also *"provides the learner with an appreciation [of] and inclusion into the cultural identity that the language presents"* (PST9), which also relates to the task of supporting transition into the new society addressed in the subsection below.

4.1.3 Supporting Transition into Mainstream Education and the New Society

Most of the PSTs define their role as involving facilitation of their students' transition into their new educational and social context. This is summarised by a participant's comment below:

> As an EAL teacher, my job is to first make my students feel comfortable in not only my class but in the school and wider community as well. (PST18)

In helping EAL learners socialise into the school community, most PSTs are concerned with the need for the EAL teacher to *"provide EAL students with the required skills to communicate with their peers and school community"* (PST3). In addition, it is also identified that the EAL teacher needs to *"work with content area teachers to assist EAL learners outside of the EAL classroom"* (PST3), and *"assist students in all their other subjects"* (PST12). These PSTs focus on two major areas, including general communication with the school community and academic studies in both the EAL classroom and content area classrooms. The PSTs identify that the EAL teacher needs to collaborate with the content areas teachers to facilitate academic transition.

Regarding the facilitation of EAL learners' settlement in the broader society outside their school, many PSTs consider developing English competency and cultural understanding as the main approach. For example, two participants write:

> My role will be to connect with each student and aim to integrate them into the community by teaching them about our culture and supporting them throughout their journey. (PST18)

> The EAL teacher assists students from non-English background to acquire and improve their English. It is essential to acquire high extent of English to fully integrate with the Australian society and succeed in any jobs students will do in the future. (PST1)

The end of PST1's comment above shows that preparing EAL learners for their future career is also considered a responsibility of an EAL teacher.

4.1.4   Understanding Learners and Providing Support

The data show that the majority of the PSTs recognise the importance of getting to know their EAL students. For example, some participants see the relevance of understanding their EAL students' backgrounds and aspirations, as well as their challenges:

> Knowing that many of them would have just arrived in Australia, it is important for me to get to know them and their backgrounds as well as their ambitions. (PST18)

> It [The EAL teacher role involves] understanding students' learning difficulties and foresee students' problems. (PST19)

Such understanding is viewed by some PSTs as a basis for an EAL teacher to support students' learning, which can be exercised in a number of ways, as shown in the following extracts:

> Acknowledging what study problems are faced by overseas students and helping them solve the problems. (PST8)

> To learn what the students need more generally from the school curriculum and implement appropriate programs. (PST12)

> They [teachers] must differentiate and take into account a range of abilities and backgrounds. This may involve cultural understanding of students' backgrounds in order to teach them social conventions in English. (PST6)

The comments above touch upon the role of the EAL teacher in understanding their learners then helping them overcome their learning challenges, implementing responsive teaching programmes and teaching culturally appropriate language. PST3 adds another dimension to the EAL teacher role:

> Australia is a diverse country with thousands of new students enrolling each year from LBOTE. I think it is important to provide support for these students and assist their on-going development in a new environment. (PST3)

While most of the comments from the PSTs' reflections above focus on supporting EAL learners in their social and academic endeavours, PST3's comment seems to touch upon the social responsibility at large of an EAL teacher in developing the capacities of a large and growing number of EAL learners in the population.

4.2 EAL PSTs' Role Identification After the Practicum

After the practicum, the PSTs responded to the question "How has the practicum altered or extended your understanding of EAL teacher work?" in a reflective writing task. Their responses again reveal their positioning in relationships with EAL learners (Anspal et al., 2012; Davies & Harré, 1990; Kelchtermans, 1993; Lasky, 2005). Following are some typical responses in their reflections:

> The practicum extended my understanding of EAL teacher work in terms of students' background, students' mixed level of English and the role of the EAL teacher as the teacher used a lot of scaffolding and modelling. (PST5)

> As students are learning English as their additional language, I think understanding prior knowledge level and culture of students is very important, and this matters to your lesson plan and teaching approaches. (PST19)

> It really became apparent that you have to work within the confines and habits of the students as well as try to get them accustomed to learning styles in Australia. Cultural knowledge and sympathy is very important. (PST4)

Their reflections show that the PSTs' understanding of their professional role grew over the duration of their practicum. Some of the PSTs recount that their perceptions of the EAL teacher role in understanding their students' backgrounds, abilities and challenges as well as providing responsive teaching and support were confirmed by their practicum experiences. However, their post-practicum reflections focused more on the pedagogical aspects of the job and the inner self. It is promising to note that in the first extract above, PST5 mentioned the instructional strategies of scaffolding and modelling as ways to respond to the diverse backgrounds and learning needs of their students. In the second comment, PST19 situates these strategies in planning and delivering EAL lessons. In the last extract, PST4 highlights the importance of EAL teaching that is not only contingent on the characteristics of the learners but also looking forward to helping them integrate into the new social and academic culture in Australia.

A couple of PSTs highlight the role of writing lesson plans as part of their EAL teacher work. While PST17 acknowledges that "*a good lesson plan takes effort and time to create,*" PST19 states, "*as long as you are prepared and do a lesson plan, it's definitely easy to manage and teach the class.*" In the second extract, PST19 shows his/her perception that lesson planning is a key factor in the effective management and teaching of EAL classes. However, another PST comments on the role of lesson planning:

> Through my placement, I have realised that teaching is not only about lesson planning and delivering lectures. Teaching is also about interaction with the students and class management using different approaches. (PST8)

Here, PST8 similarly recognises the importance of lesson planning but adds that effective EAL teaching also requires various approaches to class management in response to different classroom situations and students' characteristics, as well as teacher–student interaction. Some other PSTs reflect on the need to use visual aids in supporting EAL learning when the learners have a limited command of English to resort to in their learning. Visual aids may include "*varieties of videos*" (PST17) or "*body language and photos*" (PST19).

The following extract summarises the common growth in the PSTs' understanding about EAL teaching depicted above, which is largely about understanding the learners and teaching contexts and implementing appropriate teaching:

> The practicum has both altered and extended my understanding of EAL teacher work because it has allowed me to apply situational approaches to classroom environment settings. I feel that I have developed a more practical, situational and ecological teaching approach to teaching and learning more broadly. (PST9)

Further new insights are revealed in the PSTs' post-practicum reflections, which show greater understanding, or rather, their thinking of themselves as teachers:

> I was less certain if teaching was right for me, but now I feel I'd enjoy it quite a bit. (PST15)

> I am more confident now. I know my strengths and weaknesses better than I did beforehand and know how to adapt to best fit them in the class. (PST7)

The two participants identify that looking inwards to understand the self is important in developing their teacher identity. This is of no less importance than efforts to understand the learners and to design and implement appropriate teaching. And in this process, "*reflection on your own teaching experience is vital,*" as PST17 writes. These PSTs indicate their self-image and self-esteem (Kelchtermans, 1993), which reflect how they define themselves to themselves (Lasky, 2005).

Perhaps PST12 adds a completely different understanding about the EAL teacher role gained through the practicum experience in comparison with the perceptions previously presented:

> My understanding of EAL teaching has been coloured by how other teachers, especially mainstream English teachers view and treat EAL teachers as inferior. This has made me even more determined to become an excellent EAL teacher and to set the record straight. (PST12)

In this extract, PST12 indicates that EAL teachers are not treated with respect by mainstream English teachers. He/she describes his/her role as an EAL teacher to act to change this view of EAL teachers as inferior to those in other discipline areas. This excerpt shows PST12's positioning of self in relationship with teachers of other subjects (Davies & Harré, 1990).

4.3   In-Service EAL Teachers' Role Identification

The ISTs' identification of role is largely concerned with their positioning of self as a teacher in relationships with EAL students and content area teachers (Anspal et al., 2012; Davies & Harré, 1990; Kelchtermans, 1993; Lasky, 2005). Several themes were identified in the data from the experienced teachers such as understanding learners and catering for individual differences, having sound grammar knowledge and the ability to teach grammar well, supporting transition into mainstream education and the new society, scaffolding learning, and being flexible as their main roles.

4.3.1 Understanding Learners and Catering for Individual Differences

There is a common finding from the interviews with the three in-service EAL teachers that understanding the learners and teaching responsively are among the most important aspects of EAL teaching. Mrs. Clarks puts it generally when asked what she thinks the most important aspects of EAL teaching is:

> Just people awareness. Awareness that they've got their own background, their own culture, their own identities. They're teenagers, so they're having their own teenage brain happening as well. And just awareness that they're not always going to respond how you think they should respond or how you want them to respond and that maybe if they're not responding then there's something else that influenced that. [....] I think empathy as well, just knowing that just really empathising that they're young and they've come in for whatever reasons. That's really really important.

Mrs. Clarks describes her awareness that the learners have their own personal histories and characteristics as the most important aspect of being an EAL teacher. She states that in teaching EAL students, it is important that the teacher is responsive and empathetic. With a similar view, but working in a school situated in a low socio-economic status area, Mr. Thomas notes more specifically the need for an EAL teacher to understand and cater for the diverse needs of students with refugee backgrounds, EAL students with traumatic experiences, those with interrupted or no prior schooling, and mixed abilities:

> I think that's common to all EAL teachers though maybe kids with traumatic backgrounds or refugee background, interrupted schooling or no school. [...] I think it's an increasingly important issue in terms of our cohort that we're expected to teach, so maybe that could be something to keep in mind. Also mixed ability classes. [....]. That's one of the real challenges I suppose. [...] I find as an EAL teacher you have to cater for those kids at the bottom but also extend and challenge the kids at the top.

Mr. Thomas further adds that, the most important aspects of EAL teaching are "*for the students to engage in the language, to provide a language rich classroom environment for the students to experience success and also enjoy learning the language, acquiring the language.*" He considers using teaching resources that EAL students can relate to as an effective way of catering for the different levels of English and fostering experience of success in EAL learning:

> I like to run a classroom using resources that the students can relate to, ideally films [...] and I found that I could cater for the very good kids and still provide activities for those S1[2] strugglers. And by doing that I found that each student could achieve success in learning the language.

---

[2]S1 refers to one of the stages of the EAL Developmental Continuum used in Victorian secondary schools to assess EAL learners.

Sharing a similar view about the importance of understanding learners and responding to their needs, Mrs. Williams comments more specifically on how she as an EAL teacher can respond to her EAL learners with individual and diverse learning needs:

> We have kids who […] come in with different levels of English. So I'd say that for [Year 11 s], […], it's more about teaching them concepts and ideas rather than the basic grammar skills. […] But the Year 9 s and 10 s need to learn how to write essays […]. The Year 7 s it might be more vocabulary or grammar based. […] But certainly in Year 8, […] they need more sort of hands-on one-on-one training even sentence structure and verbs and all sort of things. [….] The majority come from […] an affluent area around this. But then […] we've got the boarders. [….]. And we have, you know, a large number of overseas students to come in as well. So there are challenges with all those sorts of things.

Here, Mrs. Williams draws attention to the highly diverse abilities of her EAL students as well as the challenges associated with their different backgrounds ranging from local wealthy students to boarding and international students.

In summary, it is commonly acknowledged by the ISTs that EAL learners have diverse social, cultural, linguistic and educational backgrounds and thus varied learning needs. Therefore, it is important that EAL teachers understand these individual differences and provide teaching that caters for this diversity. This understanding is classified as pedagogical reasoning skills and decision making in discussions about second language teacher knowledge (Richards, 1998).

4.3.2 Having Sound Grammar Knowledge and Teaching Skills

Having good knowledge of grammar and the ability to teach grammar well is also found to be an important element of the EAL teacher's role, as Mrs. Williams comments:

> In general, I think […] EAL is such a difficult one. I think they really need to have a very good knowledge of grammar. Okay, because I find that invariably the kids are going to say 'Why can't you write something like that? Why do you say this? Why is it like this? And this situation, why is it not like that?' And they need, you know, they need a hold into the language and if you don't feel very confident with grammar, it's very hard to say 'Oh that's how it is.' […] Those are the bits where the extra learning come in into every class, you know.

Mrs. Williams also notes that an EAL teacher needs to be able to teach grammar well:

> Grammar can't be taught like a lesson by itself like 'OK let's move to page 24 and let's do this verb.' You know, it's got to be part of something else in order for those kids to get it. [….] I think some people come in and they think, 'Oh, we're going to do this one unit and it's going to be from *Headway.*[3]' That's not it. You know it's about you have to think so quickly about 'Okay, the kids haven't got this bit of sentence structure. I've got to help them.' [….] So I think to have […] the ability to really teach grammar well is the one for EAL.

---

[3]*Headway* is the title of an English text book published by Oxford University Press.

228 M. H. Nguyen

Through this comment, Mrs. Williams' view is that in order to teach grammar well, EAL teachers need to use an integrated approach where grammar teaching arises from the teachable moments within lessons rather than as a lesson by itself. The view that EAL teachers need to have a good grammar knowledge and an ability to teach grammar effectively in context seems to correspond to an influential conceptualisation of the knowledge base for second language teaching by Richards (1998), which emphasises the importance of having sound subject matter knowledge and pedagogical reasoning skills and decision making in teaching a second language.

4.3.3 Supporting Transition into Mainstream Education and the New Society

The ISTs commonly point out the important task of preparing EAL students for their transition into mainstream education and the new society in Australia. This is the main function of teaching them the English language in EAL provision programmes. Mrs. Clarks summarises this aspect of the job:

> It's to give them the language or to give them the basics of the language depending on what level of the language they come into prepare them for mainstream school. So we teach through contents. We teach [through] SOSE, maths, science, English. We do the VCE preparation. So there's the academic side of it.

In Mrs. Clarks' school, EAL education is provided intensively at an English language centre before the students move on to mainstream education with less, or sometimes no, further EAL support. Therefore, to best prepare EAL students for this transition, Mrs. Clarks' job involves developing their English proficiency via the use of mainstream content. She further comments on this:

> We kind of try and keep it [EAL teaching] in step with what we're teaching in the college, but we can choose within that framework because obviously you can't do everything in two terms. So for example, someone might be teaching World War II or something like that. And when I'm teaching SOSE for example I like to do immigration […]. I can do a lot of different things with immigration and narrative and you know it brings in the whole complete programme really. And immigration is part of Year 9 and Year 10 and stuff like that. So that's how we do, we work with VELS and curriculum. […] And Science again, the Science programme is based on mainstream Science, so we choose topics that we want to do.

Here, Mrs. Clarks also points to other important aspects of EAL teaching; that is, the need for understanding and working with the content area curricula as well as collaborating with content area teachers in developing programmes of support for EAL students. Similarly, Mrs. Williams sees EAL teaching as preparing EAL students for meeting the academic demands of content area subjects:

> At this school, certainly it [EAL teaching] is to provide students with the possibility of bridging the gap between where they're at educationally and being able to function and survive, I guess, in the mainstream environment. [….]. You know, they have to be able to do the academic work required of them very quickly. And they are expected to perform really well and quickly.

In the ISTs' definition of role, another important aspect of their job is teaching VCE EAL classes in years 11 and 12, which involves *"preparing them for the VCE exam, which is fairly challenging"* (Mr. Thomas).

In addition, attending to the students' social functioning and welfare in support of their transition to the new society is also considered an important element of EAL teaching. Mrs. Clarks elaborates on this below, followed by a supportive comment by Mr. Thomas:

> So there're lots of different elements about teaching languages. One of them [is] the functional side for the lower levels would go out into the street asking for help and phone numbers and catching buses and things like that and that's really the functional side of being in a new place. [….] There's also trying to make them feel safe. Making them feel safe is really important, building their confidence, creating friendships and then there's the language side as well. (Laugh). [….] So you can see I'm […] always focused on the social and the welfare side and then I kind of bring the language in as well. […] I don't think they're going to learn as well if they don't feel safe and relaxed.

> And, you know, they left the classroom with big smiles on their faces. Yeah, I think just providing a happy, safe and enjoyable classroom environment.

In these extracts, the ISTs highlight the importance of helping the EAL students, especially the low level ones, with the ability to perform social exchanges in English as part of their daily life and making them feel safe and happy in their educational context.

4.3.4   Scaffolding Learning

The ISTs also identify scaffolding as an important part of a teacher's role. Mrs. Clarks notes that EAL teaching involves using content similar to mainstream subjects but scaffolding through little steps to build confidence for students' immersion in content areas education:

> I think the scaffolding is, you know, scaffolding and using very similar content to what is in mainstream school but you just take all those steps together. And that, I think, builds their confidence because they understand the little steps. As when they get it big, OK, they're going to read this article, you know, or read this novel, […] you know, straight away their mind can't do this. So I think you know as every EAL teacher, we'll say if there's anything in small pieces can make a big picture in the end. So I think that's the best strategy, scaffolding and about mainstream content.

Mrs. Clarks further comments on the importance of providing scaffolding to pre-VCE EAL students so that they are ready for VCE studies by the time they finish the EAL provision programme:

> So if they're pre-VCE, I think the boundaries need to be a little bit stricter on the requirements of their work and their class participation and things because they've only got two terms and when they're going to VCE. [….] So, kind of scaffolding, scaffolding, a lot of scaffolding tasks that are up to that Year 10, Year 11 level. So they kind of get the same materials but how we get there, a little bit longer and then, you know, maybe pull apart and put back together again.

From a similar point of view, Mrs. Williams reflects on her approach to scaffold EAL students:

> Well, being able to think, 'Okay, they're not understanding it'. Look into their faces; they don't understand this point. [....] And then, you know, I'll take them through different things till I get that 'Oh!'. You know, until I get that, I'll keep going. I can pace myself to go faster 'cause I know they get it. But that takes time [...]. So I think that's really important with EAL, more so than history or subjects where everything's quite defined.

In Mrs. Williams' approach, it is really important to adapt her teaching based on her students' responses and perseveres until they understand the issue.

4.3.5 Being Flexible

In the ISTs' views, an EAL teacher needs to be flexible in terms of what they teach in their EAL class, as noted by Mrs. Williams:

> It was more about being flexible with their needs and moulding what you were doing around what they were doing. [....] Every every week is different because the support requires you to be speaking to what their other teachers are doing as well because those kids need support in History or Geography. So [...], the other teachers will come to me and say, 'Look, this is what they are doing, can you help them with that.' So there's that. And also there isn't a guideline, [...] a document. Okay, there isn't something for me to say 'This is what we're doing week by week' because I run a support programme.

Here, Mrs. Williams mentions the necessity for an EAL teacher to consider the learning needs of EAL students in content areas and to develop EAL support contingent on these needs. Part of her job is speaking with content area teachers to find out what the EAL students are studying in other subjects and what areas they need support in. Another point raised by Mrs. Williams is that these emerging needs define EAL teaching rather than a pre-written curriculum document.

Being flexible is also about being responsive to emerging teaching moments such as what Mrs. Williams describes below:

> If the students come up with something, like they're genuinely asking a question, I would then go and branch off into that and that could be a mini lesson within itself. You know, and I think that the best thing about teaching EAL is that ability to be really flexible and to be really quick [....] You know, what happens to EAL is all these things come up and they're like little jewels if you like. You know you can take them and you can really go with it 'cause you've got the kids in that space and time at that point.

Mrs. Williams indicates that effective EAL teaching does not need to always follow a fixed lesson plan, and the teacher needs to be flexible enough to grab opportunities to teach new things that are not planned beforehand but relevant to the emergent needs of the learners. Being flexible to side track or go slower than the plan to accommodate emergent teaching is also acknowledged by Mr. Thomas when he says, *"If I don't finish it, I don't panic. I just, well, we leave it there and we come back to it tomorrow."*

4.4 Before and After Practicum: Role Identification at Different Stages of Teacher Education

While the practicum experiences confirmed some of the responsibilities the PSTs previously identified, their post-practicum reflections focused more on the pedagogical aspects of the job and themselves as teachers. The two previously identified aspects of the role, namely understanding learners and providing contingent teaching and support, were again found in the post-practicum reflections. The PSTs' consistent identification of these responsibilities at the two stages of teacher education shows that these core tasks are well presented and perceived in the coursework components and reinforced during the placement. This corresponds well to the national EAL teachers' resources (ACARA, 2014).

However, the other two aspects, including developing cultural understanding and supporting transition into mainstream education and the new society, were not mentioned in the PSTs' post-practicum reflections. While these two aspects have been defined by the Department of Education and Training (2015) as the main goals of EAL provision programmes and EAL teachers are expected to carry out these tasks, the realities of the practicum might have had the PSTs focus on other aspects of their role, such as the pedagogical processes. Previous research has shown that while on practicum, under the supervision and assessment of mentor teachers, PSTs tend to focus more on the mechanical side of teaching because that is what the assessment criteria and mentoring feedback usually focus on (Nguyen, 2017; Trent, 2013). In fact, similar to the past research, after the practicum, the PSTs recognise writing lesson plans and using visual aids as two other important elements of EAL teaching.

Two additional tasks, including reflecting on practice and acting as an advocate to promote EAL teaching among the school community, are understood by the PSTs after the practicum as important to their professional role. Reflection on practice has been established as an important factor in teachers' ongoing professional development (Farrell, 2015), and advocacy for EAL teaching and learning has been increasingly recognised as an important part of an EAL teacher role (Linville, 2016). The findings are encouraging because they show that through teacher education, the PSTs have developed an understanding of some of the main aspects of their professional role.

4.5 From Preservice to in-Service: Role Identification at Different Career Stages

The study found that most of the elements of the EAL teacher role identified by the PSTs and ISTs are similar. In general, both groups of participants similarly identify some key tasks involved in EAL teaching, including teaching the language, supporting transition into mainstream education and the new society, understanding the learners and providing support.

However, within these common understandings, there exist some variations in the two groups' conceptualisations of the tasks. Firstly, although both groups identify teaching the language as the utmost important responsibility of an EAL teacher, the PSTs seem to have a more generic understanding while the experienced teachers express a more nuanced, complex view in which teaching the language is interconnected with the other aspects of their role. After a short practicum, the PSTs had most likely experienced only some "discursive practices" involved in the role (Davies & Harré, 1990, p. 43). These practices shape their positioning (Davies & Harré, 1990); therefore, their self-positioning as an EAL teacher might have been partially formed, and they were yet to see the connections between multiple practices of the role.

Secondly, the two groups of participants share a similar view about understanding learners as an element of the role, but the experienced teachers focus more on learners' individual differences and are more specific about the their backgrounds and learning needs. Based on their more contextualised understanding of learners, the ISTs also suggest support and teaching that are contingent on the needs of learners. The PSTs' conceptualisations, however, are more about the theoretical necessity for understanding their learners. This might be the case that the PSTs have acquired the surface label of this aspect of the role but still lack the skills for needs analysis (TEMAG, 2014). Another possible explanation is that the PSTs had spent only three weeks in the schools and were still building their understanding of the learners, so their role definition in relation to EAL learners (Kelchtermans, 1993; Lasky, 2005) was yet to be well informed.

Moreover, the ISTs' role identification is concerned with their positionings in relationships with both EAL learners and mainstream teachers, while the PSTs are mostly concerned with their role in relationships with learners. Specifically, both groups consider supporting EAL students' transition into mainstream education and the new society as their key responsibility, but the ISTs are more specific about a whole school approach to this. They especially emphasise the importance of teaching EAL through mainstream contents and collaborating with content areas teachers in doing their job. This theme is only evident from two PSTs' reflections. In contrast, one PST identifies a subordinate role of the EAL teacher in relationships with content area teachers, which is considered a complicating issue by Harper, Cook, and James (2010).

In addition, some of the elements of role identified by the experienced teachers are not found in the PSTs' conceptualisations. For example, teaching VCE EAL classes seems to be recognised only by the ISTs. This could be because PSTs are often not assigned to teach VCE classes due to the high-stakes nature of the VCE examinations. The experienced teachers also claim being flexible as an important part of EAL teaching while this is not identified by the PSTs. From the data, it can be inferred that with greater autonomy and higher level of experience and contextual understanding, the ISTs were able to exercise this flexibility. The PSTs, however, spent only three weeks in the practicum school, so their contextual understanding was not as developed. This lends support to previous research findings that PSTs, especially international PSTs, often lack contextual knowledge (Nguyen, 2014). Also,

PSTs are often under supervision and had to meet certain requirements that might constrain their autonomy, authority and practice (Nguyen, 2014, 2017; Trent, 2013).

5   Conclusion and Implications

The study reveals a number of similarities and differences in terms of role conceptualisation between EAL teachers at different stages of teacher education and career. It was based on a small sample of one cohort of 28 PSTs at one university and three ISTs. Although the findings were not aimed for generalisability to a broader population, they offer a number of implications for different stakeholders. It is unrealistic to expect PSTs to demonstrate the same level of expertise and professionalism as experienced teachers. However, identifying role conceptualisations by teachers at different stages of teacher education and career enables consolidation of teacher education programmes to narrow the gaps.

First, university teacher educators need to establish strong contextual knowledge regarding the complexity and diversity of EAL teaching through coursework and links with field experiences. Teacher education needs to equip teacher candidates with skills for analysing the learning needs of their students. School mentors could assist with contextual knowledge development by providing more guidance on the different aspects of EAL teaching specific to contexts. This could be done through guest talks at university and mentoring during the practicum. PSTs would also benefit from guided reflections on their professional learning which focus more on the contextualised role of EAL teachers.

Second, it is important for PSTs to develop good understanding of the school curriculum including VCE and mainstream curriculum. Teacher education activities should enhance this understanding for PSTs because it has a significant influence on the way they teach and position themselves as teachers. While it is less likely that PSTs have VCE classes during their practicum, it is important to discuss and raise awareness about this responsibility in preparation for their future role.

In addition, the study shows that the PSTs hardly identify collaboration with content areas teachers and a whole school approach to EAL education as elements of their future role. In contrast, the experienced teachers recognise this as a key part of their work. Therefore, teacher education needs to develop such an understanding and create opportunities for PSTs of EAL to collaborate with PSTs of content areas in learning to address the needs of EAL learners in mainstream education. Despite a small sample size, future research could build on the findings of this study by, for example, surveying role identification among PSTs across different universities and a greater number of ISTs.

234   M. H. Nguyen

References

ACARA. (2014). *English as an additional language or dialect teacher resource: EAL/D overview and advice.* Sydney: Australian Curriculum, Assessment and Reporting Authority.

Anspal, T., Eisenschmidt, E., & Löfström, E. (2012). Finding myself as a teacher: Exploring the shaping of teacher identities through student teachers' narratives. *Teachers and Teaching: Theory and Practice, 18*(2), 197–216. https://doi.org/10.1080/13540602.2012.632268.

Australian Bureau of Statistics. (2017). 2016 Census: Multicultural. Retrieved 2 January, 2019, from http://www.abs.gov.au/ausstats/abs@.nsf/lookup/Media%20Release3.

Barkhuizen, G. (Ed.). (2017). *Reflections on language teacher identity research.* New York: Routledge.

Davies, B., & Harré, R. (1990). Positioning: The discursive production of selves. *Journal for the Theory of Social Behaviour, 20*(1), 43–63. https://doi.org/10.1111/j.1468-5914.1990.tb00174.x.

Department of Education and Training. (2015). *The EAL Handbook: Advice to schools on programs for supporting students learning English as an additional language.* Melbourne: Victoria State Government.

Department of Education and Training. (2018). EAL Annual Reports. Retrieved 26 April, 2018, from http://www.education.vic.gov.au/school/teachers/support/diversity/eal/Pages/ealonlinereports.aspx.

Farrell, T. S. C. (2015). *Reflective language teaching: From research to practice.* New York: Bloomsbury Publishing.

Gross, L. A., Fitts, S., Goodson-Espy, T., & Clark, A.-M. (2010). Self as teacher: Preliminary role identification of the potential teaching candidate. *Australian Journal of Teacher Education, 35*(2), 1–19.

Harper, C., Cook, K., & James, C. K. (2010). Content-language integrated approaches for teachers of EAL learners: Examples of reciprocal teaching. In C. Leung & A. Creese (Eds.), *English as an Additional Language: Approaches to Teaching Linguistic Minority Students.* London: SAGE.

Johnson, K. E. (2009). *Second language teacher education: A sociocultural perspective.* New York: Routledge.

Kelchtermans, G. (1993). Getting the story, understanding the lives: From career stories to teachers' professional development. *Teaching and Teacher Education, 9*(5), 443–456. https://doi.org/10.1016/0742-051X(93)90029-G.

Lasky, S. (2005). A sociocultural approach to understanding teacher identity, agency and professional vulnerability in a context of secondary school reform. *Teaching and Teacher Education, 21*(8), 899–916. https://doi.org/10.1016/j.tate.2005.06.003.

Linville, H. A. (2016). ESOL teachers as advocates: An important role? *TESOL Journal, 7*(1), 98–131. https://doi.org/10.1002/tesj.193.

Nguyen, M. H. (2014). Preservice EAL teaching as emotional experiences: Practicum experience in an Australian secondary school. *Australian Journal of Teacher Education, 39*(8), 63–84. https://doi.org/10.14221/ajte.2014v39n8.5.

Nguyen, M. H. (2017). Negotiating contradictions in developing teacher identity during the EAL practicum in Australia. *Asia-Pacific Journal of Teacher Education, 45*(4), 399–415. https://doi.org/10.1080/1359866X.2017.1295132.

Oliver, R., Rochecouste, J., & Nguyen, B. (2017). ESL in Australia—A chequered history. *TESOL in Context, 26*(1), 7–26.

Phillips, J., & Simon-Davies, J. (n.d.). Migration—Australian migration flows and population. Retrieved 2 January, 2019, from https://www.aph.gov.au/About_Parliament/Parliamentary_Departments/Parliamentary_Library/pubs/BriefingBook45p/MigrationFlows.

Richards, J. C. (1998). *Beyond training: Perspectives on language teacher education.* New York: Cambridge University Press.

TEMAG. (2014). *Action now: Classroom ready teachers.* Victoria: Department of Education.

Trent, J. (2013). From learner to teacher: Practice, language, and identity in a teaching practicum. *Asia-Pacific Journal of Teacher Education, 41*(4), 426–440. https://doi.org/10.1080/1359866X. 2013.838621.

Dr. Minh Hue Nguyen is a lecturer in TESOL Education in the Faculty of Education at Monash University. Her research, supervision, teaching and engagement are in the areas of second language teacher education and second language teaching and learning. Underpinned by a sociocultural theoretical framework, her publications have focused on preservice EAL teachers' professional learning, emotions, identity, pedagogical learning, and the role of mentoring and the teacher education curriculum in preservice EAL teachers' professional learning. Her most recent research project examines collaboration between EAL teachers and content areas teachers in supporting EAL learners in the mainstream classroom.

Printed in Great Britain
by Amazon

10347415R00141